UNION POWER AND AMERICAN DEMOCRACY

Union Power and American Democracy

The UAW and the Democratic Party, 1935–72

Dudley W. Buffa

Ann Arbor   The University of Michigan Press

To my parents, Harold and Beverly Buffa

Copyright © by The University of Michigan 1984
All rights reserved
Published in the United States of America by
The University of Michigan Press and simultaneously
In Rexdale, Canada, by John Wiley & Sons Canada, Limited
Manufactured in the United States of America

1987 1986 1985 1984   4 3 2 1

Library of Congress Cataloging in Publication Data

Buffa, Dudley W., 1940–
  Union power and American democracy.

  Bibliography: p.
  Includes index.
  1. International Union, United Automobile, Aerospace,
and Agricultural Implement Workers of America—Political
activity—History. 2. Trade-Unions—United States—
Political activity—History. 3. Democratic Party (Mich.)
—History. 4. Michigan—Politics and government.
I. Title.
HD6515.A8B83 1984   322'.2'0973   83-21594
ISBN 0-472-10042-4

Preface

In the fall of 1962, a political era came to a close. George Romney's defeat of Governor John B. Swainson ended fourteen years of Democratic control of the executive branch of the Michigan state government. No one then could know—and no one then would have believed—that fully twenty years would pass before the election of Michigan's next Democratic governor.

Though the Republican governor was reelected in 1964, the Democratic party elected majorities to both houses of the state legislature. The Seventy-third Michigan Legislature operated with what, relatively speaking, was a marvelous efficiency. Programs advocated for years by the Democratic minority were adopted by the Democratic majority, and the platform of the Democratic party was made a prominent part of the legislative agenda.

The majority power that made possible the passage of Democratic legislation, however, also produced a serious and damaging division between the leadership of the Democratic party and the leadership of organized labor, as they battled over how best to employ it. Zolton Ferency, the state party chairman, insisted it be used to pass a state income tax. August "Gus" Scholle, president of the Michigan AFL-CIO, argued against a measure he believed would jeopardize Democratic control of the legislature. In what became open warfare between Ferency and Scholle, labor held the allegiance of the legislature and Ferency lost control of the party.

The dispute between labor and the Democratic party raised an interesting question: How had labor come to acquire its power, and precisely how far did its power extend? It was clear that nothing labor opposed would be adopted by the Democratic majority in the legislature. Joseph Kowalski was Speaker of the House, but he remained an international representative of the UAW, and he never decided anything of major importance without the prior approval of Gus Scholle. But did labor's power stop at the legislature or did it reach into the organization of the party itself?

The answer to that question begins with an observation about political parties and interest groups in general. Numerous studies have been made of the two separately, but the relationship between them has only rarely been examined. This is at least partly because of the belief that interest groups generally avoid involvement with either of the major parties in order to be free to pursue limited and specific aims with both of them. Still, many interest groups find themselves more closely attuned to the programs and policies of one party than to those of the other. Perhaps the most frequently cited instance of this phenomenon is the American labor movement. Labor, or at least sizable segments of it, has been considered one of the major constituent elements of the Democratic coalition since the early days of the New Deal. As part of a broad coalition that provided electoral support for the Democratic party, labor was able to elect officeholders sympathetic to its cause, and by virtue of that assistance managed to keep them sympathetic. Labor and the Democratic party, in other words, developed a reciprocally beneficial relationship. Unlike other groups with which the Democratic party entered into alliance, labor developed its own political apparatus, which rather quickly became part of the party organization. This strengthened the Democratic organization but it also began to blur the distinction between labor and the party.

From 1965 until the fall of 1967, I worked as an administrative assistant to the Michigan Speaker of the House. A year later I found that I was myself, by a curious irony, the embodiment of at least part of the answer to my own question about the political strength of labor. During the 1968 campaign I was placed on the payroll of the UAW as a temporary international representative and spent all of my time working for the acting chairman of the Michigan Democratic party, Sander Levin, as director of the party's legislative campaign. Thus it was difficult for me not to believe that there was a very close relationship between the UAW and the Michigan Democratic party. Later, as special assistant to U.S. Senator Philip A. Hart and as the senator's representative in the Democratic party, I was given an even closer view of, and a different perspective on, the political activity of the UAW. I became convinced that it was a mistake to believe that the UAW was simply a participant—if the most powerful one—in a coalition of interests that made up the party. I no longer had any doubt that the UAW had a stranglehold on the Michigan Democratic party.

This book begins with the earliest political activity of the UAW and ends with the 1972 Democratic state convention, in which for the first time the union instead of the party leadership chose the slate of candidates ultimately nominated by the party. A subsequent book will detail the development of the UAW's domination of the Michigan Democratic party from 1972 through the 1982 gubernatorial election in which James Blanchard put an end to twenty years of Republican control of the executive branch of government and began a new chapter in the story of the UAW's involvement with the Democratic party.

Acknowledgments

It would take more pages to thank adequately all of those who helped on this project than it has taken to tell the story. Three people, however, must be singled out. Joseph Cropsey of the University of Chicago, the best teacher, and one of the best friends, I have ever had, supplied encouragement and advice. Sam Fishman of the UAW provided access to union personnel and materials, and, of at least equal importance, served as a reliable guide through the labyrinth of Michigan politics. Sidney Woolner, who served as administrative assistant to both Governor G. Mennen Williams and, some years later, Senator Philip A. Hart, read the manuscript in its entirety and saved me from more errors than I care to recall. This is only the latest of the debts I owe him.

Contents

PART 1
The Liberal-Labor Coalition

CHAPTER 1

Labor Joins the Democratic Party

Although his tactics may have varied, Samuel Gompers never altered his opinion that government should abstain from involvement in the relations between labor and management. During the depression adherence to this doctrine became more difficult; in 1932 the American Federation of Labor (AFL) broke with its long-standing opposition to governmental intervention and lent support to demands for an unemployment insurance program. It was passage of the Norris-LaGuardia Act in that year, however, that brought about a fundamental reconsideration of labor's political interests. Insofar as the act brought under control the use of both the yellow-dog contract and the labor injunction, it removed some of the more injurious forms of state intervention and was consistent with the "voluntarism" advocated by Gompers. Nevertheless, the act was legislation—legislation that had been passed with the support of labor—and "the idea that political institutions might not only be neutralized but might even be seized began to be thinkable."[1]

The Norris-LaGuardia Act was followed by the passage of the National Industrial Recovery Act in 1933. Section 7(a) of the act guaranteed the right to bargain collectively through representatives chosen by the members without employer interference.[2] Passage of the two acts almost immediately gave rise to "a burst of new organizing activity."[3] In the judgment of what until then had been a weak and struggling United Auto Workers union (UAW), "nowhere in the United States has the right to organize in their own unions met with greater response than in the auto industry in Michigan."[4] The infusion of large numbers of auto workers into the ranks of organized labor was seen as constituting a difference not only in degree but in kind: "The hang-dog look has disappeared and without fear, they look into the eyes of their fellow men and women, for they are no longer individuals, living in fear, but thirty thousand strong in the city of Flint, one for all and all for one. . . ."[5] In their new-found enthusiasm and self-confidence, the auto workers let it be known in the first issue of their first published paper that political activity was a major concern.

Although the A.F. of L. is a non-partisan organization, the professional politician
had better watch his step and those seeking public office will be thoroughly
checked as to their attitude toward organized labor. Many of those now holding
public office will find that labor united is of some consequence and the voting
power of unified labor is not a thing to be despised and passed over lightly.[6]

Two years later the auto workers' interest in political activity had not
abated; if anything, it had become more ambitious. At a national conference
held in Detroit in January, 1935, a four-point program was adopted. The
fourth point called for independent labor activity and politics. Labor, if the
auto workers had anything to say about it, would no longer be a "non-partisan
organization."[7] Shortly after this convention, the United Auto Workers became part of the new Committee for Industrial Organization (CIO), and the
emphasis on independent political action grew even more intense. By 1936
this feeling had become "so strong among UAW members . . . that CIO
officials had to pressure the delegates to the 1936 auto workers convention
before they could be persuaded to endorse Roosevelt."[8] When the CIO held
its first state convention in 1939, it was clear that Roosevelt and the New
Deal had still not managed to attract the unanimous support of industrial
workers. Though a "majority of the delegates . . . fought off attempts at
independent third-party political action on the ground that the New Dealers
deserved support," the convention clearly distinguished this from any "all-
out endorsement of the Democratic Party as a whole."[9] Support for the New
Deal, as distinguished from the Democratic party, was again evidenced in
July, 1940, when the UAW's executive board approved a resolution endorsing
Roosevelt for reelection that called him "the greatest friend of labor ever to
hold the office of President of the United States."[10] It was during the New
Deal that the unions "emerged as a party campaign organization. And organized labor's formal endorsements of Democratic presidential candidates
accurately symbolized this major alteration in its political behavior. . . ."[11]
   One of the major labor endorsements of a Democratic presidential candidate had come in 1936 when the CIO supported Roosevelt. "Mindful that
an unfriendly president in the White House might spell the doom of his dream
of organizing the unorganized," John L. Lewis, through a combination of
loans and outright contributions, supplied the Roosevelt campaign with nearly
half a million dollars.[12] Lewis, however, did not identify the New Deal with
the Democratic party, and believed that after Roosevelt the Democratic party
would "revert to its pre-depression, pre-Roosevelt character, and there would
then be no substantial difference between the Democratic party and the Republican party."[13] As he saw it, labor should carry the New Deal "to a point
where a solid progressive labor-farmer base could be developed" that would
provide the means to control the Democratic party if possible or to begin a

third party if necessary.[14] By 1939, "Lewis was becoming increasingly interested in the establishment of a third political party."[15]

Lewis's plans for a third party never materialized; Roosevelt's decision
to seek a third term, combined with Lewis's anger over what he considered
the president's perfidious neutrality toward labor and management, drove
Lewis into his famous endorsement of Wendell Wilkie. Immediately after that
endorsement, Walter Reuther, then a member of the UAW executive board
responded in a thirteen-city radio address, assuring his listeners that "American labor will take Roosevelt!"[16] There is a certain irony in the fact that
Reuther, who was attacking Lewis on behalf of Roosevelt, would very soon
be entertaining the same fears and considering the same alternatives that had
led Lewis toward third-party politics. The irony was to be compounded when
Reuther's contemplation of third-party politics, like Lewis's, was ended by an
unexpected and unforeseen event in electoral politics.

In February, 1951, *Fortune* magazine published an article describing the
apparent reconciliation of Walter Reuther to the established, capitalist scheme
of things. The contract Reuther had negotiated with General Motors (GM)
was said to be the first

> that unmistakably accepts the existing distribution of income between wages and
> profits as "normal" if not as "fair." As such it was the first major union contract
> that explicitly accepts objective economic facts—cost of living and productiv-
> ity—as determining wages, thus throwing overboard all theories of wages as
> determined by political power, and of profit as "surplus value."[17]

Reuther's agreement to the GM contract was seen as marking a departure
from the Walter Reuther who had "believed in the class struggle, in some
form of socialism, and in a labor party to bring about the 'necessary change
in the system.' "[18] The departure was not so great as *Fortune* imagined.

Reuther's adherence to both socialism and third-party politics had been
considerably more tentative than was alleged. It is true that in 1932 both
Walter and Victor Reuther supported Norman Thomas for the presidency,
believing that a strong socialist showing that year would lead to victory in
1936. The basis for this expectation, however, was not a sectarian commitment but a belief that the two major parties would be discredited.[19] Roosevelt
and the New Deal caused Reuther to reconsider what labor's political approach
should be. According to one of Reuther's earliest allies,

> [the] New Deal in fact met the program of immediate demands that the Socialists
> were concerned with. Once they, and I include myself in this, were convinced
> that Roosevelt was for the same things the Socialists were for, then the pursuit

of short run objectives overshadowed long range aims. That Roosevelt wasn't going to nationalize the means of production was ignored precisely because there was now a fighting chance to get something that was worthwhile.[20]

Not every socialist was persuaded that Roosevelt and the New Deal required that third-party politics give way to support for the Democratic party. In 1938 Reuther split from "more doctrinaire Socialists" who "preferred to back their own candidate" rather than endorse the reelection of Michigan Governor Frank Murphy.[21] Murphy had played what was perhaps the decisive role in the successful, and peaceable, settlement of the 1937 sit-down strike.[22] Having witnessed the importance of at least political neutrality, if not political support, to the union's organizational efforts, Reuther had "pressed for all-out support of the Democratic governor."[23] Reuther failed to obtain vigorous union support for Murphy, and the Republican candidate, Frank Fitzgerald, became Michigan's new governor.

The risks involved in third-party politics were apparent, at least to those who were coming to have the means by which to exercise influence within the existing political arrangements. The New Deal, by taking over the immediate demands of the socialists, had obtained the loyalties of some, but by no means all, of the third-party socialists. Those whose loyalties it did attract were mainly those who, like Reuther, were fast coming into positions of power and responsibility within the trade union movement. By permitting and even encouraging the growth of unions, the New Deal, whether deliberately or not, had given many of those who would otherwise have become the leading elements of the socialist movement great encouragement to remain in the mainstream of American politics. Years later Victor Reuther explained his own and his brother's loss of interest in the socialist party:

> I think it was the feeling that you really can't do anything significant in the political field unless you've got some kind of organized base to operate from. And the trade union movement offered far greater possibilities for social gains and legislative improvement than did the vehicle of a political party.[24]

By 1944 the question of third-party politics seemed settled in the mind of Walter Reuther. That year a number of secondary UAW leaders, most of whom still believed that only a labor party would represent working-class demands, organized the Michigan Commonwealth Federation (MCF). On the assumption that blue-collar workers would support third-party candidates who had a realistic chance of success, the MCF entered candidates for both a state senate and a congressional seat in a district where a majority of the voters were union members. Along with the rest of the UAW executive board, Reuther went on record as opposing the attempt of the MCF to establish a third party.[25] The MCF did not succeed. Attracting less than 1 percent of the vote cast in the state senate contest and only 1.5 percent in the congressional election, it disappeared as an organized political party.[26]

Shortly after his refusal to support the MCF's third-party bid, Reuther made it clear that he also rejected collective bargaining techniques in which labor consulted only the immediate interests of its membership. During the 1946 contract dispute with GM, "Reuther set forth the philosophy that the UAW could move ahead only 'with the community and not at the expense of the community.' "[27] That this sentiment was not rooted in simple altruism is evidenced by Reuther's assertion that the success of a strike against General Motors, "will in large part, depend upon public opinion."[28] Reuther believed the union could secure improvements for its membership, whether through collective bargaining or political action, only if it were able to attract allies from the broader community. In collective bargaining, this meant convincing the public that what labor obtained from management need not bring about higher prices. Thus, in the 1946 GM negotiations Reuther proposed, much to the consternation of management, that the company agree not to raise prices as a result of any wage increase. He also proposed that the company open its books so that the public might determine the validity of GM's insistence that it could not afford a 30 percent increase in wages.[29] In political action, the ability to attract allies depended on participation in an electorally effective coalition.

Labor's rejection of third-party politics was based on the belief that Roosevelt and the New Deal were the best allies it had ever possessed. With the passing of Roosevelt, however, the New Deal seemed more and more in jeopardy. In the judgment of the UAW's leadership, this was occasioned not so much by the resurgence of Republicanism as by the refusal of President Harry S. Truman to pursue the progressive policies of his predecessor. In an internal document, the UAW placed full responsibility for the Democratic defeat in the 1946 congressional campaign on Truman's apparent apostasy: "The few congressmen who campaigned on a real New Deal program had to apologize or ignore the head of their party, President Truman. They had to explain the disgraceful failure of Truman and his administration."[30] Disillusionment with Truman did not begin with the results of the 1946 congressional campaign; it had become evident to Reuther months earlier that a continuation of the New Deal was not likely in the post-Roosevelt Democratic party. It appeared that the coalition of interests that had been called into being by the New Deal, and that had in turn become its main support, would have to begin to look to itself rather than to the existing Democratic organization for a progressive political party. Therefore, on April 25, 1946, Reuther submitted to the executive board "A Program for UAW-CIO Members" advocating precisely this.

Recognizing the need for a reorientation of political forces in America along lines that truly reflect basic economic, social and political issues, we stand for independent political action. Labor should join hands with farmers, professionals, small business and other functional groups to work toward the eventual formation of a broad new progressive party which will truly represent the needs of our nation and its people.

To avoid creating the impression that he was willing to support a labor party of the sort fashioned by the founders of the MCF and to underline his intention that this new party be in fact a continuation of the New Deal Democratic party, Reuther added: "Such a movement cannot succeed if it is launched prematurely and on a narrow basis."[31]

After the 1946 election, sentiment for a third party remained. It continued to be accompanied, however, by an insistence that it not be launched prematurely—that is, not without the active support of those who had joined together under the New Deal. "A basic condition for a successful third party movement must be the agreement and unity of labor, liberal and minority groups; also farm organizations and progressive independent political groups along with their leaders who supported Roosevelt."[32] Though support within the UAW for a third party may have been at its zenith in 1936, as Irving Howe and B. J. Widick argued in *Walter Reuther and the UAW*,[33] the period between the 1946 congressional elections and the 1948 presidential election was clearly the high-water mark of third-party sentiment within the UAW while Walter Reuther was its leading force. In March, 1948 the UAW international executive board adopted "as its official political objective the formation after the 1948 national elections of a genuine progressive political party."[34] Though the UAW followed the CIO's endorsement of Truman, it did so without enthusiasm and without unanimity; Emil Mazey, for example, announced he would once again cast his ballot for Norman Thomas.[35] The executive board did not even wait for the election to schedule an educational conference for January 19, 1949, the date on which nearly everyone expected Thomas Dewey to be inaugurated President of the United States, to prepare for the formation of a third-party movement.[36]

While Walter Reuther and the UAW were exploring the possibilities of third-party politics, the CIO, of which the UAW was a part—if in this respect a somewhat independent part—was firmly reasserting its intention to remain within the traditional two-party system. When the CIO's Political Action Committee was formed on July 11, 1943, Sidney Hillman had expressed at least tentative opposition to a third party: "We are opposed to the organization of a third party at this time because it would divide the forces of progressives throughout the nation."[37] Nor did this opposition disappear with the succession of Harry Truman to the presidency. Shortly before the 1946 congressional election, Jack Kroll, then director of the CIO Political Action Committee, wrote: "The CIO-PAC from its inception, and of today, is not a third party movement."[38] Kroll reiterated this policy in the 1948 presidential campaign, stating, "It has been the policy of the CIO Political Action Committee not to support a third party."[39] By a thirty-three to eleven vote, the CIO executive board decided it was "politically unwise to inject a third party into the political scene of 1948."[40]

The head of the Michigan CIO-PAC was in something of a predicament. On the one hand, the national CIO-PAC had consistently adhered to a policy of opposition to third-party politics. On the other hand, the UAW, which had a working majority on the state CIO-PAC, was seriously considering formation of a third party. It would appear, on the basis of the record alone, that the state CIO-PAC decided in 1948 to follow the direction set by the UAW rather than that announced by the national CIO. At the state CIO convention in 1948, a resolution was introduced and adopted that called for a national conference to discuss political realignment and the possibility of a third party. That a qualifying phrase stating that the call for a conference would issue only in the event Truman was defeated was added at the end of the resolution did not seem very important. It was, nevertheless, the key to the tactic adopted by the president of the state CIO, August "Gus" Scholle.

Scholle had never been an advocate of third-party politics. Why he agreed to a resolution advocating a third party is perhaps best explained by one of Scholle's closest associates, Tom Downs:

> Scholle and Emil Mazey were close friends. There was no essential disagreement between them with respect to political objectives. They differed, however, over the question of a third party. Mazey wanted it and Scholle didn't. They differed on something else. Mazey and just about every other labor leader knew Truman was going to lose. Gus somehow or other knew he was going to win. So when Mazey started pushing this third party resolution, Gus said he wanted to add a little qualifying language, sort of clean it up so they wouldn't be embarrassed if Truman won. Mazey told Gus that if he wanted to do it go ahead but he knew Truman would lose. I suppose you could say Gus and Emil compromised and Gus took all the marbles. He had a funny way of working things out like that.[41]

Scholle's reasons for opposing the formation of a third party went beyond the immediate question of the 1948 presidential election. He had already begun work that would involve labor in a coalition that had as its principal objective the capture of the Michigan Democratic party.

When Franklin Roosevelt was elected to the presidency in 1932, it marked the end of Republican and the beginning of Democratic dominance. The party that had saved the union from permanent political division was seen as incompetent to solve the problem of economic depression. Through four successive elections, Roosevelt and the New Deal commanded majority support in the country, while Democratic majorities were regularly returned to the Congress. What was true of the nation as a whole, however, was not always true of some of the states. Not every state voted Democratic, and not every state Democratic organization eagerly embraced the New Deal. In Michigan, in fact, the election of Roosevelt and the advent of the New Deal were accompanied neither by regular Democratic majorities nor by a transformation of the state Democratic party into an organization imbued with the liberal principles of the New Deal. If anything, the election of Roosevelt in 1932 brought about an intensification of the principle that had informed the state party organization for three quarters of a century.

Since 1856 Michigan had been a one-party state. With few exceptions, the most notable of which was the election and reelection of Governor Woodbridge Ferris in 1912 and 1914, the Republican party dominated state politics. With little hope of electing Democrats to state offices, those who involved themselves in the party organization had as their sole inducement for doing so the prospect of whatever patronage might become available under a Democratic national administration. After the 1932 election it seemed that the public trough was about to run over. When the new Congress convened, each congressman found on his desk a 421-page document listing some 150,000 jobs in the federal government not subject to the civil service. Eight hundred of these, exclusive of postmasterships, were located in Michigan.[42] The state party was not slow to acquire the fruits of victory. "The party organization, truly, presents a curious spectacle in that virtually every one of its officials either has cornered a public job for himself or is engaged in the pursuit of one."[43] Having obtained positions more lucrative than those they had possessed before, party officials wanted nothing so much as to keep them. This interest in their own economic well-being had a really remarkable political consequence.

The quest for and enjoyment of patronage have often been cited as the lifeblood of an electorally effective political machine.[44] In Michigan during the New Deal the availability of federal patronage had the peculiar effect of motivating party members to do even less than before to elect Democrats to statewide positions. The logic, if perverse, was persuasive. Federal patronage was awarded in conformity with the wishes of the highest-ranking Democrat in a state. Where, as in Michigan, neither the governor nor either of the U.S. Senators was a Democrat, the national committeeman became the conduit of federal largess. Unlike a governor or a senator, the national committeeman was under the control of the party organization, and, as it was the party organization that had supplied so many worthy individuals with public employment, any alteration of the arrangement was unlikely to engender feelings of security in its beneficiaries.

Throughout the Roosevelt administration the Michigan Democratic party had as its sole preoccupation the reelection of the president. The two Democrats who were elected to the governorship, Frank Murphy in 1936 and Murray Van Wagoner in 1940, both succeeded without any apparent assistance from the state party organization. Murphy was elected almost without an organization of any kind and did little to create one during his single two-year term as governor. Van Wagoner, on the other hand, had a well-developed political apparatus at his disposal, but it was not the state party. As state highway commissioner, he had built what the *Detroit News* called "one of the most powerful political machines Michigan has ever seen."[45] Van Wagoner's organization, however, built upon the state patronage available to the head of the highway department, dissolved under the combined impact of Republican victory in 1942 and civil service reform.[46]

The importance attached to the position of national committeeman was perhaps best exemplified in 1944 when the political demise of Van Wagoner led to a contested gubernatorial primary. This was "an almost comic campaign . . . among three candidates each of whom appeared to be little more than a front man for an aspirant to the national committeemanship."[47] It was more than mere appearance. E. Cyril Bevin, a supporter of Edward J. Fry who won the nomination, became the new national committeeman. In November Fry became the defeated candidate for governor.[48]

With a party organization interested almost exclusively in the maintenance of federal patronage, the Michigan Democrats were as unprepared as they were uninterested in contesting elections with Republicans. The 1946 campaign in Michigan was little less than a Republican landslide. Arthur Vandenberg was returned to the U.S. Senate with a more than 300,000-vote margin over his Democratic opponent. Kim Sigler was reelected by a margin almost as great in his contest with former Governor Van Wagoner. Democrats failed to reelect some of their incumbent congressmen and after the election found themselves with only three of Michigan's seventeen members of Congress. All the state offices were taken by Republicans, and Democratic representation in the state legislature was virtually nonexistent. Of the one-hundred-member House of Representatives, only five were Democrats. In the state senate twenty-eight of the thirty-two members were Republicans. Perhaps most distressing to those who had any concern about the electoral future of the Democratic party was its failure even to carry Wayne County, which in 1944 had supplied seven-and-one-half times as many voters as the second largest county in the state and had supported the Democratic gubernatorial candidate, Edward Fry, by a margin of nearly three-to-two.

The overwhelming Democratic defeat was seen by the Republican party, and the automobile companies that had come to control much of it, as an opportunity to further erode the strength of the already weak Michigan labor laws. Though they had participated in an occasional political campaign before, the auto companies "made their first systematic attempt to influence the selection of county convention delegates and thus gain a share of interest and control" within the state Republican party in 1940.[49] In Genesee County, Arthur Summerfield, one of the largest Chevrolet dealers in the country, gained control of the county organization. In Wayne County, the Ford people became active. The notorious Harry Bennett "provided a number of Ford employees to run for delegate under the ostensible leadership of old-timer John Gillespie whose insurance company handled a good deal of Ford business."[50] By 1946 the influence of the auto companies was considerable, not only within the party organization but among Republican members of the state legislature. General Motors and the Ford Motor Company may not have "run the legislature," as some Democrats charged, but on legislation that mattered to them they got what they wanted. What they wanted when the newly elected legislature met in January, 1947, was the virtual emasculation of the Workmen's Compensation Act. Lawyers, most of whom were in the employ of GM, drafted what came to be known as the Bonine-Tripp amendments to the Michigan labor law. The automobile lobby "helped jam the amendments through the legislature," and Governor Sigler signed them into law.[51]

Though it was little noted at the time by what seemed an omnipotent Republican party, the Bonine-Tripp amendments were viewed by the state CIO as a provocation, and served to propel them into the state Democratic party. According to Neil Staebler, who eventually would do as much as anyone, and considerably more than most, to fashion a new Democratic party in Michigan, Gus Scholle of the state CIO "was much aroused by this; he vowed then to do something about throwing the Republicans out."[52] Passage of the Taft-Hartley Act by the Republican Eightieth Congress "stimulated labor political action" on the national level[53] and served to intensify Scholle's belief that defeating the Republicans was the only course for the labor movement in Michigan.

Antilabor legislation at both the state and federal levels increased Scholle's determination to bring at least the Michigan CIO into the Democratic party. Unlike Reuther and the UAW, Scholle never had the slightest interest in third-party politics.[54] "A lot of UAW people were inclined toward a Socialist party. They sort of lived in another world. Scholle was always a Democrat."[55] Scholle's lack of interest in third parties is attributable, at least in part, to the position he held within the CIO. While Reuther spent years involved in a factional struggle for control of the UAW—a struggle, moreover, that was often conducted as a battle between socialists and communists—Scholle held a more secure position within what was, relatively speaking, a more settled organization. In addition, almost from the beginning of his career with the Michigan CIO Scholle was not engaged in the more specifically economic activities of unions; he never was really involved in collective bargaining, for example. Instead, he was almost constantly involved in political activities. While Reuther was engaged first in acquiring and then in exercising control of an international union, Scholle devoted himself almost exclusively to Michigan politics.

Sensing very early what Marx and Engels had noted in the nineteenth century, that workers, whether organized or not, were unlikely to throw away their votes on candidates of minor parties, Scholle viewed the involvement of labor in the state Democratic party as his main objective. This involvement, he believed, would strengthen the party's prospect for electoral success, and, at least as important, would bring it into compliance with the political principles prominently articulated in the New Deal. According to one of the early organizers of the UAW, and one of the earliest supporters of Walter Reuther, the "UAW was never very clear about their aim in politics. Gus, on the other hand, knew what his aim was." Although Scholle was almost alone in the labor movement in his early and consistent recognition of the need to assert labor's interests in the state Democratic party, a new and growing group of liberals shared his belief that the existing state organization was neither liberal nor effective.

The 1946 elections had been at least as upsetting to a young Detroit attorney as they had been to Gus Scholle. G. Mennen Williams, who had served under Frank Murphy both when Murphy was governor and when he was U.S. attorney general, had long since exchanged the views he had held as head of the Young Republicans of Princeton for those of an ardent New Dealer. Along with his law partner, Hicks Griffiths, Williams began searching for a means by which to revivify the Democratic party. Informal discussions among a small group of friends led to a suggestion by Williams that "they ought to enlarge the discussion group and get a wider sampling of political opinion."[56]

As a consequence, the first organizational meeting of liberal Democrats was held on November 21, 1947, in the basement of Hicks Griffiths's home. Among those attending were several who would later rise to positions of prominence in the state party and in Michigan politics. Neil Staebler, who would serve as state chairman for almost ten of the twelve years that Williams was governor, came from Ann Arbor. Noel Fox, whom Williams would appoint to the bench, came from Muskegon. Hicks Griffiths would serve as the first state chairman under the newly formed liberal-labor coalition, and his wife Martha would serve twenty years as a member of Congress and be elected Lieutenant Governor in 1982.[57] One person in attendance had already achieved a certain measure of political success. John Gibson, assistant secretary of labor, had come from Washington to see what could be done to rebuild the state party. Before becoming assistant secretary of labor, Gibson had been head of the Labor Department in Michigan during the Van Wagoner administration. He had also been at one time chairman of the Wayne County CIO, and numbered among his closest friends Gus Scholle. Thus at the very first meeting of the liberal group, it was evident that they were interested in labor as an ally and that labor was interested in them.

On what seemed the realistic assumption that capture of the party organization would require at least a decade of hard work, the liberal Democrats decided to begin organizing Democratic clubs throughout the state. As the liberals' organizational base, the clubs would sponsor precinct delegate candidates in order to acquire influence at county and district conventions of the regular party. The liberals hoped that the clubs would enable them eventually to acquire majorities of precinct delegates and therewith control of the state party organization. To assist these efforts, Williams inquired whether it might help if he ran for governor. There was a division of opinion, but the group finally decided to "talk up Mennen Williams as a possible candidate for governor."[58]

The November meeting was followed by several others. In early December it was decided to hold meetings anywhere it appeared they could make inroads "on decadent organizations."[59] The first of these was held that same month in Ann Arbor, and more than a hundred people turned out. The next month in Flint and the following month in Grand Rapids, the liberals went about the business of organizing the dissident Democrats. In each city they established a Democratic club and "made contacts with labor groups."[60] By March the liberals had formally organized themselves as the Michigan Democratic Club and elected a board of directors. With Hicks Griffiths working as a full-time organizer, clubs were soon established in Detroit and in most of the other large cities.[61] At the time of the spring convention of the state Democratic party, Democratic clubs were solidly ensconced in a dozen cities. But although "the movement was a definitely recognizable threat to the party management," it was still only a minority, if a rather bothersome one.[62] To have any real prospect of taking over the formal mechanism of the state party, the liberals needed a strong ally, and in March, 1948, they got it.

According to one account, as early as 1947 the reform Democrats invited Gus Scholle "to join in discussions aimed at combining liberal forces and seizing the Democratic party machinery."[63] Though Scholle had not attended the liberals' initial organizational meeting at the Griffiths' home, he was well aware of their plans and progress. In addition to John Gibson's participation, the Michigan CIO had been directly represented in the liberal group by Webb Magner and Harold Marsh of Jackson.[64] Scholle's first meeting with Williams took place at the beginning of 1948, when Williams invited him to drive to Bay City, where both were scheduled to address a convention of the Brewery Workers. It was during this trip that Williams mentioned to Scholle that he was considering the possibility of becoming a candidate for governor.[65] Scholle did not believe a Williams candidacy would have a prayer.[66] He was very interested, however, in securing liberal allies with whom to reclaim the state party from its conservative leadership.

Scholle then took what was to be the most important single step for the formation and the success of the incipient liberal-labor alliance. At the state CIO-PAC conference in Lansing on March 13, 1948, a formal resolution was approved which brought the CIO into the state Democratic party:

> Progressives and liberals within the Democratic party have often been out-numbered by conservative and reactionary elements. The PAC is unanimous in its opinion that the best way of supporting liberalism within the Democratic party, to conform to the national CIO policy, and to serve the best interests of Michigan labor is to join the Democratic party.

In fact, the intention was not to join the party as it then existed but to change it.

> It is our objective in adopting this policy to remold the Democratic party into a real liberal and progressive political party which can be subscribed to by members of the CIO and other liberals.

The resolution then indicated the method the CIO would use to effect the requisite change.

> We therefore advise CIO members to become active precinct, ward, county, and congressional district workers, and to attempt to become delegates to Democratic conventions.[67]

With passage of the PAC resolution, the state CIO and the newly-formed liberal Democratic clubs were allied in pursuit of a double purpose: the election of G. Mennen Williams as governor and the seizure of the regular Democratic party machinery. In both endeavors the major obstacle was not the strength of the regular party organization as such, but the political ambition of another segment of the trade union movement.

From 1928 to 1940 the Republican party in Wayne County was under the control of Edward N. Barnard, an attorney for the Detroit and Wayne County Federation of Labor. With the assistance of the Wayne County AFL's president, Frank X. Martel, Barnard "recruited his candidates for delegates from the local AFL membership and after their election held them in line with entertainment, food, and drink, which were hard to come by in Depression days."[68] Martel's Republican affiliation ended in 1934, when, "having been heaved bodily out of the Wayne County Republican convention" during a factional struggle, he endorsed the Democratic slate.[69] Martel, however, was unable then or later to give political direction to the AFL as a whole. The traditional structural independence of the AFL unions, along with the personal ambitions of some of the leaders of the affiliated unions, made any attempt to exercise control extremely difficult.[70] Nevertheless, Martel tried. The Wayne County AFL was little more than a forum for the discussion of common problems, but Martel saw in it the means by which he

> could become a big frog in a small puddle. He wanted to control every union. He did not represent union members; he represented organizations. But Martel was very capable and ruthless and he was able to control people who headed up some of the unions. He got the building trades, for example, by picking his own people to take it over. Martel once said "the way to become a big man is to have a lot of little men working for you."[71]

Martel's method, based as it was on the assumption that he could control "little men," led him to believe that he was the only "big man" in the Wayne County AFL. This in turn caused what was perhaps the greatest error of judgment he ever made, an error that more than anything else prevented the AFL from exercising even a semblance of unified political influence. In the late thirties he remarked to an ambitious young union officer, "Someday you'll make a good business agent."[72] Jimmy Hoffa never forgot it.

In 1931 Hoffa, along with a few others, obtained a charter from the AFL and formed a local union. The next year "they moved into the Teamsters Union and a year later Hoffa was in charge of Local 299 of the International Brotherhood of Teamsters in Detroit."[73] Having begun as the leader of a union with only a few hundred members, Hoffa had by the early 1940s "formed and headed the Michigan Conference of Teamsters and pulled all of the locals in the state into his widening power base."[74] After World War II, the Teamsters appeared to be seeking influence within the state Democratic party. "Many members of that union were elected to the county convention of 1946," and at the party's 1947 spring convention John Franco of Pontiac was elected state chairman with Teamster support.[75]

A year later Hoffa's intention seemed clear both to liberal Democrats and the CIO. "Working through carefully selected delegates and apparently expending an enormous sum of money, Hoffa succeeded in electing his personal attorney, George S. Fitzgerald, as the Democratic National Committeeman."[76] Convinced that Hoffa had expended as much as $65,000 in order to have one of his lieutenants in a position to quash federal indictments against him, the liberal Democrats believed the Teamsters had embarked upon the utter corruption of the state Democratic party.[77] The CIO "recognized this as a drive to seize the state Democratic party to exercise influence through it at the national level."[78] The reaction of the liberals and the CIO to Fitzgerald's election as national committeeman presupposed not only that Hoffa sought to capture the state party, but that Fitzgerald was nothing more than Hoffa's legal and political mouthpiece. Fitzgerald, however, denied both assumptions. According to Fitzgerald, "Hoffa was a lot like a mischevious boy, like a boy who would break a couple of windows and run behind the barn and laugh."[79] In Fitzgerald's judgment, Hoffa's main political interest in 1948 was to cause as much trouble as he could for Walter Reuther and Gus Scholle, especially Scholle. His antagonism toward Scholle was rooted in jurisdictional disputes between the Teamsters and the CIO. A few years earlier Hoffa had decided to organize not only truckers but food workers, a tactic which, if successful, would enable the Teamsters to take control of warehouse workers. The next step would be the organization of workers in retail outlets. This strategy brought Hoffa into direct conflict with Scholle, who had no choice but to support the claims of the CIO retail workers against those of the AFL retail workers. Hoffa saw that as a CIO move aimed at eventually wresting control of the warehouse workers from the Teamsters. The antagonism intensified when the state CIO leaders entered into an alliance with Frank Martel to stop Hoffa's rise in "labor politics."[80] And when Scholle led the CIO into the state Democratic party, Hoffa saw yet another personal challenge. When it was clear that Scholle was backing Williams for the Democratic gubernatorial nomination, Hoffa was prepared to lend his support to Victor Bucknell as a possible opponent. Unlike Scholle, however, Hoffa was not a political organizer.

> Hoffa was more of an adventurer in politics. The Teamsters had moved into the Democratic party in 1946 but never really got involved; they always kept themselves somewhat independent. The whole theory behind Teamster political action was to support individual candidates. Hoffa went with Bucknell because he thought it would raise some hell for Scholle and Reuther who were supporting Williams. Reuther and Scholle held themselves out as "holier than thous," as opposed to the "racketeering" Hoffa. When Bucknell got in they painted him as the racketeering candidate."[81]

Convinced that Bucknell was owned by Hoffa, the liberal-CIO coalition was certain that Fitzgerald's candidacy for national committeeman was a well-designed move by Hoffa to assist Bucknell's gubernatorial campaign. Fitz-

gerald's victory at the national convention, however, owed at least as much
to a politically fatal decision by E. Cyril Bevin as it did to Teamster influence.
As the Michigan national committeeman, Bevin, along with a number of
others, including Chicago's Jake Arvey, became involved in an attempt to
nominate Dwight Eisenhower instead of Harry Truman.[82] His involvement
with the anti-Truman forces had been covert, and when the story broke he
"looked like Brutus to Caesar. Anybody could have beaten Bevin after that."[83]

Despite the fact that it had been Bevin's own unsuccessful machinations
that had made him politically vulnerable, Democratic liberals in Michigan
remained convinced that Fitzgerald had been elected by, and was directly
accountable to, Jimmy Hoffa. Hoffa seemed to share this opinion. Almost
immediately after his election as the new national committeeman, Fitzgerald
was asked to endorse Bucknell's gubernatorial candidacy. He had reservations.
In the first place, he was dubious about some of the support Bucknell was
receiving, especially the endorsements of John Franco and Viola Henderson,
chair and vice-chair of the state party organization. He was suspicious of their
motives and was also concerned about Hoffa's involvement. He had begun
to believe that Hoffa had gone too far into "this political thing." Unlike almost
everyone else who was ever around Hoffa, Fitzgerald was willing to tell him
what he thought and get away with it. "Our relation by this time was more
than that between lawyer and client. It was something like that between an
older and a younger brother."[84] With reservations about some of the people
backing Bucknell, and with the belief that Hoffa was overextending himself
politically, Fitzgerald refused to endorse Bucknell's candidacy.

At almost the same time that Fitzgerald was refusing to go along with
Hoffa's gubernatorial choice, several people who had supported Fitzgerald
for national committeeman decided to put a third candidate in the field. At
four in the morning following his election, Fitzgerald received a telephone
call from Frank Kelley, Sr., of Wayne County. Kelley, who was the chairman
of the Michigan delegation, thought very little of Williams and Bucknell.
Kelley informed Fitzgerald that a group had decided that Bernie Abbott of
Albion should run. He wanted to know whether Fitzgerald would have any
objection if they asked Abbott to enter the race. Fitzgerald "told them that
I had no objection and would not oppose their support for Abbott." Fitzgerald
refused to endorse Bucknell and refused to oppose Abbott; Hoffa was livid.
"Jimmy and I had a very bitter quarrel about this."[85]

Abbott's candidacy may very well have made the difference between
victory and defeat in the gubernatorial primary. William's biographer refers
to Abbott's entrance into the primary contest as "an unexpected break." "His
entry confused and to a degree split up the groups supporting Bucknell, the
Teamsters' candidate, and in some instances Teamster unions gave Abbott
their support."[86] Abbott, who was reluctant to run in the first place, did not

care much for campaigning and did very little of it. He managed, nevertheless, to take votes away from Bucknell in the outstate area. With his two opponents hurting each other, Williams was able to win the primary with a plurality of 8,000 votes, but with less than 39 percent of the total votes cast. Even with this indirect assistance, however, Williams's victory depended on the vote in Wayne County. His margin of victory was 8,000 votes, but his plurality in Wayne County was 12,000. That plurality was in large measure the direct result of the organizational activities of the CIO.

Unlike Hoffa, Scholle was a brilliant political organizer, and unlike Reuther, he clearly understood why he wanted a political organization. Scholle, as we have seen, had managed in the early spring of 1948 to put the state CIO on record in favor of both entrance into the state Democratic party and the gubernatorial candidacy of G. Mennen Williams. In the summer Scholle took personal charge of a drive to recruit precinct delegate candidates in Wayne County. Of the 1,240 petitions filed for precinct delegate in the county, approximately 80 percent, or 1,000, "were representatives of CIO members and cooperating liberals."[87] Of the 1,000 candidates representing the liberal-labor coalition, no less than 75 percent ran at the behest of the state CIO. Recruitment of candidates was an important contribution of the CIO leadership to the construction of a political organization in the county, but it was not the only one. The CIO supplied every candidate with campaign literature that tied the particular candidate to the endorsed Democratic slate and to the general liberal principles the new coalition stood for. The most frequently used pamphlet or flyer had an American flag on the cover and displayed the name of G. Mennen Williams, as the gubernatorial candidate, along with the name of the particular precinct delegate candidate. Thus in every precinct in Wayne County where a CIO-recruited candidate was running, that candidate became the primary campaign worker not only for himself but for the liberal-labor slate as a whole. More than half of the precincts in the county had such candidate-workers. This was "the first time that any party group had ever organized people to run for precinct delegate and had tied them in with a program and a gubernatorial candidate."[88]

There is little doubt that it was successful. Seven hundred and twenty of the 1,000 liberal-labor candidates were elected. Perhaps more important for the future of the liberal-labor coalition was the fact, which emerged from a study conducted by the CIO after the primary, that it was precisely in those precincts where precinct delegate candidates used a flyer that connected them with Williams that Williams gained his margin of victory. "Where we had guys running for precinct delegate, Williams came out first. Where we didn't, he didn't."[89]

Williams had won the primary, but nearly everyone expected him to lose the general election. No Democrat was thought to have any chance against the incumbent Republican governor Kim Sigler, who in an unopposed primary had brought out to the polls 430,965 voters, while the three-man Democratic primary had attracted only 283,113.[90] Even the state CIO was reported as having decided that any expenditure of resources on the Williams campaign would be a useless extravagance. Less than two weeks before the general election, *Newsweek* magazine reported that the "CIO's Political Action Committee is devoting little attention to its local [Michigan] political candidates. The candidates the PAC supports, it supports casually [Frank Hook, Democratic candidate for the senate, and G. Mennen Williams, Democratic candidate for governor] and really gives them no chance of winning." For this reason, the PAC "is devoting its time, energy, and money to the congressional races."[91]

Not everyone believed that Sigler was invulnerable. One of the state's most prominent Democrats attended a meeting in the early part of 1948 at which Sigler was scheduled to be the principal speaker.

> Sigler was late. He finally rolls up in a limousine with a motorcycle escort. He took the mike away from the fellow then speaking and announced melodramatically that he had been warned not to come. But he was there to defy the Communists. I told my wife that if after that kind of performance Sigler could win an election I shouldn't be in politics.

Democrats were not the only ones who found Sigler's overweening manner offensive. Very serious schisms had opened and widened within the ranks of the Republican party because of Sigler's singularly arrogant treatment of party matters.[92] Still, Sigler was governor, and Williams, while not a political neophyte, was publicly an unknown. That he nevertheless managed to defeat Sigler rather quickly became in party lore the political equivalent to the biblical account of David and Goliath. In a party tract published in connection with the beginning of Williams's fourth term as governor, the "young man from nowhere" is described as having "in a weary convertible, swept across Michigan like a fresh breeze in politics. They [Williams and his wife] covered more than 12,000 miles, talking sense directly to the people, and the people recognized it."[93] Unlike David, however, Williams had not declined the armor offered by others.[94]

Four years earlier, in 1944, the "astonishing activity and efficiency of the CIO Political Action Committee in support of President Roosevelt was a major sensation. . . ."[95] Still, in the judgment of one observer, the work that year had been "sporadic, superficial, resting on Roosevelt."[96] In Michigan, labor had done little in Wayne County and even less outstate. "The CIO-PAC had made some inroads in the industrial area in and around Detroit but was ineffective in much of the rest of the state."[97] By the August, 1948, primary, however, it was clear that the state CIO-PAC, with remarkable speed and efficiency, had called into being a Wayne County organization fully capable of carrying the day for candidates it supported. It was this precinct-level organization that permitted Williams to conduct what appeared to many a quixotic journey to the far corners of the state. Williams simply ignored Wayne County until the very end of his campaign against Sigler. He concentrated instead on farm areas that the Republicans had taken for granted for years and on the industrial areas outside of Wayne County. Williams left "until the last the Detroit–Wayne County industrial region where the AFL-CIO union forces were helping to carry the campaign."[98] But matters there were well taken care of. In 1944, 875,119 votes had been cast for governor in Wayne County, 504,581 of these for the Democratic candidate, Edward J. Fry.[99] In 1946, 650,056 were cast, and the Democratic candidate received only 300,091, the first time in years that a Democrat had failed to carry the county. In 1948, with the new organizational power of the CIO-PAC, Wayne County alone supplied Williams with 47.9 percent of his total statewide vote.

The political organization created by the state CIO was designed to transform the state Democratic party into a vehicle for the perpetuation of the New Deal. With the election of Williams, it seemed that at least the single most important elective office in the state was about to be filled by a man with an identical goal. Shortly after his election, Williams, in response to an Associated Press story that claimed the governor-elect had no plans to bring a New Deal to Michigan, stated matter-of-factly, "Whoever said that didn't talk to me."[100] But while Williams clearly agreed with the CIO about the desirability of a New Deal in Michigan, the formal structure of the state party was still under the nominal direction of John Franco, for whom political issues were nothing so much as a bothersome distraction from the really important objectives of patronage and influence. Franco, however, was now a lame duck. With the capture of four of the six Wayne County congressional district organizations in the fall, the liberal-labor coalition had acquired the power to remove Franco at the regular spring convention of the state party. The new coalition had elected a governor and was in position to control a party. The prodigious CIO political organization had enabled the fledgling liberal-labor alliance to go much further than anyone a year earlier would have dared imagine.

Notes

1. Grant McConnell, *Private Power and American Democracy* (New York: Alfred A. Knopf, 1966), p. 299.
2. Charles Rhemus, Doris B. McLaughlin, and Frederick H. Nesbitt, *Labor and*

American Politics rev. ed. (Ann Arbor: University of Michigan Press, 1978), p. 155.

3. McConnell, *Private Power,* p. 303.

4. *United Auto Workers Weekly* 1 (October 3, 1933): 1.

5. Ibid.

6. Ibid., p. 2.

7. B. J. Widick, *Detroit: City of Race and Class Violence* (Chicago: Quadrangle Books, 1972), p. 65.

8. Doris B. McLaughlin, *Michigan Labor: A Brief History from 1818 to the Present* (Ann Arbor: Institute of Labor and Industrial Relations, 1970), p. 126.

9. Ibid., p. 127.

10. Quoted in Frank Cormier and William J. Eaton, *Reuther* (Englewood Cliffs, N.J.: Prentice-Hall, 1970), p. 165.

11. J. David Greenstone, *Labor in American Politics* (New York: Alfred A. Knopf, 1969), pp. 8–9.

12. Saul Alinsky, *John L. Lewis: An Unauthorized Biography* (New York: Putnam and Sons, 1949), p. 163.

13. Ibid., p. 170.

14. Ibid., p. 177.

15. Ibid., p. 170.

16. Quoted in Cormier and Eaton, *Reuther,* p. 169.

17. "The U.S. Labor Movement," *Fortune,* February, 1951, p. 92.

18. Ibid.

19. Cormier and Eaton, *Reuther,* p. 19; Victor Reuther, *The Brothers Reuther and the Story of the UAW* (Boston: Houghton Mifflin Co., 1976), p. 65.

20. All quoted material not otherwise referenced is drawn from confidential interviews conducted by the author.

21. Cormier and Eaton, *Reuther,* p. 144.

22. For a comprehensive treatment of the strike and Murphy's role in it, see Sidney Fine, *Sit-Down: The General Motors Strike of 1936–1937* (Ann Arbor: University of Michigan Press, 1969).

23. Cormier and Eaton, *Reuther,* p. 144.

24. Quoted in Cormier and Eaton, *Reuther,* p. 124.

25. Ibid., p. 278.

26. In the December, 1945, issue of *Fortune,* Reuther was quoted as stating that "instead of from Marx, the American political concept must grow from American soil." "Reuther: F.O.B. Detroit," *Fortune,* December, 1945, p. 282.

27. Jack Stieber, *Governing the UAW* (New York: John Wiley and Sons, 1962), p. 10.

28. Quoted in Cormier and Eaton, *Reuther,* p. 219.

29. See Walter P. Reuther, "This is your Fight," *Nation* 162 (November, 1946): 35. See also Department of Research and Education, CIO newsletter, *The Truth About the CIO,* November–December, 1945, p. 7, where it is argued that "From its formation, the CIO has concerned itself with the social and economic welfare of the nation as a whole, and has steadfastly refused to adopt a purely business unionism outlook."

30. Richard T. Leonard, *Report of the Political Action and Legislative Department, UAW-CIO to the Executive Board,* December, 1946.

31. Walter P. Reuther, *A Program for UAW-CIO Members,* memo to the International Executive Board, UAW-CIO April 25, 1946, p. 11. See also the December, 1945, issue of *Common Sense,* in which Victor Reuther, impressed by Atlee's victory over Churchill, argues for a new party.

32. Leonard, *Report,* p. 7.

33. Irving Howe and B. J. Widick, *The UAW and Walter Reuther* (New York: Random House, 1949), p. 272.

34. Summary of the UAW International Executive Board Meeting, March 1–5, 1948, quoted in Stieber, *UAW,* p. 37.

35. Ibid.

36. Howe and Widick, *UAW and Reuther,* p. 277.

37. Quoted in Matthew Josephson, *Sidney Hillman, Statesman of American Labor* (Garden City, N.Y.: Doubleday and Co., 1952), p. 596.

38. Jack Kroll, "Why Labor Is in Politics," *New York Times Magazine,* October 27, 1946, p. 15.

39. Quoted in Philip Taft, *Organized Labor in American History* (New York: Harper and Row, 1964), p. 612.

40. Ibid.

41. Tom Downs, interview with author, July 14,1971. A somewhat different version is supplied by Fay Calkins in *The CIO and the Democratic Party* (Chicago: University of Chicago Press, 1952), p. 142.

42. *Detroit News,* January 24, 1933.

43. *Detroit News,* May 7, 1933.

44. See for example Harold Gosnell, *The Machine* (Chicago: University of Chicago Press, 1937); Edward C. Banfield and James Q. Wilson, *City Politics* (Cambridge: Harvard University Press, 1963); James Bryce, *The American Commonwealth* (London: Macmillan and Co., 1891).

45. *Detroit News,* September 15, 1939. Quoted in Stephen B. Sarasohn and Vera H. Sarasohn, *Political Party Patterns in Michigan* (Detroit: Wayne State University Press, 1957), p. 47.

46. Cormier and Eaton, *Reuther,* p. 280.

47. Sarasohn and Sarasohn, *Party Patterns,* p. 34.

48. Ibid.

49. Ibid.

50. Ibid. For a more elaborate treatment of Ford's involvement see Keith Sward, *Henry Ford* (New York: Rinehart, 1948); Bennett's version can be found in Harry Bennett, *We Never Called Him Henry* (New York: Fawcett Publications, 1951).

51. Frank McNaughton, *Mennen Williams of Michigan: Fighter for Progress* (New York: Oceana Publishing, 1960), p. 151.

52. Neil Staebler, interview with author, May 1, 1971.

53. V. O. Key, Jr., *Politics, Parties, and Pressure Groups* (New York: Thomas Y. Crowell, 1964), p. 64; see also Taft, *Organized Labor,* p. 613.

54. However, Cormier and Eaton assert in their biography of Reuther that "A. Philip

Randolph, Gus Scholle, and others toyed with establishing a People's Party in 1946,"
Reuther, p. 279.

55. Adelaide Hart, interview with author, August 31, 1971.

56. McNaughton, *Mennen Williams,* p. 99.

57. Sarasohn and Sarasohn, *Party Patterns,* p. 55; McNaughton, *Mennen Williams,* p. 100; Neil Staebler, interview with author, May 1, 1971.

58. McNaughton, *Mennen Williams,* p. 101.

59. Ibid.

60. Ibid., p. 102.

61. Ibid.

62. Ibid., p. 103.

63. Cormier and Eaton, *Reuther,* p. 280.

64. Neil Staebler, interview with author, May 1, 1971.

65. McNaughton, *Mennen Williams,* pp. 104–5.

66. August Scholle, interview with author, September, 1971.

67. Quoted in Sarasohn and Sarasohn, *Party Patterns,* p. 55, and Cormier and Eaton, *Reuther,* p. 280.

68. Sarasohn and Sarasohn, *Party Patterns,* p. 27.

69. Ibid., p. 49.

70. Ibid.

71. George Fitzgerald, interview with author, June 22, 1972.

72. Ibid.

73. Walter Sheridan, *The Fall and Rise of Jimmy Hoffa* (New York: Saturday Review Press, 1972), p. 13.

74. Ibid., p. 14.

75. Sarasohn and Sarasohn, *Party Patterns,* p. 54; McNaughton, *Mennen Williams,* p. 96.

76. McNaughton, *Mennen Williams,* p. 103.

77. Neil Staebler, interview with author, May 1, 1971.

78. McNaughton, *Mennen Williams,* p. 103.

79. George Fitzgerald, interview with author, June 22, 1972.

80. Ibid.

81. Ibid.

82. Cabell Phillips, *The Truman Presidency,* (New York: Macmillan Co., 1966), p. 200. See also Margaret Truman, *Harry S. Truman* (New York: William Morrow, 1973), p. 7; Arthur Krock, *Memoirs: Sixty Years on the Firing Line* (New York: Funk and Wagnalls, 1968), pp. 242, 243; Harry S. Truman, *Years of Trial and Hope* (New York: Doubleday and Co., 1956), p. 185; Wilfred E. Binkley, *American Political Parties: Their Natural History* (New York: Alfred A. Knopf, 1963), p. 403.

83. George Fitzgerald, interview with author, June 22, 1972.

84. Ibid.

85. Ibid.

86. McNaughton, *Mennen Williams,* p. 111.

87. Sarasohn and Sarasohn, *Party Patterns,* p. 56.

88. Tom Downs, interview with author, June 13, 1973.

89. Tom Downs, interview with author, June 14, 1971.

90. Sarasohn and Sarasohn, *Party Patterns,* p. 56.

91. H. Levine, "Labor in Politics," *Newsweek,* October 25, 1948, p. 37.

92. Conservatives were particularly annoyed. See Neal R. Pierce, *The Megastates of America* (New York: W. W. Norton and Co., 1972), p. 419.

93. Michigan Democratic State Central Committee, *The Michigan Democratic Story 1948–1954* (Lansing, Mich.: Michigan Democratic Party, 1955).

94. See Niccolò Machiavelli, *The Prince,* (New York: St. Martin's Press, 1964), p. 115.

95. Binkley, *Political Parties,* p. 393.

96. Claire Neikind, "Ringing Doorbells with PAC," *New Republic,* October 25, 1948, p. 11.

97. Ibid.

98. McNaughton, *Mennen Williams,* p. 120. McNaughton incorrectly links the AFL and the CIO. The two organizations did not merge until 1955.

99. State of Michigan, *Official Canvass of Votes, General Primary and November Elections, July 11 and November 7, 1944* (Lansing, 1945), p. 52.

100. *Battle Creek Enquirer,* November 14, 1948.

CHAPTER 2

The Coalition in Power

In his political autobiography former Michigan Secretary of State James M. Hare claimed that by the middle of 1948 G. Mennen Williams "was able, with the help of Hicks Griffiths, Martha Griffiths, Horace Gilmore, James Lincoln and the Reuther brothers, Frank Martel of the AFL and the leaders of the black community, to take control of the Democratic party."[1] Hare is incorrect in two important respects. First, the labor contingent in the new liberal-labor alliance was represented not by the Reuthers, or even by Frank Martel, but by Gus Scholle. Second, it was not before but only after Williams's election as governor that the state Democratic party was taken over by the coalition. This is not to argue that the existing party organization under its chairman, John Franco, was anything like an effective political apparatus. The ability of the CIO-led forces to capture four of the six Wayne County congressional district organizations in 1948 had demonstrated not only the efficiency of the CIO-PAC but the absence of any real strength in the regular party organization. In the election campaign itself, Franco, along with the rest of the party elements who heeded his direction, was simply ignored.[2] After the election there was little question which faction of the party possessed predominant strength. That Franco remained in the chairmanship after Williams's victory was due solely to the fact that the next election of party officers would not take place until the winter of 1949.

Franco had no illusions about his political prospects; it was clear that the next state convention would replace him with a Williams supporter. For a time it appeared that Franco and the pro-Teamster forces who had elected him in 1947 would simply refuse to issue a convention call. Instead, two calls were issued, one by Franco and one by "The CIO-liberal group."[3] Since the convention was to select not only new party officers but candidates for positions on the state's administrative board, the possibility of two separate conventions raised the prospect of two different party slates, a prospect few Democrats cared to contemplate.[4] This consideration seems finally to have been persuasive; Franco and his allies decided against pursuing a strategy of competitive conventions. That did not mean, however, that Franco was interested in participating in his own political execution. When the convention convened in Grand Rapids during the first week of February, he was there, but only to observe. "Chairman John R. Franco . . . watched his own liquidation from the sidelines."[5] The Democrats "today pronounced him 'politically dead.' "[6] Hicks Griffiths, who had directed Williams's gubernatorial campaign, succeeded Franco as party chairman. Thus, in considerably less than the ten years that had been anticipated when it first came into being, the liberal-labor alliance had assumed control of the regular state party apparatus.[7]

It would be an understatement to assert that the convention was controlled by the liberal-labor alliance; it was entirely owned by it. There was no bargaining with other groups; there were no other groups with which to bargain. The regular organization was not captured; it was destroyed and replaced with an entirely new one. Every one of the sixty-eight members elected by the convention to the newly constituted Democratic state central committee was a member of the liberal-labor coalition.[8] Actually, it is more precise to say that the great majority of the members elected to the central committee were liberals. At first it seems astonishing that labor, which had almost single-handedly taken over the Wayne County Democratic party and carried the county for Williams in both the primary and general elections, received so little formal recognition in the new party organization. According to the newspaper accounts of the convention, "of the 68 members of the new state central committee, not more than 15 or 20 could be identified with unions."[9] Labor's minority position on the central committee seems stranger still in light of the fact that in "every top strategy conference, August Scholle, president of the Michigan CIO council and Robert Scott, secretary of the Michigan Federation of Labor were present or represented by spokesman."[10] It could not really have been a situation in which labor was outmaneuvered by a perfidious ally. In fact, liberals seem to have been quite aware of the importance of maintaining the support of labor in the convention, as evidenced in the selection of a slate of candidates for the spring election. "All through the sessions shaping the ticket, conferees were careful to avoid candidates to whom either Governor Williams or the CIO could object."[11] It seems a fair conclusion that power in the convention was equally distributed between the liberals and labor, and that the assent of both was required for the action of either. It follows that the disproportionate number of liberals on the central committee was an arrangement to which labor had willingly agreed. This would account for the manner in which labor relinquished the claim to an equal representation; it does not supply the reason that guided labor's decision.

Three years after the liberal-labor coalition came to power in the Michigan Democratic party, Fay Calkins argued that labor had necessarily to moderate its claims in such an arrangement. According to Calkins, "interest groups . . . provide objectives; parties provide a means of reaching these objectives."[12] Because it is beyond the resources of a single interest group to build a majority, it has to combine with others. This, however, requires each group to modify its own objectives to some degree. "They have to compromise and accommodate to each other."[13] At least in the beginning, however, the liberal-labor coalition in Michigan evinced virtual unanimity in its objectives and in the methods by which to attain them. Scholle and Williams were both ardent New Dealers who shared an overriding commitment to apply in Michigan what FDR had begun in the nation. The mutual attraction of liberals and labor was based not on the net benefit to be derived from the political power that would be gained when separate political aims were discarded, but on the identity of interests that already existed. Because the interests of the two members of the coalition were identical, the question of which of them had greater representation on the central committee had far less relevance than it would have had if the groups had been adversaries. More important, however, was the fact that whatever the size of its contingent on the central committee, labor's power within the new party organization was not likely to be underestimated. All of the members elected to the new central committee had reason to know that a substantial proportion of the votes that put them there were responsive to the CIO leadership.

Labor's minority representation on the central committee did not diminish its real power within the party. Indeed, there were reasons to believe that minority representation would benefit both the CIO and the Democratic party—reasons that were persuasive at least from the perspective of the CIO's political leadership. The political organization August Scholle had created was made up of union members for whom Scholle's leadership was an institutional given; as president of the state CIO, he wielded power over those below him in the union hierarchy. His influence in the Democratic party depended on his power over the union political organization, and as other members of that organization assumed elected positions in the party, a potential danger arose for both Scholle himself and the CIO as a whole. To the extent to which a CIO member played an independent part in the party leadership, Scholle's position in both the party and the union organization would be threatened. It would demonstrate to liberals that Scholle did not speak for a united labor movement, and for unionists it would open up the prospect of competing avenues of advancement within labor's political organization. Thus a rationale for minority representation on the central committee becomes clear. The larger the number of unionists holding party offices, the greater the potential danger to Scholle's position. With a relatively small group of trusted allies on the committee, Scholle could better protect himself. This was not by any means simply self-serving. Scholle's ability to assemble and to direct an effective—and indispensable—union political apparatus had been proven, to the extreme satisfaction of the liberals. They viewed the continued, and even improved, performance of the Michigan CIO-PAC as a necessary prerequisite for preserving and increasing their newly acquired political strength. Far from being the result of a necessary accommodation to the interest of other groups, labor's position as a distinct minority on the new central committee was a tactic for securing maximum, undivided CIO influence in the state party.

Much of the literature on American political parties conveys at least the impression that the dominant, if not the sole, concern of party leaders is the acquisition of enough support to win elections. According to Clinton Rossiter, for example, the "task that they have uppermost in mind is the construction of a victorious majority."[14] This understanding was formulated—if not originally, perhaps most persuasively—by Lord Bryce. Discussing "The Parties of To-day" in 1891, Bryce argued:

> Neither party has any principles, any distinctive tenets. Both have traditions. Both claim to have tendencies. Both certainly have war cries, organizations, interests enlisted in their support. But these interests are in the main the interests of getting or keeping the patronage of the government. Tenets and policies, points of political doctrine and points of political practice have all but vanished. They have not been thrown away but have been stripped away by time and the progress of events, fulfilling some policies, blotting out others. All has been lost, except office or the hope of it.[15]

His discussion, however, was concerned (as the chapter title indicated) with parties as they existed at a particular period—a period, moreover, that was in fact somewhat peculiar. It was characterized by an influx of immigrants into the larger cities on the Eastern Seaboard, unprecedented industrialization, and a concentration on private affairs in the aftermath of the Civil War. This combination produced political organizations based on the votes of an ignorant urban proletariat, staffed by men of limited perspective, and at least tolerated by those for whom personal gain and public service were irreconcilable. Within a few years of its publication Bryce's description of political parties in the United States in *The American Commonwealth* needed qualification. Although the urban machines did not disappear, the twin forces of populism and progressivism infused American politics and American political parties with a concern for matters beyond the acquisition of patronage.

Emphasis on principle did not replace patronage once and for all as the moving force in American party politics. Yet the temporary emergence of parties based on principle seems to be a recurrent and therefore constant phenomenon. It has been argued with considerable force that at fairly regular intervals a critical election takes place. A critical election is precisely one in which a great issue is decided. That decision in turn establishes the framework within which or the assumptions upon which political debate is conducted until the next critical election takes place.[16] As the vehicles through which candidates and their opinions contest elections, political parties may be expected to undergo similar recurrent transformations. Aroused by the prospect of a fundamental alteration in the existing scheme of things, large numbers of the previously uncommitted enter existing parties or new ones, and the parties quickly become the embodiment of the ruling passion or principle of their membership. After the issue has been decided, the critical election enthusiasm dissipates, the range of public debate narrows, the number of active participants in the party diminishes, and patronage once again becomes the main incentive to political involvement.[17]

After the election of Williams and the capture of the party chairmanship, the liberal-labor coalition was still very much caught up in the enthusiasm of reform. Rather than concentrating on ways to make the party more inclusive, which an organization that desired place and position would have done, the group began preparing "for the party housecleaning they intended to make in September in the county and district conventions."[18] Housecleaning meant quite simply the complete destruction of the Teamsters' political influence. What had become an intensely emotional commitment to the elimination of the Teamsters and their allies from participation in the Democratic party was caused only in part by the fact that Hoffa had inspired political opposition to Williams. The major cause was the repugnance with which the members of the liberal-labor coalition had witnessed the methods employed by the Teamsters to work their will. Gus Scholle, for example, claimed that the Teamsters had distributed close to forty thousand dollars among the Michigan delegation to the 1948 Democratic national convention to secure the election of George Fitzgerald as national committeeman, and that to enforce the obligations of contract several of Hoffa's lieutenants made themselves and their pistols visible at all times.

There were more witnesses to the behavior of the Teamster faction during the district convention battles of that year. The Seventeenth District provided a clear example of how the Teamsters operated politically. When the convention opened it was evident that this silk-stocking district, which regularly voted three-to-one Republican, contained some very able and effective new Democratic activitists. Two of them, Al Meyer and Adelaide Hart, were momentarily bewildered by what was taking place. The district chairman was Charles Nugent, a professor of law and an ally of the Teamsters. He was doing his best, or his worst, to negate a liberal-labor majority among the assembled delegates. On the crucial issue of the election of a permanent convention chairman, Nugent called for a voice vote. The liberals, refusing to cooperate with what seemed to them a blatant attempt to "railroad the convention," demanded a recorded vote. Nugent refused. For Al Meyer, a young teacher, that was unbelievable. "I couldn't understand how a law professor could refuse to have a recorded vote."[19] Despite Nugent's recalcitrance, a recorded vote was finally obtained, and to the surprise of absolutely no one, the Teamster faction was too small to prevent the election of Hicks Griffiths as chairman.

If the Teamsters had proven themselves difficult to trust, their decision to attempt, in 1950, to reverse the results of the party battles of 1948 did nothing to lessen suspicion. By the spring of 1950, the CIO and the liberals were convinced that their desire to eliminate the Teamsters was matched by an equal determination on the part of Hoffa and Fitzgerald to seize a position of dominance in the party. As the great majority of delegates to Democratic state conventions were from the six Wayne County congressional districts, the war would hinge on the outcome of the battle there. In May the "CIO and the liberals . . . began a countrywide roundup of delegate candidates."[20] No less than "3,600 candidates were entered in the county's 1,735 precincts, with contests in 1,113 precincts."[21] One attempt, and only one, was made to avert the impending confrontation between the Teamsters and the liberal-CIO alliance. Jack Kroll, head of the national CIO-PAC, and Joseph Kennan, of the AFL's League for Political Education, brought Hoffa, Fitzgerald, and Scholle "to a Washington peace conference."[22] A few days after this conference, the last vestige of hope for a negotiated settlement of differences vanished, "when the CIO and the liberals claimed to find evidence of wholesale violation of the laws governing nomination petitions."[23]

Liberals gave every evidence of genuine moral outrage when the fraudulent petitions were uncovered. It would seem they had good reason. The number of such petitions was staggering: 1,009 of them were challenged.[24] Many of them contained names written in an identical hand, in strict alphabetical order, lending support to the allegation they had simply been copied from the telephone book by a few people working in George Fitzgerald's office.[25] There is no reason to doubt that however they were obtained, most if not all of the petitions submitted on behalf of precinct delegate candidates committed to the Teamster cause were illegitimate.

Failure to comply with the letter, or even the spirit, of Michigan's election law in securing signed petitions for candidacy as a precinct delegate had not, however, been uncommon.[26] In the view of George Fitzgerald, it was "traditional that you screwed up petitions to run for district delegate." Fitzgerald, at least, was not inclined to break with tradition.

Jerry Cavanagh worked out of my office. He was part of what was called the Irish Mafia in the Fourteenth and Fifteenth Districts. I heard of one guy who worked his way through the phone book and got names for the petitions. No question there was a lot of that sort of thing, but it was done on both sides. The

CIO did the same thing. The petitions were silly. It's better to let a guy pay a fifty buck filing fee. Scholle and the rest of them though built the whole thing up to claim that Hoffa was trying to take over the Democratic party. It wasn't true.[27]

Liberals, however, believed it was, and were outraged by the attempted fraud and astonished at the scale of the attempt.

If Fitzgerald saw nothing terribly wrong in submitting fraudulent petitions, the last man in the state who could honestly claim ignorance of the practice was Gus Scholle. He had full knowledge that fraudulent petitions had been used before, and used on a rather large scale. In 1949, the CIO had endorsed George Edwards in the Detroit mayoral contest. With Scholle's help Edwards also obtained the endorsement of the Democratic party organization. In the Thirteenth Congressional District a mailing was sent to each elected Democratic precinct delegate. The post office returned most of the letters with the notation that no such person existed. "We realized then that a lot of false petitions were being made."[28] Scholle, then, was aware of what had been going on. Moreover, it was precisely because he had discovered the prevalence of the practice in 1949 that the liberal-labor coalition was in a position to detect and to disclose the large-scale forgeries committed by the Teamsters in 1950. Scholle may even have been aware of the Teamster effort before the Washington meeting with Hoffa and Fitzgerald but didn't mention it until the petitions were submitted and Hoffa could more easily be discredited in the eyes of the national labor leaders.

In a shrewd tactical maneuver designed to avoid having the issue determined by the Republican-controlled State Elections Division, Neil Staebler, who had replaced Hicks Griffiths as state chairman when Griffiths was appointed to the probate court by Governor Williams, brought suit in circuit court to compel the Wayne County Clerk to throw out the fraudulent petitions.[29] The court "prescribed a procedure too complicated to follow in the limited time between the filing deadline and the date upon which the ballots had to be presented."[30] In effect, the court refused to decide the issue one way or the other. Nevertheless, it did supply the liberal-labor coalition with a legal rationale for the exercise of political power, indicating in dictum that in its judgment "the eligibility of these persons to act as delegates may properly be determined by the county conventions in their respective districts in the event that they are elected to office."[31] Despite the court's refusal to throw out the forged petitions, the statement that the matter was one for the party organization to decide meant, from the point of view of the Williams-Staebler group, that it was not at all an unfavorable decision. Four of the six Wayne County districts were controlled by the liberal-CIO coalition, and in all four no delegate whose candidacy had been based on a fraudulent petition was allowed to attend the district convention.[32]

The exclusion of those delegates was not accomplished with the decorum of a legal proceeding. The CIO and AFL "furnished men and women . . . to act as 'screening committees' to examine delegate petitions and issue challenges at the door."[33] More specifically, the screening committees were established "to prevent those who perpetrated the frauds from illegally seizing control of the party."[34] The Teamsters and their allies looked on the committees not as impartial arbitrators of a legal dispute, but as physical obstacles placed in the way of their right to enter the conventions. In the Seventeenth District, the screening committee decided to lock the doors of the hall and allow delegates to enter two or three at a time after their credentials had been verified. Charles Nugent, demonstrating once again a well-developed ability to ignore his own understanding of legal procedure, rushed the doors from the inside in an attempt to let his friends and allies in, and tore from the hands of Al Meyer the list of certified delegates. In retaliation, Meyer grabbed Nugent by the neck and reclaimed the delegate list. In the scuffle, Adelaide Hart was thrown down a flight of stairs. The doors held, Meyer retained the list, and Adelaide Hart survived; the Seventeenth District remained in the control of the liberals.

It was in the Fourteenth District that the showdown fight took place.[35] When the district convention, held at the Briggs Body UAW Union Hall, was opened by its chairman, Nick Rothi, it was clear that things were going to be difficult. Seventy-five delegates who had used fraudulent petitions pushed their way into the hall. Fistfights broke out and some blood was spilled. Rothi, who hadn't been able to find a gavel, used instead what the Teamsters and the *Detroit News* called a sawed-off baseball bat and what the liberals called "an eight-inch wooden pestle." George Fitzgerald, convinced that only Rothi's rulings from the chair were preventing a Teamster takeover of the district, began making remarks designed to draw the chairman onto the floor of the convention. "I was trying to get Rothi off the dais and drop the bat so I could kick the hell out of him."[36] One of the things Fitzgerald said that night was taken down by Herb George, a reporter from the *Detroit Free Press,* and it had considerable consequences for the liberal-labor coalition. Having failed to entice Rothi from the chair, Fitzgerald, who was still the Democratic national committeeman, exclaimed: "I have just seen the Democratic party taken over by Socialists using Communist methods." Though in Fitzgerald's mind the whole episode "didn't amount to much," he was not unaware that "the newspapers really loved it." Fitzgerald's accusations were seized upon by the Detroit papers as a confirmation of the allegations they had been making for several years: that the CIO and socialism were indissolubly linked.

The liberal-labor coalition withstood the Teamster challenge to its dominance in four of the six Wayne County districts, took control in a fifth and showed power in the other. Only George Fitzgerald now stood between the liberal-labor coalition and complete control of the party machinery. Fitzgerald, however, could not be replaced as national committeeman until the next Democratic national convention, still two years away, and until then he gave the coalition all it could handle. From the very beginning of his term as national committeeman, he displayed an almost unique ability to torment his adversaries in the party. Shortly after Williams was elected governor, Williams, Hicks Griffiths, and Fitzgerald met to discuss how patronage would be handled. Fitzgerald, who admired Williams but viewed Griffiths as the "original Mr. Prick," said, "for the hell of it, that I would give them 50 percent of the federal patronage if I got 50 percent of the state patronage. They didn't want to do it, so I left. I would have been able to work the thing out with Williams alone, but Griffiths I really hated." Griffiths and the rest of those who had supported Williams in the 1948 primary continued to regard Fitzgerald as a major threat; eventually they offered him a judicial appointment as an inducement to give up his position. When it was clear that he was not going to step aside, then, according to Fitzgerald, "the Williams crowd wanted to debase the office. But I always was giving them this bullshit that the national committeeman was like the cardinal of the Catholic church. You had to respect the office."[37] Respect for the office, however, yielded to the desire to control federal patronage. Williams and Staebler met with President Truman and "agreed appointments would lie with the Governor."[38]

For four years Fitzgerald kept it up, as did his opposition. Fitzgerald was repeatedly called a stooge for Jimmy Hoffa, even though, according to Fitzgerald, Hoffa asked him to appoint someone only once, and he refused. Whatever the nature of Fitzgerald's relationship with Hoffa, few if any of the national committeeman's adversaries in the party were willing to put any but the worst interpretation on it. When the 1952 national convention met, the intensity of the liberal-labor coalition's desire to replace George Fitzgerald had not in the least diminished. Ernest J. Lacey, Wayne County chairman and a member of the liberal-labor coalition, was elected the new national committeeman. The last position of importance within the state party apparatus had finally been brought under the coalition's control. Yet during the preceding year, an event had occurred that ought to have made suspect any prediction of an untroubled and a unified existence for the liberal-labor alliance.

When George Fitzgerald stood on the floor of the Fourteenth District convention in the summer of 1950 and announced that the Michigan Democratic party had that evening been taken over by socialists employing communist tactics, he struck a chord in Detroit editorial writers and a nerve in the liberal-labor coalition. The trade union movement in Michigan, and the UAW in particular, had only recently emerged from very serious factional struggles in which communists had been involved. Walter Reuther, in alliance with the socialist wing of the labor movement, had successfully driven the communist faction out of positions of authority in the union. However, the difference between communist and socialist, though obvious to the unionists, was often ignored by the public. This was especially true in the early 1950s, when many Americans believed the differences between the various groups on the political left were insignificant: to be anywhere on the left was tantamount to treason. Though ardent New Dealers, the leaders of the liberal group in the liberal-labor coalition understood the political consequences of too close an identification with a labor movement which, whatever its own political aims, was characterized by the press and looked upon by much of the public as a repository of socialists and incipient socialism. Republicans viewed precisely such an identification as their most potent weapon against the Democrats in general and G. Mennen Williams in particular.

With less than a week remaining before the 1950 gubernatorial election, while Williams was charging that the Republicans planned to add new taxes if they were elected, his opponent, former Governor Harry F. Kelly, insisted that the "kings and the kingmakers are getting ready to turn loose 5,000 paid workers to try to stampede Michigan into Socialism." Kelly identified Williams as the king and Walter Reuther and Gus Scholle as the kingmakers.[39] This strategy very nearly succeeded. Williams did manage to be reelected, but only after a recount that took ten days, and only by a margin of 1,154 out of 1,879,382 votes cast, which gave Williams 49.8 percent of the vote to Kelly's 49.7 percent.[40] For Williams and his supporters there must have been a certain poetic justice in the fact that the recount had been directed by George Edwards, who had lost the Detroit mayoral race the preceding year largely because the Detroit papers had labeled him a socialist and a subversive. Edwards, however, would find more irony than justice in the fact that his political career would continue to be influenced more by what had been said about him by conservatives than by what he had done for liberals.

When Williams was reelected to his second term, Michigan was still represented in the U.S. Senate by two Republicans. One of them, Arthur Vandenberg, had acquired a national reputation as an opponent of partisanship on the great questions of foreign policy. On questions of domestic policy, the senator had a rather different perspective. On the great question of who should replace the retired postmaster in Grand Rapids, for example, the senator informed the Democratic national committeeman that appointing the labor-supported candidate would generate large amounts of unfavorable publicity from the newspapers he controlled. Grand Rapids got a postmaster the senator could approve. When the senator died in 1951, the liberal contingent in the state Democratic party and its leader, Governor Williams, were confronted with both a political opportunity and a very difficult political problem. Appointing a Democrat to the unexpired senatorial term would improve considerably the prospects of electing a Democrat to a full term in the 1952 election. The problem, however, was to select from a number of actual and potential claimants an appointee who would be supported by the party as a whole and who would have a decent prospect of success in 1952.

In what was clearly going to be the single most important appointment of his administration, Williams moved with caution. At the suggestion of state chairman Neil Staebler, the Democratic county chairmen were polled. Stephen Roth, who had been elected state attorney general in 1948 and defeated two years later, had the greatest support among the county chairmen, but others were also mentioned, among them Noel Fox, twice Democratic candidate for secretary of state. Williams, however, remained "inscrutable." For those around him at the time, it was "difficult to know what he was thinking. He listened a lot and did not disclose whom he was leaning toward. This was his normal procedure. It enabled him to get a good cross-section of opinion."[41] One opinion that did not wait for an invitation was that of the state CIO.

It seemed at first as if every member of the CIO had sworn a blood oath to obtain the appointment of George Edwards to the U.S. Senate. The state CIO council and the UAW executive board both endorsed him without a single dissenting vote. No one was more committed to any prospective appointee than Gus Scholle was to George Edwards, and Scholle, after all, had no little influence among the party's rank and file. But whether he or anyone else had any influence with G. Mennen Williams was another question. Some of those who worked with him for years came to believe that the governor's sole criterion in making any appointment was competence. As one of them expressed it: "The governor's intent was always to get the best man. The best Democrat if that was possible, but a 'neuter' if he was that much better. In all his appointments he took infinite pains to make sure he got the best."[42] This at first suggests a vigorous independence of judgment, an independence which ought not to be suspect simply on the grounds that many of the witnesses to it were Williams's most loyal and dedicated followers. Independence and the appearance of independence were not always politically compatible, however. The distinction is important to an understanding of the way Williams treated labor. In a section of his very friendly biography of Williams, Frank McNaughton, attempting to display the inability of labor to influence the governor, inadvertently demonstrates something significantly different. "Some groups of labor have repeatedly urged the appointment of outstanding labor lawyers to the Wayne County Circuit Bench. Their demands have been vigorous, insistent and pressing. In each instance, the demands have been rejected."[43] The conclusion seems clear. Independence of judgment was best demonstrated by rejecting absolutely ("in every instance") the recommended appointment of "outstanding" labor lawyers. Maintaining a public position of independence from the labor movement, no matter how he relied on it for electoral support, seems to have at least influenced the governor's ostensibly independent judgment.

Williams was faced with a political problem fraught with danger. The liberal-labor coalition he had helped to create, and from which he had benefited more than anyone else, was divided on the question of the proper replacement for Senator Vandenberg. Labor seemed united in its advocacy of George Edwards; the liberal element, though not united behind a single candidate, had shown by its support for Roth and Fox a preference for one of its own rather than one of labor's. Pleasing one side would mean antagonizing the other. Both together were barely sufficient to provide statewide majorities; losing one would guarantee electoral disaster. Still, it was not inevitable that choosing the candidate preferred by one side would cause such extreme dissatisfaction in the other. It seems doubtful that liberals would have deserted Williams in any appreciable numbers if George Edwards had been appointed, especially since Edwards's liberal credentials had been clearly established during his distinguished career on the Detroit Common Council. Edwards, after all, had been a public advocate of open housing legislation when that required not only moral but physical courage. The selection of Edwards would have pleased labor without in any significant sense alienating the liberals. In other words, the coalition could have been maintained. It would not, however, have increased its electoral prospects. Selecting Edwards, indelibly labeled by the newspapers as the CIO's ally, if not its creation, to replace Vandenberg, who had demonstrated the ability to transcend party allegiance, would make the Democratic party seem indifferent to interests greater than partisan advantage. In what many at the time considered a stroke of political genius, Williams ignored the claims of the CIO, put out of mind the preferences of the party's county chairmen, seemed even to forget political party—and appointed a Detroit newspaperman who had never before held or even been a candidate for public office.

As a Detroit newspaperman, Blair Moody was almost unique. He wrote a widely read and decidedly liberal column for the widely read and decidedly conservative *Detroit News*. Both liberals and labor had a high regard for him as a man and as a newspaperman. No one, however, had publicly proposed that Moody be considered as Vandenberg's replacement, and few had any idea he was being considered until his appointment was announced. According to a story in *Time* magazine, "Soapy, on Hicks Griffiths' advice, rejected Edwards and told the CIO he was going to pick Detroit newsman Blair Moody, an old, personal friend."[44] Griffiths was not alone in his opposition to Edwards. On a Sunday morning soon after Vandenberg's death, Congressman John Dingell, Sr., called George Fitzgerald and told the national committeeman he wanted to mention Moody to Williams as a possible replacement. Dingell thought the Edwards-Scholle-Reuther axis was too far to the left and that Moody was more moderate. Fitzgerald, for reasons of his own, also thought Moody would make a good senator.[45] Though he never knew for certain, Fitzgerald tended to believe that Dingell also made his argument directly to Williams. Whether he did or not, opposition to Edwards was scarcely an opinion the governor had not heard before.

More damaging for the prospects of George Edwards than the opposition of either Griffiths or Dingell, to say nothing of Fitzgerald, was the absence of any real support from someone who "should have been pushing very hard for George Edwards," and who, in fact, was bound by a vote of his own organization to do precisely that. When the state CIO council and the UAW executive board had given their unanimous endorsement to Edwards a rumor had already been circulating that the proceedings were really designed merely to give a public expression of loyalty to Edwards rather than to initiate an all-out fight on his behalf. There was no doubting the sincerity of Scholle's commitment to Edwards, but there was a growing suspicion that Walter Reuther would prefer to see Blair Moody chosen to fill the Vandenberg vacancy. Though Reuther may not have taken any direct action to support Moody, he did nothing to help the cause of a man with whom he had been associated in the formative years of the union and with whom he very nearly shared a common violent death when gunmen entered his home while Edwards was a guest, lined everyone up against a wall, and asked which of them was Walter Reuther.[46] When Williams announced his decision after Moody had been sequestered for two days in Neil Staebler's home,[47] "the CIO publicly beat its breast over this 'defeat' but had no really serious objection."[48] The UAW did not complain, and until the day he died Walter Reuther never once discussed the Moody appointment with his friend of forty years, George Edwards.

Reuther's failure to support Edwards made Williams's choice easier. The rejection of Edwards carried with it no danger of any serious repercussions from the labor movement. It is considerably less clear what Reuther's own motivations were. There may have been several. Reuther was aware that almost every day the newspapers were charging that Williams was a labor stooge, and appointing Edwards would scarcely undermine these accusations. Reuther seems also to have been persuaded that Moody, during his career as a Washington correspondent, had developed a proper grasp of foreign affairs and Reuther, it is to be remembered, found nothing inconsistent in the combination of domestic liberalism and militant anticommunism. Moody gave every indication of sharing both points of view. There is also the possibility that another, more private motivation had some influence. Reuther, more than any other leader in the union before or since, had come to represent the UAW as a whole, and it has been suggested that he was not perfectly indifferent to the way in which power was distributed. Had Edwards been appointed to the Senate, Reuther perhaps would not have stood out so clearly. It had happened once before. When Reuther left the presidency of Local 174 Edwards had wanted to succeed him. Reuther, however, swung his support to Mike Manning, an older man with a less promising future. Edwards decided not to run.[49]

There seems little doubt that if Edwards had been appointed in the frenzied days of the early fifties, something other than unanimous approval would have followed. In December, 1951, when Williams did appoint Edwards to a position—a seat on the district probate court—the reaction was vicious. Jack MacGriff, managing editor of the Detroit suburban newspapers, in a pamphlet with the engaging title "Presenting Some Facts on Michigan's Governor G. Mennen "Soapy" Williams—a Fellow not to be Followed— Giving the Low Down on the Gang from Michigan," described the newly appointed judge as "Socialist-follower George Edwards, who is notorious in Michigan as a pal of pinkos and himself a vice president of the ADA-ers." Comment in the more prestigious press was typified by an editorial in the *Detroit Free Press*, where Edwards's main qualifications to deal with "matters of juvenile problems and delinquency" were to be found, according to the editors, in the fact that he

> was one of the first organizers and leaders of the notorious and riotous sit-down strikes in Detroit in which private property was seized by a band of goons; he set the law at defiance and spent 30 days in jail for contempt of court. He once declaimed that the real seat of government in Detroit was a soap box in Cadillac Square.[50]

The reception would appear to supply convincing evidence that selecting Moody as the successor to Senator Vandenberg enabled Williams and his liberal-labor coalition to avoid the intensely partisan attacks to which Edwards was continually exposed. But more than most human endeavors, political calculations are subject to an inherent incertitude. It might reasonably have been assumed that Moody's past conduct would protect him from ridicule and abuse, and that his immunity would in turn provide the Democratic party with at least a semblance of respectability. The commingling of the reputations of Blair Moody and the liberal-labor coalition, however, served only to decrease the public regard for Moody without alleviating the calumny directed toward the Democratic party. Less than six months after his appointment to the Senate, Blair Moody was described by W. H. Hall, secretary of the Detroit Board of Commerce, as "the socialist CIO junior senator from Michigan," and his bill to increase unemployment payments as "another step toward the socialist state with Walter Reuther, his sponsor and director."[51] Nor did the attack on Moody diminish the abuse directed toward Williams. In the early months of 1952, Republican state chairman Owen Cleary "dug back into the record . . . to support charges that Governor Williams has hindered moves to outlaw the Communist party in Michigan." According to Cleary, Williams led an administration filled with "commie-coddlers."[52]

The two major political advantages of the Blair Moody appointment had been his independence of both labor and the Democratic party and his stature as a well-known journalist, advantages which, it was reasonable to expect, would markedly improve the chances to retain the senate seat in the 1952 election. However, as we have seen, the public soon replaced its perception of his past independence with the conviction that he was intimately connected with the liberal-labor coalition. This, in turn, negated whatever benefit might have accrued to an ostensibly nonpartisan candidate in the senatorial election of 1952. Nominated by the Democrats as their candidate for a full term, Moody was beaten by the Republican candidate, Congressman Charles Potter, by 44,000 votes. Moody's selection had done little if anything to restrain either the newspapers or the Republicans in their attacks on Williams and the Democratic party. Moreover, Moody had been unable to use successfully the advantages of incumbency in the quest for election to a full term. The ironies that emerged from the appointment of Blair Moody instead of George Edwards had only begun to reveal themselves.

With the election of 1952, G. Mennen Williams remained governor but Michigan was once again represented by two Republicans in the United States Senate, the newly elected Charles Potter and the very conservative Homer Ferguson. Ferguson faced reelection in 1954, and for a time Williams gave some thought to running against him. Even at the beginning of 1954 it was uncertain exactly what he would do. When eight hundred labor leaders attended a Michigan CIO dinner in Lansing in the latter part of January, the toastmaster asked whether they wanted Williams to run for reelection. "There was a roar of assent. He then asked how many would prefer that Governor Williams run against Homer Ferguson, the Republican senator. . . . The answer seemed to those present to be in about equal measure to the first voice tally." Williams, keeping his own counsel, responded to the voice vote with mischievous restraint. "'It is obvious you want me to run for something,' said the Governor, smiling, when he finally rose to speak."[53] Blair Moody also continued to insist that he had not yet decided whether to try his fortune a second time.[54]

Although the CIO leaders had evidenced equal support for Williams as either a gubernatorial or a senatorial candidate, the leader of the Michigan CIO-PAC labored under no comparable ambiguity of sentiment. Williams might be as effective a campaigner for the senate as he had been for the governor's chair, but it seemed unlikely that any other candidate could retain the governorship for the Democrats, and Gus Scholle "early made it clear that he hoped Williams would seek to retain his office for another term."[55] Nevertheless, it was not until April 20 that Williams publicly announced his plans. In a brief statement he "ended months of speculation" by stating simply, "My decision is to run for Governor."[56] His decision to seek an unprecedented fourth term opened the way for the second senatorial candidacy of Blair Moody.

With Williams and Moody occupying its two highest places, the liberal-labor slate of candidates seemed assured of victory in the Democratic primary. The major threat to this hegemony came once again from the Teamsters. After their decisive defeat in the 1950 district disputes, George Fitzgerald withdrew from regular participation in party activities; he even refused to attend the Democratic state convention.[57] He had been replaced as national committeeman in 1952, but he was not yet prepared to retire from political life. Two years later, in what was seen as another attempt by Hoffa and the Teamsters to secure influence in the party, he filed as a candidate for the Democratic nomination for lieutenant governor and became the sole opponent of Governor Williams's legal counsel, Philip A. Hart. For members of the liberal-labor coalition the issue was clear. It was simply a question of whether the state party would continue to be liberal in its principles or become corrupt in its politics. Hart labeled Fitzgerald a threat to the party, and Williams, abandoning even the pretense of neutrality, endorsed Hart and made speeches on his behalf.[58]

Fitzgerald was not the only candidate fighting the liberal-labor coalition in the primary election. Blair Moody also found himself with a primary opponent—an opponent, however, who did not come from the Teamsters and was not expected to be anything but a minor annoyance. More than anything else Patrick V. McNamara was a very independent man. Though an executive with a contracting company, he also served as honorary president of the AFL Pipefitters Union.[59] Largely through the efforts of the UAW, McNamara had successfully run for positions on both the Detroit Common Council and the Detroit Board of Education. His unwillingness to follow the normal conventions of political life was exhibited in an incident that is hard not to enjoy. Discovering that the members of the Common Council were other than distinguished statesmen, McNamara resigned, supplying in defense of his action the statement that the council members were "a bunch of jerks."[60] Despite this early evidence of extreme independence, few expected McNamara to enter the Democratic senatorial primary in 1954 and fewer still extended to his candidacy any possibility of success; it is doubtful that McNamara himself seriously thought he could win. Robert Perrin, a reporter for the *Detroit News*

who covered the campaign and later became McNamara's administrative assistant, never was able fully to understand his reasons for entering the contest
against Moody. Based on a long acquaintance with McNamara's character, he
came to believe that it was "perhaps because the building trades wanted to
have some fun with the UAW and the state CIO."[61] This same explanation
was put forward by Charles W. Edgecomb, a Wayne County auditor who had
originally entered McNamara's name. Edgecomb, who had had his differences
with the UAW since 1945, claimed that he and McNamara had been interested
in "just having a lot of hell-raising fun."[62]

Whatever McNamara's initial motivations might have been, his candidacy
was not viewed by the liberal-labor coalition with even a semblance of good
humor. Recalling their past support of McNamara, but failing to remember
his fierce independence, labor attempted to dissuade him from continuing his
candidacy. Though they had never been close, Walter Reuther was induced
to make a direct appeal to McNamara.[63] It would have been difficult to invent
a tactic less likely to succeed. Had there been any hesitation in McNamara's
mind about prosecuting his campaign with vigor, Reuther's overture effectively removed it. "McNamara was an extreme individualist. If he decided
he wanted to be the U.S. Senator, he would run regardless, and he would
run even harder if anyone suggested to him it wasn't the thing to do."[64] Unable
to prevent McNamara from running, labor put its political resources into the
Moody campaign.

The official party organization faced a more difficult situation. The men
and women who, along with labor, had contributed to the creation of a new
Democratic party in Michigan were genuinely persuaded that those they had
opposed and finally eliminated from positions of party influence in 1948 and
1950 were the self-interested practitioners of a venal politics. They, on the
other hand, meant to reform not only the party but politics generally. In what
they believed to be a new politics, a central tenet was the obligation to do
nothing that would in any way discourage those who sought to run for public
office as representatives of the Democratic party. A corollary was an insistence
that the party organization exercise the strictest neutrality in primary elections.
That this injunction was being violated in 1954 by the organized opposition
to George Fitzgerald's candidacy was defended on the grounds that Hoffa's
associate represented a clear and present danger to the very principles upon
which the recently refashioned party depended for its integrity and support.
Fitzgerald after all had directed the scheme to produce fraudulent petitions,
an act that had resulted in the criminal conviction of one of his associates in
that ill-starred venture.[65] Even here, however, the suspension of the neutrality
principle was at first less than forthright. Williams's early support of Hart
was "not blatant. The governor would simply find himself on the same platform with Hart and naturally say a few things about him."[66]

In light of the campaign rhetoric McNamara employed, it would not have been astonishing if the coalition had suspended its neutrality in the primary campaign for senator as well. He vigorously "attacked 'the present ADA, CIO boss and egghead' party leadership—not to mention Staebler, Scholle, and National Committeeman Lacey, whom he accused of 'throwing a roadblock' in front of other candidates."[67] McNamara's anger at the absence of party neutrality, however, was in a certain sense contrived. As a procedural matter, the state party organization made its facilities available to both candidates, and McNamara chose not to accept its invitation precisely in order to keep the neutrality issue alive. This was not, it must be added, simple deception on his part. The issue was a very real, though a complicated one. In the strict sense, party neutrality meant the party organization's abstention from involvement in the campaign of a contender for the party nomination. The party organization, however, was made up of men and women who in their capacity as individual citizens were free to support whomever they would. McNamara clearly understood that this rather fine distinction was politically untenable. Party leaders who as individuals supported Blair Moody were rather more important than other individuals for the obvious reason that their leadership positions supplied them with a wider influence. And with the notable exception of G. Mennen Williams, who was "careful to play the public role of a neutral,"[68] those who comprised the party leadership were almost unanimous in their support of Blair Moody. Nevertheless, no matter how often McNamara might call attention to the substantive partisanship exhibited by the state party, the issue seemed unlikely to have any great political impact. With two weeks remaining in the primary campaign, it seemed virtually certain that Moody would be the Democratic nominee for the senate. Then, on July 20, Blair Moody died.

McNamara easily captured the Democratic nomination,[69] and, on the surface at least, he and the liberal-labor coalition appeared united in their efforts to dispel any suggestion of lingering animosity. At the state convention, Williams went out of his way to praise McNamara, while the senatorial candidate ceased entirely to refer to Williams and the other members of the liberal-labor coalition with the invective he had only recently employed. Both Williams and McNamara had an obvious interest in obtaining party unity; factionalism during the campaign would only benefit the Republicans. Of the two, McNamara had the strongest incentive to gloss over former differences. Not only did Homer Ferguson have the advantage of incumbency, he had, with the help of Jimmy Hoffa, received the endorsement of the Michigan Federation of Teamsters. It was clear, at least to McNamara, that Ferguson would lose only if Williams won by a substantial margin. Two years earlier, Williams had won by 8,518 votes and Blair Moody had been defeated by 45,000 votes. In McNamara's judgment, his own victory hinged on the governor's ability to amass a plurality of at least 75,000 votes.[70] One reason McNamara had to depend on Williams's success for his own was the decided lack of enthusiasm with which the UAW embraced his candidacy. According to one of McNamara's supporters, "about all you can say is they didn't campaign against him."[71] As it turned out, their enthusiastic support was not required.

If McNamara's chances were tied to the margin of victory Williams achieved, that margin was in turn bound up with the total number of voters who turned out. Two weeks before the election a spokesman for party chairman Neil Staebler stated that "the Democrats' main hope for victory for Mr. McNamara and the rest of the state ticket was that there would be more than 2,000,000 votes cast."[72] More than the requisite two million votes turned out. Williams received an unprecedented quarter-million plurality and Patrick V. McNamara, who began his campaign by attacking the liberal-labor alliance, became the first U.S. senator elected by the coalition-controlled Democratic party. Walter Reuther, who had attempted to convince McNamara to withdraw, reported to the UAW membership: "In Michigan . . . labor's good friend, Senator Patrick McNamara, defeated the extremely reactionary spokesman for big business and the auto industry—Senator Homer Ferguson."[73]

The 1954 election was an unqualified success for the liberal-labor coalition. "In an off-year election, the party equalled its 1934 triumph when it had had the advantage of Franklin Roosevelt's ample coat tails."[74] The entire Democratic slate of statewide candidates was elected. From then until the end of Williams's twelve-year tenure as governor, the Democrats remained in control of the executive branch. Nor was their electoral success limited to the statewide campaign; by managing to secure 55 of the 110 seats in the lower house, the Democrats, for the first time in twenty years, were not the minority party in both houses of the state legislature. Having carried so many Democratic candidates into office by accumulating what was then considered an astonishing margin of victory, G. Mennen Williams had become the most powerful politician in the state and a potential power in the nation.

The electoral power Williams exhibited in the 1954 election was matched by the great political strength of labor in the state party organization. The *Detroit Free Press* reported that in the spring of 1956, according to "Michael Novack, CIO county chairman, the organization (CIO-PAC) reaches down to 55 percent of Wayne County in 2,007 voting districts. It has precinct captains, zone leaders, district chairman and coordinators just like the slick machines of professional politicians. In fact, it outdoes most of them."[75] This precinct-level organization provided the means for labor to exert great influence in the state party. "Delegates from six Wayne County congressional districts, Oakland, Macomb counties all bound by the unit rule constituted a majority at the Democratic state convention held in the latter part of the spring of 1956. In practically every instance, they were responsive to UAW-CIO influence and desires."[76] Voluntary one-dollar contributions to the CIO-PAC were estimated to bring in between $180,000 and $200,000 annually.[77]

The same issue of the *Detroit Free Press* that described the CIO-PAC apparatus carried an interview with Walter Reuther concerning the political aims of the UAW. For all practical purposes the Republican party was excluded as a political alternative for labor. According to Reuther, the UAW had supported individual Republicans, but "it becomes more difficult all the time because it is becoming harder and harder to find a good Republican worthy of our support." This was particularly true in Michigan. "Nobody denies the fact," Reuther asserted, "that the Michigan Republican party is dominated by big business. General Motors and Ford dominate it."[78] Reuther, however, was no longer interested in the development of a labor party. "The whole historic development of the American political structure is such that it doesn't lend itself to the kind of narrow class party structure that Europe has reflected. Therefore, we don't believe the Labor Party as such is the answer." Nor was the existing national Democratic party completely acceptable. The attitudes of Senator James Eastland and others like him in the South were not, in Reuther's judgment, an asset to the Democratic party; their presence was not even considered advantageous during campaigns. "I think you can win without him and I think you can win only if you don't have him." What Reuther wanted was precisely what he had advocated in the closing years of the previous decade, a restructured Democratic party.

> We need a broad party that will reflect interests of workers, farmers, white collar groups, small businessmen, professional groups . . . those who generally share the same basic economic and social problems.

Reuther, in short, was advocating the realignment of the parties on the basis of political ideology, a realignment that he believed possible.

> I think that ultimately American politics will evolve in that direction where the people of America will get a real likeness of the two-party system, so that you have a liberal party and a conservative party.[79]

It is clear that Reuther was far from being a political ideologue for whom such practical considerations as the possibility of winning elections had no significance. A labor party was doomed to political oblivion, but a party based on liberal principles could become, in Reuther's judgment, a successful competitor in American politics. This required an understanding of liberal principles that was broad enough to include individuals and groups who could supply the necessary electoral base. This in turn meant that labor would not necessarily consider the most liberal candidate the best candidate. The possibility that labor, in the interests of liberalism as it understood it, would withhold its support from the most liberal candidate available became in fact the principle the UAW followed at the 1956 Democratic national convention.

In November, 1955, shortly after announcing his intention to seek the nomination of his party for the presidency for the second time, Adlai Stevenson said in an address to a Democratic rally in Chicago, "moderation is the spirit of the times."[80] G. Mennen Williams, who had been mentioned with some frequency as a possible favorite-son candidate for the nomination, quickly and rather vigorously denounced the Stevenson statement. In a speech to the Colorado Young Democrats he said, "Democrats would be guilty of 'the most craven cowardice' if they allowed the 1956 presidential campaign to 'degenerate into a spineless and self-defeating formality.' "[81] Williams, after extolling both the patriotism and abilities of Stevenson, went on to suggest, at least implicitly, that he was something less than the kind of Democrat needed to lead the party in the impending presidential campaign.

> I would remind you that the temporizers, those who look backward, those who are satisfied with the status quo, those who today grudgingly yield to the necessities of yesterday and hence never progress but always and everywhere slide back, are traditionally on the other side, not ours.[82]

Williams, it was clear, was now on record in opposition to the nomination of Adlai Stevenson.

By the early spring of 1956, it was widely reported that Williams was very much available for the first place on the national ticket and would probably not decline an invitation to occupy the second. There seemed little doubt that Williams believed it was precisely his brand of liberalism that ought to provide the guiding direction for the party as a whole.

> I feel it is the national heritage of the Democratic party to be liberal, progressive and forward-looking. Democrats have won when they have had a bold progressive program. We can win again on that kind of a platform, and we must have it.[83]

The bold, progressive program Williams envisaged was exemplified in his civil rights position. On April 29, in an address to the St. George Association of the New York Police Association, he argued that the foreign policy of the United States was hindered by a failure to deal adequately with the problem of equality at home. The world's view of the United States, according to

Williams, was shaped less by the principles espoused in the Declaration of Independence than by a

> picture of a little colored boy murdered without rebuke in Mississippi, a mob throwing a man's furniture through the windows of his apartment outside Chicago because he happens to be a Negro, and stones being thrown at a co-ed because she insists upon the right to the kind of education she wants in a university of her own choosing.[84]

When the Michigan Democratic party held its state convention in June, Williams's strong civil rights position received the unanimous support of the state party. The UAW, which was "adamant for an uncompromising stand by the parties on the civil rights question," was in complete agreement with his position.[85] Among other proposals, the civil rights planks included demands for the elimination of discrimination in federal employment, creation of a civil rights division in the Department of Justice, and abolition of the poll tax.[86] The convention then proceeded to indicate that its support of Williams went beyond approval of his civil rights position. Despite some evidence of support for the presidential ambitions of both Adlai Stevenson and Estes Kefauver, Williams was designated Michigan's favorite-son candidate for the Democratic nomination. Eighty-eight delegates and fifty-two alternates were selected to cast Michigan's forty-four votes for G. Mennen Williams.[87]

Williams, however, had already concluded that he had little if any chance for the nomination. This did not diminish his opposition to Stevenson's moderate approach as incompatible with "the kind of ringing New Deal and Fair Deal philosophy the next standard bearer of the party should have in order to represent the party or to win."[88] Much closer to the liberalism Williams advocated was Averill Harriman, governor of New York. Williams had worked with Harriman on civil rights matters, and New York had been the first state to establish a fair employment practices commission. Together the two governors had at one point set up regional conferences on civil rights.[89] Harriman was more likely than Stevenson to support a civil rights plan even if adopting it might entail the loss of the southern states. At the national convention, however, Walter Reuther and the UAW argued that the Michigan delegation ought to declare for Stevenson. Williams was reluctant to follow Reuther's suggestion because of the civil rights issue. He even expressed some hesitation about whether Stevenson would "vigorously pursue a liberal program if elected."[90] According to one source, the disagreement between Williams and the UAW was resolved by the intervention of a third party: "When it became impossible to reconcile the apparent deadlock, Chester Bowles was called in; after an all night argument at the Congress Hotel, in Chicago,

Bowles finally convinced Williams to vote for Stevenson, accomplishing what Reuther could not bring about."[91]

Williams had wanted the most liberal candidate even if that meant losing the South. Reuther wanted a liberal candidate, but he also wanted to win. As demonstrated during the 1956 national convention, Williams and Reuther did not completely agree on the most effective political tactic to advance the principles of Democratic liberalism. Nevertheless, throughout the twelve years Williams occupied the governor's office, labor gave him its unstinting political support. There was never even a suggestion that it do anything but endorse his gubernatorial candidacies. For twelve years Williams constituted the central fact of the liberal-labor alliance. He could not win without labor's support, but neither could labor have defeated him in a primary had it ever thought of trying. But in 1960, after an unprecedented six terms as governor, Williams was not a candidate, and for the first time since the liberal-labor coalition came into being labor had to decide what it would do in a gubernatorial primary.

Notes

1. James M. Hare, *With Malice Toward None* (East Lansing: Michigan State University Press, 1972), p. 13.

2. Stephen B. Sarasohn and Vera H. Sarasohn, *Political Party Patterns in Michigan* (Detroit: Wayne State University Press, 1957), p. 57.

3. Ibid.

4. Under the Michigan Constitution of 1908, which was then in force, a number of different administrative positions were elected statewide at two-year intervals. Instead of running with the gubernatorial candidates in the fall elections, however, they were elected in April during odd-numbered years.

5. *Detroit News,* February 2, 1949.

6. Ibid.

7. Sarasohn and Sarasohn, *Party Patterns,* p. 57; Doris B. McLaughlin, *Michigan Labor: A Brief History from 1818 to the Present* (Ann Arbor: Institute of Labor and Industrial Relations, 1970), p. 130.

8. Sarasohn and Sarasohn, *Party Patterns,* p. 57.

9. *Detroit News,* February 2, 1949.

10. Ibid.

11. Ibid.

12. Fay Calkins, *The CIO and the Democratic Party* (Chicago: University of Chicago Press, 1952), p. 9.

13. Ibid. See also Clinton Rossiter, *Parties and Politics in America* (Ithaca: Cornell University Press, 1960), p. 24, where it is asserted: "The whole process of American politics appears as the give-and-take of interests in search of realization. Nowhere is the true nature of that politics more clearly revealed than in the unique tie-up of the parties and the interest groups."

14. Rossiter, *Parties,* p. 11.

15. James Bryce, *The American Commonwealth,* vol. 2 (London: Macmillan and Co., 1891), p. 220.

16. V. O. Key, Jr., "A Theory of Critical Elections," *Journal of Politics* 17 (February, 1955): 3.

17. An interesting discussion of this phenomenon in city politics is found in James Reichley, "Philadelphia: 'Good Government' Leads to Moral Frustration," in *Urban Government,* ed. Edward C. Banfield (New York: Free Press, 1961), pp. 357–64. The problem Reichley takes up is how to continue the spirit, as distinguished from the institution, of reform in city politics—that is, how to preserve the existence of reformers when reform has been accomplished. Reichley concluded that in Philadelphia, at least, the problem was insoluble. An interesting parallel can be found in the literature on the Russian Revolution, where the problem was perceived in terms of retaining the revolutionary spirit in those who by virtue of revolution had become possessed of political power—that is, how to retain the revolutionary spirit when place and position had become the guiding force in the lives of the party membership. (See Leon Trotsky, *The New Course* [Ann Arbor: University of Michigan Press, 1965].) The problem of retaining the spirit of a revolution after it has taken place received its most profound expression in Lincoln's Lyceum speech. Lincoln's concern with the problem of preserving the principles that informed the founding are closely connected with the phenomenon of recurrent alterations between principle and patronage exhibited by American political parties. The founding established the principles on which the American regime would exist. In other words, it established the assumptions on which political parties could legitimately operate. Parties became acceptable in the United States only when it was generally recognized that they posed no threat to those fundamental principles, but in fact were devoted to both political liberty and republican government. (See Richard Hofstadter, *The Idea of a Party System* [Berkeley: University of California Press, 1969]. See also Harvey Mansfield, Jr., *Statesmanship and Party Government* [Chicago: University of Chicago Press, 1965].)

18. Frank McNaughton, *Mennen Williams of Michigan: Fighter for Progress* (New York: Oceana Publishing, 1960), p. 112.

19. Al Meyer, interview with author, August 27, 1971.

20. Sarasohn and Sarasohn, *Party Patterns,* p. 59.

21. Ibid.

22. Ibid.

23. Ibid.

24. Ibid.

25. Adelaide Hart, interview with author, August 31, 1971.

26. Ibid.

27. George Fitzgerald, interview with author, June 22, 1971.

28. Tom Downs, interview with author, June 13, 1973.

29. McNaughton, *Mennen Williams,* p. 113.

30. Sarasohn and Sarasohn, *Party Patterns,* p. 113.

31. Quoted in ibid.

32. Ibid., p. 61.

33. McNaughton, *Mennen Williams,* p. 113.

34. Michigan Democratic State Central Committee, *The Michigan Democratic Story: 1948–1954* (Lansing, Mich.: Michigan Democratic Party, 1955).

35. McNaughton, *Mennen Williams,* p. 113.

36. George Fitzgerald, interview with author, June 22, 1971.

37. Ibid.

38. Neil Staebler, personal communication with author, February, 1982.

39. *Detroit Free Press,* November 3, 1950.

40. McNaughton, *Mennen Williams,* p. 132.

41. Adelaide Hart, interview with author, August 31, 1971.

42. Ibid.

43. McNaughton, *Mennen Williams,* p. 153.

44. "Prodigy's Progress," *Time,* September 15, 1952, p. 29.

45. George Fitzgerald, interview with author, June 22, 1971.

46. Sidney H. Woolner, interview with author, March 8, 1982.

47. Neil Staebler, personal communication with author, February, 1982.

48. "Prodigy's Progress," *Time,* September 15, 1952, p. 29.

49. Tom Downs, interview with author, June 13, 1973.

50. *Detroit Free Press,* December 5, 1951.

51. Quoted in B. J. Widick, *Detroit: City of Race and Class Violence* (Chicago: Quadrangle Books, 1972), p. 129.

52. *Detroit Free Press,* March 2, 1952.

53. *New York Times,* January 31, 1954.

54. Ibid.

55. Sarasohn and Sarasohn, *Party Patterns,* p. 66.

56. *New York Times,* April 21, 1954.

57. McNaughton, *Mennen Williams,* p. 115.

58. Ibid., p. 116.

59. Sarasohn and Sarasohn give the erroneous impression that McNamara was a full-time union official. See *Party Patterns,* p. 66.

60. Quoted in *Detroit News,* October 25, 1954.

61. Robert Perrin, interview with author, March 31, 1973.

62. Quoted in Sarasohn and Sarasohn, *Party Patterns,* p. 66.

63. Mildred Jeffries, interview with author, September 1, 1971.

64. Adelaide Hart, interview with author, July 26, 1971.

65. Neil Staebler, personal communication with author, February, 1982.

66. John Murray, interview with author, July 26, 1971.

67. Sarasohn and Sarasohn, *Party Patterns,* p. 66.

68. Ibid.

69. Sarasohn and Sarasohn suggest that an attempt was made to encourage a vote for Moody. See *Party Patterns,* p. 66. However, though "there was some discussion by individuals of a proposition to encourage a Moody vote (which would have thrown the election into the hands of the Democratic State Central Committee) . . . no serious consideration was given to such a plan." Sidney H. Woolner, interview with author, March 8, 1982.

70. *New York Daily News,* October 25, 1954.

71. Robert Perrin, interview with author, March 31, 1973.

72. *New York Times,* October 24, 1954.

73. Walter Reuther, "Report to the UAW-CIO Membership," *United Automobile Worker* (March, 1955).

74. Sarasohn and Sarasohn, *Party Patterns,* p. 67.

75. H. M. Gurge, "The UAW Comes of Age in Politics," *Detroit Free Press,* June 3, 1956.

76. Ibid.

77. Ibid.

78. *Detroit Free Press,* June 3, 1956.

79. Ibid.

80. *New York Herald Tribune,* November 27, 1955.

81. Quoted in ibid.

82. Ibid.

83. Quoted in *Louisville Courier-Journal,* March 27, 1956.

84. Quoted in *New York Times,* April 30, 1956.

85. Quoted in *New York Times,* June 3, 1956.

86. Ibid.

87. Ibid.

88. *New York Post,* July 20, 1956.

89. John Murray, interview with author, July 26, 1971.

90. McNaughton, *Mennen Williams,* p. 152.

91. Ibid.

CHAPTER 3

Defeat and Division

When G. Mennen Williams announced at the beginning of March, 1960, that he would not seek a seventh term, James M. Hare, secretary of state, quickly declared his readiness to pursue higher office. This was not unexpected. Since the 1958 election, when he ran 45,000 votes ahead of the governor, Hare had been seen as Williams's logical and likely successor. It was his demonstrated ability to attract votes and not his unvarnished liberalism which occasioned the expectation of Hare's political advancement. Many Democrats were rather uneasy with his casual attachment to party principle.

> When he goes into the hinterlands for political meetings, he talks about the noncontroversial topic of traffic safety instead of the state's tax dilemma. . . . Some Democrats think that as governor he would butter up to the Republican controlled legislature and the state's newspaper publishers—two of Governor Williams favorite sparring partners over the past decade.[1]

Someone who appeared to be more committed to the sort of liberalism espoused by Williams was the thirty-four-year-old lieutenant governor, John B. Swainson. Elected to the state senate in 1954 and again in 1956, Swainson realized that the Williams era in Michigan politics was drawing to a close. When Philip A. Hart decided to run for the U.S. Senate, Swainson became a candidate for lieutenant governor. Elected to that position in the fall of 1958, Swainson awaited with impatience the opportunity to exchange the second position in state government for the first. The withdrawal of Williams, however, removed only one of the obstacles that stood in the way of his ambitions.

Faced with the prospect of a contested primary, both the party and the labor leadership sought ways to avoid serious division within the party. The first attempt to maintain internal peace took the form of suggestions to Swainson that Hare should be allowed to have the governorship a few times before Swainson took over.[2] The implied promise of future support might have appealed to someone with less ambition or more confidence in the future, but

Swainson remained unmoved. A battle for the nomination could not be avoided, but the party leadership sought to reduce the possibility of party schisms by adopting a position of strict neutrality. Throughout the primary campaign, neither Williams nor the state party chairman, Neil Staebler, made a single public statement that could be construed as advocating the candidacy of either contender. What was done in private was another matter.

Shortly after Williams announced his decision not to run, the leadership of both the party and labor met to devise a common strategy. Among those in attendance were Neil Staebler, G. Mennen Williams, and Gus Scholle.[3] The working assumption was that Hare was far too strong to be challenged seriously by Swainson. As Swainson was clearly going to lose, any support given him would be wasted; worse yet, it would no doubt anger the next governor. An open endorsement of Hare, on the other hand, would present another set of difficulties, risking division within the party. Not only those who might support Swainson but those who believed in the principles of open competition would become at least apathetic and perhaps even antagonistic in the general election. An endorsement by labor might also hinder the electoral prospects of the Democratic candidate in the general election. The newspapers would seize on the endorsement as another manifestation of labor's dominance of the party and of the candidate. For precisely this reason, Hare himself had asked that no labor endorsement be given.[4] Neutrality was adopted as the best possible policy. The private decision of the liberal-labor leadership corresponded to the public posture of the party, but only because it was seen as the measure most likely to make James Hare the successor of G. Mennen Williams.

Labor adopted a position of neutrality with the intention of easing the way for Hare in the general election, but neutrality allowed Swainson to win the primary. Neutrality meant that everyone in the labor hierarchy could do whatever he wished. For the top leadership of the UAW, this had little actual consequence. Since the press and the public might view their support for a particular candidate as representative of the union position, they abstained for the most part from active participation in the campaign of either one. Among the secondary leadership, however, neutrality exercised less restraint on personal involvement. This was particularly true of several of the local union presidents. Three of them, Russell Leach of UAW Local 155, Harry Smith of Local 174, and Barney Underwood of Local 235, believed Hare would not be the kind of governor they wanted.[5] With the freedom of action granted through the neutrality policy, they began to lay plans for a campaign to acquire the labor vote for John Swainson. The major element in their strategy was to gather the support of as many of the union locals as possible. Solidarity House was not in the least enthusiastic over the prospect of local unions becoming involved in a contest in which the UAW was supposedly neutral.

Ed Purdy, director of the UAW citizenship department, suggested that it would be unwise for the locals to do what the union as a whole would not.[6] His advice was ignored. With Russ Leach advising and advancing him, Swainson proceeded to canvass the union locals and to win converts among them. Although his voting record as a state senator was unblemished in the judgment of a labor audience, Swainson's ability to persuade local after local that he, and not James Hare, was their best hope for an ally in the governor's office was the result of his own forceful presentation and their sympathetic admiration for the underdog.

Several things contributed to Swainson's success in using his position as a challenger with doubtful prospects to secure the sympathy and the support of local unions. During World War II, Swainson lost both legs in a land mine explosion. However, his vigorous and forceful appearance made his use of artificial limbs scarcely noticeable. He could be seen as someone of character without having to utter a word. Moreover, he had worked his way up from circumstances much like those common among union members; it was easy for them to regard him as one of their own.

Leach and others also shrewdly advanced the attitude that the membership now had an opportunity to show the leadership whose union it was.[7] The local unions saw Swainson as the challenger to the Democratic establishment and support of him as a gesture of defiance to the established union leadership. This brotherhood of mavericks increased its size with each passing day. Within two months of announcing his candidacy, Swainson had secured the allegiance of at least half of all the UAW locals in the state, and nearly 80 percent of the larger ones. The newspapers began to report Swainson's activities among the locals and to suggest that the local union presidents were taking on the president and the officers of the international, but the union leadership remained convinced that Hare would easily win.[8] Then, in May, the state AFL-CIO convention met in Lansing and Swainson acquired at least the acknowledgment that his candidacy was a serious one.[9]

In keeping with its official policy of neutrality, the state AFL-CIO invited the Democratic candidates for governor to address its May convention. Hare, Swainson, and Ed Connor all accepted. Connor, it should be mentioned, had been persuaded to enter the race by Joe Kowalski, one of the Democratic leaders in the state house of representatives and an international representative of the UAW. Kowalski had no great love for Hare and considered Swainson to be "just a kid."[10] All three candidates spoke to the convention, but two of them might more profitably have spent their time elsewhere. Though the state AFL-CIO professed neutrality, its convention did not. Even before he began his speech Swainson was given an enthusiastic, spontaneous demonstration— which, like almost all spontaneous demonstrations, had been very carefully arranged. Russ Leach, who had guided Swainson through the canvass of local unions, used his wide acquaintance with members of the local union delegations to the state convention to great advantage. What is known in political circles as a "wire job" was consummated with considerable dexterity and an unusual attention to detail. Swainson, acting on Leach's instructions, entered the convention hall at the rear and proceeded down the middle aisle. Also following Leach's direction were several hundred delegates, who immediately pressed toward Swainson from both sides of the aisle with outstretched hands. Precisely the same procedure was followed as Swainson left the hall after his address. Gus Scholle, who was presiding over the convention, repeatedly hammered the gavel to restore order. At one point Scholle added to the appearance of spontaneity by shouting to Swainson: "John you are disrupting the convention."[11] The state AFL-CIO retained its official neutrality position, but the delegates to its convention used the freedom that policy permitted to campaign with energy and effect for John Swainson. Nor was it only the rank and file that he carried with him. Despite an agreement with Neil Staebler and others that he would not oppose Hare, Gus Scholle soon began to support Swainson.[12]

Without the efforts of organized labor's secondary leadership, Swainson would not have defeated the secretary of state in the gubernatorial primary. In areas where union membership was concentrated—areas where the union lieutenants directed their campaign—Swainson found his margin of victory. Hare carried fifty-eight of the state's eighty-three counties, but the twenty-five taken by Swainson included all six of those in the Detroit metropolitan region.[13] Of these six, Wayne County alone accounted for 266,737 of the 540,743 votes cast in the Democratic gubernatorial primary.[14] Swainson outpolled Hare in the county, 145,800 to 87,682.[15] His vote there supplied more than half of his state total of 274,743.[16] Moreover, the margin of 88,118 by which he outdistanced Hare in the county exceeded by 18,461 the 69,657 vote margin by which he defeated Hare in the state altogether. Wayne County gave Swainson the Democratic nomination; and the secondary leadership of the UAW, set free to follow their own counsel by the union's policy of nonintervention, gave Swainson Wayne County.

In the general election, Swainson was opposed by Paul D. Bagwell, who had run against Williams in 1958 and lost by what was viewed as the remarkably small margin of 147,444.[17] Two years earlier, in the face of the Eisenhower landslide, Williams had defeated Detroit Mayor Albert Cobo by 290,313.[18] After the 1958 campaign, Bagwell's nomination by the Republican party for a second run at the governorship was a certainty. The absence of G. Mennen Williams, in combination with the bitterly contested Democratic primary, appeared to give Bagwell an excellent chance to end twelve years of Democratic domination. Confronted for the first time in more than thirty years with the necessity to select both a president and a governor without an incumbent seeking reelection to either position, Michigan voters, who had three times split their ballots to vote for a Republican for president and G. Mennen Williams for governor, decided to cast a party vote. Kennedy defeated Nixon by 1,687,269 to 1,620,428 in the Michigan vote and Swainson beat back the Bagwell challenge by almost the same margin, 1,643,634 to 1,602,022.[19] Swainson's first election as governor, however, was his last. Two years later he was opposed not by Paul Bagwell, but by George Romney; and Romney, who proclaimed partisanship a vice and considered opposition partisanship, was not to be denied. For the first time in fourteen years, the Democrats found themselves out of office.

A significant group within the Democratic party had already felt deprived of power for two years. The party apparatus that had been so carefully built up during the long tenure of G. Mennen Williams had been largely dismantled and replaced at the direction of John Swainson after the general election in 1960. Before his inauguration, a meeting of Swainson supporters was held to begin deliberations on the ways and means by which the newly elected governor should construct a political organization. Among those present were Al Meyer, chairman of the Seventeenth District, who had been one of the first to urge Swainson to run against Hare, John J. "Joe" Collins, who had been in charge of Swainson's outstate campaign, and Mitch Tendler, who had handled much of the public relations work during the campaign.[20] As governor, Swainson had the power to determine who would and who would not hold office in the state party, and he intended to use it. Joe Collins was chosen to be the next state chairman, and Harriett Phillips, the chairman of the Oakland County Democratic party and one of Swainson's earliest adherents, was picked to be vice chairman. Mitch Tendler was appointed the governor's executive secretary.

It is at this point that one of the most colorful and most controversial Democrats in Michigan history makes his appearance. While John Swainson was winning his primary battle, Zolton Ferency was losing his. An unsuccessful candidate for the Fourteenth District congressional nomination, with $9,000 in campaign debts and without employment, Ferency began to practice law in Detroit in September.[21] Having been a member of two state boards, the Workmen's Compensation Appeal Board and the Liquor Control Commission, Ferency had more than a passing knowledge of state government. As both a congressional candidate and vice-chairman of the Fourteenth District Democratic organization, Ferency also had a decent understanding of Democratic politics in Wayne County. This combination of political and governmental experience proved to be precisely what was lacking in Swainson's first executive secretary. Mitch Tendler very quickly lost the support of both Swainson and the new party chairman, Joe Collins.[22] No other position was as important to the governor's prospects of running the government and controlling the party. For example, the executive secretary had the responsibility of finding people who had both the necessary competence and the requisite political loyalty to be placed on 142 boards and commissions. He was also to serve as the governor's chief of staff and his immediate contact with the appointees who would serve on the various boards and commissions. One hundred seventeen appointments were yet to be made when Collins and Dave Lebenbom, an influential member of the Wayne County Democratic committee, suggested to Ferency that he ought to consider taking over as the governor's executive secretary.[23] In March, Ferency had dinner with Swainson. Swainson had no direct knowledge of Ferency's abilities, but had been told by a number of people that this was someone who could extricate him from what had become an administrative morass.[24] On April 14, Zolton Ferency became the governor's executive secretary.

During the two years Ferency worked for Swainson, he developed serious doubts about the ability of Joe Collins to lead the Democratic party organization. Collins displayed a much keener interest in becoming what he eventually became, an insurance salesman who made a million dollars, than in devoting time and energy to political organization. Doubts about the chairman's desire to protect and promote the political fortunes of John Swainson seemed confirmed when Ferency learned that Collins was making discreet overtures to Staebler and his group during the 1962 campaign.[25] It seemed clear, to Ferency at least, that Collins had decided Swainson was going to lose, and that he could retain the chairmanship only by reaching an understanding with the segment of the party he had been chosen to replace.[26]

After the 1962 election, Swainson left Michigan for a period of rest and recuperation in the South. Ferency was left behind to bring fourteen years of Democratic rule to an end and make way for the incoming Republican administration. During the two months between the election and the actual transfer of power, there was considerable discussion about what should be done with the state party organization. Those who were close to Swainson found no virtue in the prospect of a party chairman who was antagonistic to Swainson and the forces he led, and any chairman who owed his election to the Staebler-Williams faction would in their judgment necessarily be hostile.[27] Moreover, the party chairman would quite clearly have at least the opportunity to exercise a broader leadership than had been possible when a Democrat sat in the governor's office. Ferency argued, and Swainson agreed, that the chairman would have to be not only an able organizer but a knowledgeable and astute political spokesman.[28] Though Swainson agreed with Ferency about the responsibilities the chairman would have while the Democrats were out of office, he displayed no real interest in leading a fight to remove Joe Collins from the chairmanship.[29] Only when Ferency declared his candidacy four days before the state Democratic convention did Swainson finally indicate his willingness to become directly involved.[30]

With barely half a week remaining before the convention, Swainson seemed only to state the obvious when he said, "We have a lot to do."[31] But much had already been done. Ferency had spent several weeks contacting members of the Wayne County Democratic apparatus, appealing for support to those who had helped him before. He had also met with UAW leaders Leonard Woodcock and Douglas Fraser. Both were willing to support Ferency, but their sentiments were not shared by all of organized labor.[32] Gus Scholle and Al Barbour, head of the Wayne County AFL-CIO council, were opposed to Ferency, whether because (as Ferency thought) they knew him too well and suspected he would be too intractable as party chairman, or because (as several labor leaders believed) Scholle "would do almost anything for Soapy,"[33] and Williams, most believed, was opposed to Ferency.

Several meetings of the labor leadership were held to resolve the issue. Scholle, along with others who were allied with the Williams-Staebler faction, argued that Collins was entitled to continue in office by virtue of the fact that in the recent election Democrats had been victorious in a majority of the statewide contests.[34] Although the gubernatorial race had obviously been the principal object of contention, its loss was clearly attributable to the failure of Swainson himself. His inability to so much as stay even with most of his Democratic running mates should properly divest him of any right to dictate selection of the party chairman.[35] This attempt to go beyond a defense of Collins's performance as party chairman to an attack on Swainson's abilities as a candidate was an essential part of any argument that was to have even a remote prospect of persuading the UAW to follow Scholle's lead. The reason is rooted in the history of the liberal-labor coalition.

Since the very inception of the coalition the UAW, on the one hand, and Gus Scholle, on the other, had had different opinions on how involved labor should be in the Democratic party. Scholle concerned himself almost exclusively with political affairs and came to exercise considerably more influence in the party than in the labor movement. UAW leaders, however, were mostly content to leave internal party matters alone. This attitude, combined with their generally good relations with Scholle, induced the UAW to give the state AFL-CIO president great discretion in the way he represented labor's interests within the party. Scholle's continuing political power depended in large measure on the UAW's adopting what was almost a policy of nonintervention, but it was also limited by that dependence. In keeping with its policy of dealing with the party as an entity separate and distinct from itself, the UAW deferred to Williams's selection of the party leadership throughout his tenure as governor. There seemed no apparent reason to depart from this arrangement with the accession of John Swainson; and even after he had been defeated, he was still, as the party's gubernatorial nominee, the titular head of the state party. Thus, in order to persuade the UAW to back Collins for party chairman despite Swainson's preference for Ferency, it would be necessary to discredit Swainson himself.

The attempt to argue a distinction between Swainson's personal failure and the success of the party under Collins's leadership, however, was not persuasive. The UAW leaders concluded that far from demonstrating an overriding reason to discard past policy, the attack on Swainson was nothing more than a political maneuver.[36] Because of its desire to remain an ally of the party instead of a regular participant in it, the UAW had become involved in an internal party matter. However, that involvement was still tentative. On the Friday evening before the convention opened in Grand Rapids, the labor caucus met, and it was evident that Scholle did not have the votes to carry the caucus for Collins. He suggested it take no position and that each member be left free to support whichever candidate he wished.[37] The fact that, even after it was clear that a majority did not support Collins, the UAW went along with Scholle instead of compelling the caucus to endorse Ferency indicates nothing so much as its continuing unwillingness to use its strength to influence decisively an internal party dispute.

With labor formally neutral, Collins seemed assured of reelection. The same evening the labor caucus met Leonard Woodcock told Ferency that the situation did not appear promising and then began a recital of the counties Collins was going to win.[38] Moreover, though Ferency knew Collins had the support of every Democratic statewide officeholder, the energy expended on his behalf by the lieutenant governor, T. John Lesinski, was surprising. The lieutenant governor was an imposing man. It was said of Lesinski, who weighed at least 350 pounds, that if he were wrapped in a sheet and put in front of a house, the first laundry truck to come by would carry him off. His attributes, however, were by no means restricted to his girth. He had a very acute intelligence, impressive political ability, and considerable ambition. It was this latter characteristic that motivated his activities in Grand Rapids. He had chosen this as the battle ground upon which he, the thrice chosen lieutenant governor, would demonstrate once and for all that his political strength surpassed that of John B. Swainson. On Friday evening Ferency's prospects seemed bleak indeed. Nothing was yet suspected of what would come to be called the "Morton House Caper."

One of the major strengths Collins had was the active support of almost every well-known Democrat. Staebler, and therewith, it was assumed, Williams, favored the incumbent chairman. Frank Kelley, Jr., the attorney general, and James Hare, the secretary of state, were firmly behind Collins, as were T. John Lesinski and Congresswoman Martha Griffiths. Gus Scholle, though he did not represent a unified labor caucus, was still presumed by many delegates to be labor's voice. At some point, it occurred to someone in the Ferency camp that although it was obviously impossible to recruit this group of influential Democratic leaders away from Collins, it might be possible to remove them, at least temporarily, from the proceedings of the convention. All the major democratic leaders backing Collins were contacted and informed that an important meeting of the leaders of both factions was about to take place at the Morton House hotel and that their attendance was indispensable. When they arrived, none of Ferency's supporters was to be found.[39]

While the major figures in the Collins campaign were on their way to the Morton House, John Swainson arrived at the convention hall. He had been ill, and on the orders of his physician, who was himself an active Democrat, was brought to the convention by ambulance. Rather than enter immediately at the stage, the former governor came into the convention hall at the rear. As he made his way through the assembled delegates to the podium, emotion began to rise. Everyone seemed transfixed by the spectacle of the recently defeated governor leaving a sickbed, or as some seemed to believe, a hospital death bed, to make a plea that the party be placed in the hands of his former assistant. If Swainson's appeal was not a sufficient threat to Collins's fortunes, someone advised Collins that his allies had deserted him. "Your support has taken a powder. Show me any of your people." Collins, who had not been notified of the Morton House meeting, looked in vain for those he had counted on most. He was then told that a tally had been taken and that Ferency had it going away. No such tally existed, but Collins was already being overwhelmed with bad news, and was susceptible to the ploy. He had earlier been told, on what was supposedly reliable authority, that G. Mennen Williams, thoroughly chagrined by the party's civil war, was flying in and would throw his support to Ferency in order to promote party unity. Believing that he no longer had even a chance to win, Collins advised the convention to elect Ferency by acclamation. It has been suggested that on a legitimate vote Collins would have won by a margin of more than two-to-one.[40]

This version of the way Zolton Ferency was first elected chairman of the Michigan Democratic party has received wide circulation. Mere mention of the Morton House Caper is enough to make those who were with Ferency chortle and those who opposed him grimace. In fact, it had very little to do with the actual result. Ferency's strength came not from a political maneuver that briefly removed the leaders of the Collins campaign from the convention, but from his ability to acquire delegates from Wayne and Oakland counties. The Oakland County delegation had initially seemed committed to Collins. Gus Scholle, who was a member of it, had worked hard to keep it out of Ferency's grasp. Others, however, like Allen Zemmol, who had been active in Swainson's primary fight with James Hare in 1960, saw in Ferency's battle against Collins a repetition of the earlier struggle, and were not eager to give up what they had already won. Though the delegation was leaning to Collins, the issue was in doubt, and that made the campaigning abilities of the candidates decisive. In such a contest, Ferency clearly had the upper hand. With a flamboyant style that had not yet lost its effect through repeated exposure, he brought the members of the caucus out of their chairs. Against Ferency's fiery rhetoric Collins could offer only the mundane generalities of an undistinguished party functionary. Oakland County moved into the Ferency camp.[41]

Most of the Wayne County chairmen were for Ferency from the outset. Whether they could deliver their districts, however, depended upon labor, and labor did not quite know what it wanted. Scholle was for Collins; Woodcock and Fraser were for Ferency; the labor caucus was for neutrality between them. In the 1960 gubernatorial primary neutrality had permitted everyone in the labor movement to support the candidate of his choice. As this policy had made it possible for Swainson to secure the Democratic nomination, it now made it possible for Swainson's choice to obtain the chairmanship of the Democratic party. Once the labor caucus declared itself neutral, the rush to Ferency began in earnest. Not only did all the UAW delegates join Ferency, but many of the other labor representatives did so as well. A majority of the steelworkers, for example, refused to follow Scholle's lead.[42] Still, despite the sizable strength Ferency obtained from the individual members of the labor caucus, the contest was far from over. It was so close that everything seemed to hinge on the Sixteenth Congressional District.

One of the few Wayne County District chairmen who had refused to endorse Ferency was Gordon Traye of the Sixteenth District. At first Traye refused even to let Ferency speak to the district caucus, but toward the end of the deliberations Ferency managed to get in. Almost immediately T. John Lesinski stormed into the room and demanded to be heard. Lesinski had been before the caucus twice previously, and what was viewed as his dictatorial manner had not endeared him or his candidate to the delegation. When Doug Fraser now stood up, listed the people who had appeared on Collins's behalf, and suggested that Ferency ought to be given the courtesy of a hearing, Traye had little prospect of obtaining support for his objections. Ferency, who had been born and reared in the Sixteenth District, managed to persuade the caucus, with the help of Fraser and those delegates who were also members of UAW Local 600, the largest local union in the world, that he and not Collins ought to lead the party.

The defeat of John J. "Joe" Collins had not been a consequence of an eleventh-hour conspiracy engineered by the Swainson-Ferency forces. It had been, instead, the result of Ferency's ability to capitalize on substantially the same support Swainson had received in his successful primary campaign two years earlier. This was possible only because the labor caucus could not agree to support either candidate. That in turn was caused by the UAW's continued reluctance to intervene in the internal workings of the party organization independently of the state AFL-CIO. Content to leave control of the party in the hands of the party leadership, the UAW, when faced with a situation in which the leadership was divided, acquiesced in a policy of labor neutrality. Nor was it simply a question of the UAW's being reluctant to impose its position on the other members of the AFL-CIO. Woodcock and Fraser had associated themselves with Ferency from the beginning, but Roy Reuther, who directed the UAW's political arm, was, in the words of one labor activist, "betwixt and between."[43] Not until a 4 A.M. meeting on the day the convention was to begin balloting did Reuther, as the result of an insulting remark made by one of Collins's supporters, begin to move in Ferency's direction.[44]

The Morton House Caper did little, if anything, to advance the prospects of Zolton Ferency. To the extent to which the episode was credited with having been instrumental in his election to the chairmanship, it provided his opponents with both a convincing excuse for defeat and a convenient pretext for future attack. A victory that had been won through such a device could scarcely be called legitimate, and those who had been deposed from power could hardly be faulted for seeing in it a rather sordid chapter in an ongoing contest for control.

Ferency had sought the chairmanship of the state Democratic party with the hope and the expectation of giving it a coherent policy and a clear voice while the Republicans held power. But early in his term Ferency discovered that what a state party could do in the absence of a Democratic state administration was seriously affected by the presence of a Democratic national administration. When the 1964 Democratic national convention opened in Atlantic City, the issue most likely to cause contention was whether to seat the regular Mississippi delegation or the delegation representing the Freedom Democratic party. There seemed to be little doubt which delegation would receive the support of Michigan Democrats; they had left the state carrying a unanimous resolution declaring their endorsement of the Mississippi Freedom party.[45] The issue for the Michigan delegation appeared to be simply racism in the South, and for Michigan Democrats support for civil rights was the indispensable prerequisite to participation in the party or respectability in politics. The issue, however, proved to be something other than a clear-cut case of virtue against vice.

Lyndon Johnson was not disposed to permit any issue to distract attention from his nomination, much less an issue that might disrupt the convention altogether. The president decided a compromise would have to be arranged before the convention was gavelled into session. With the acquiescence of Martin Luther King, a bargain was struck. A promise that the procedures by which delegates were selected would be improved in the future was given in exchange for the seating of the regular Mississippi delegation.[46] This was not what the Michigan delegates had come to do, and the question at first seemed to be whether to accept the president's decision or to comply with the state party's original instructions. Then, at a strategy meeting of nearly two dozen of the most influential members of the delegation, it became apparent that the real question for most of them was not what to do about the president's compromise solution but how to obtain for it the willing consent of the delegation as a whole. Walter Reuther, who had helped arrange the compromise,[47] was going with the president, as were both U.S. senators, the congressmen, including black Congressman Charles Diggs, Gus Scholle, Neil Staebler, and almost everyone else in the room. But Zolton Ferency would have nothing to do with it. He announced, "Deliberate all you want, I know where I'm going."[48] Ferency's argument, that Johnson's compromise could be beaten on the floor was met with the reply that the wishes of the president could not be ignored. Only two others stated their intention to side with the party chairman; one of them was John Swainson. With Scholle speaking for the compromise and Ferency against it, the issue was debated in a caucus of the full delegation. Ferency lost two-to-one, and the Michigan Democratic party, contrary to its own resolution, voted for the seating of the Mississippi regular Democratic delegation.[49]

Scholle had opposed Ferency in his fight for the chairmanship in 1963. That defeat had not been nearly so annoying to the head of the state AFL-CIO as was Ferency's unsuccessful opposition in Atlantic City. Reasonable men might differ over the selection of a state party chairman, but to disagree with and actually fight against a decision of a Democratic president of the United States went beyond the bounds of requiring, or even permitting, tolerance. The first rebuke Ferency received turned out to be a favor. Before Atlantic City the chairman had been mentioned, with what he perceived to be growing frequency, as a possible running mate for Neil Staebler, the party's gubernatorial candidate. A combination of Staebler and Ferency would have neatly brought together the factions that had been in opposition since Swainson succeeded G. Mennen Williams as governor. After Atlantic City whatever possibility there had been that Ferency would be asked to run with Staebler disappeared. Instead the nomination was given to the state solicitor general, Robert Derenkowski, who brought to the ticket the advantages of a name that, if not well known, was still Polish. Staebler, it turned out, needed more than a Polish running mate. Despite the huge plurality rolled up by Lyndon Johnson, despite the first Democratic majorities elected to both houses of the state legislature in thirty years, despite the greatest overall Democratic sweep in Michigan history, George Romney defeated Neil Staebler in 1964 and began his second term as the state's governor.

After the election there seemed to be two obvious and unavoidable political facts. The first was the availability of potentially formidable Democratic candidates for higher office. Frank Kelley, Jr., for example, had been reelected attorney general by a wide margin and appeared to have a solid base from which to mount a campaign for the governorship in 1966. The other fact, however, offset the first. George Romney's ability to withstand the Johnson landslide made him seem, especially to those like Kelley who would have to give up an important office to run against him, invulnerable. As 1966 approached, many names were mentioned as a possible Democratic adversary for the Republican governor, but no one announced a candidacy. Everyone wanted to be mentioned for an honor that no one really prized. The Democratic state chairman understood the real reluctance that accompanied the apparent interest of the long line of prospective nominees. In the early months of 1966, when there was still no declared candidate in the field, the press began to ask the chairman whether the Democrats were simply going to concede the election. Ferency would respond by insisting that there were a great number of qualified potential candidates and would mention the names of several, few of whom, as he well knew, had any desire to challenge George Romney. As the party chairman could scarcely conceal the absence of a gubernatorial candidate, the possibility developed that Ferency himself might become the Democratic standard bearer. When reporters began to ask him whether this possibility was a real one, Ferency would answer that it was an eventuality he had every hope would not come to pass. Only if there were no candidate available that he could support without reservation would he consider seeking the nomination himself.

Each time Ferency proposed as a possible candidate someone with no interest in running and accompanied the suggestion with a repetition of his own reluctance to do so, those who had little love for the chairman grew more alarmed; they feared the Ferency gubernatorial campaign might have begun in earnest. This was a source of discomfort for reasons that went beyond personal animosity. In the judgment of his enemies, Ferency was not to be trusted, and if they could not rely on him as party chairman they probably would not be able to rely on him as a candidate. What would have been a serious concern in any event was a matter of extreme urgency in light of the new plans of G. Mennen Williams. The six-term governor, who seemed to have been banished to the political wilderness first by Kennedy and then by Johnson, had decided to relinquish the ambassadorship to the Philippines in exchange for the opportunity to succeed Patrick McNamara, who had grown very ill, in the United States Senate. Someone more sympathetic to Williams and his followers than Ferency had to be found if there was to be any chance of conducting a coherent and cooperative campaign.

Two alternatives to Ferency seemed to be available. The first was John

Mackie, who, after achieving wide electoral support as the state's highway commissioner, had been elected to the Congress. It seemed likely he could be persuaded to forgo reelection to a second term and become a candidate for governor. Several leading Democrats prompted him to do precisely that. Romney was formidable, but, they argued, with Williams on the ticket far from invulnerable. Mackie, though refusing to make a firm commitment, did nothing to dispel the hope that he might do as asked. Uncertainty came to an end when Mackie, at a press conference he had called in Flint, which everyone expected was for the purpose of declaring his gubernatorial candidacy, announced he would remain in Congress. He did not remain very long. A young Republican, Donald Riegle, defeated him in a stunning upset in November.[50] The other alternative was the young mayor of Detroit, Jerome P. Cavanagh, who had already acquired something of a national reputation. Cavanagh, however, was not interested in becoming governor. He had become mayor, to everyone's astonishment, at the age of thirty-two, and he had unlimited ambitions. Elected as a young Irish Catholic within a year of another young Irish Catholic's capture of the presidency, the mayor noticed the parallels many people were drawing and believed them. The next, but not the last, step for Cavanagh would be not the state capitol but the Senate of the United States. The next obstacle for him was not George Romney but G. Mennen Williams. Everything seemed possible.

The failure to obtain a candidate who had sufficient stature to preclude a Ferency campaign did nothing to diminish the outrage that met Ferency's first disclosure of his intentions. In the early weeks of 1966, Ferency met with Gus Scholle at the state party headquarters in Lansing. Scholle was informed of what he already had ample reason to expect, that Ferency was going to be a candidate for governor. He was livid. One of Ferency's closest assistants knew what Scholle was going to be told and placed himself near enough to the closed door of the chairman's office to hear everything that went on. Scholle, who had a great facility with the more colorful parts of the English language, outdid himself. He used every uncomplimentary name imaginable and invented new forms of profanity on the spot. The episode finally came to an end with a declaration that Ferency could run for governor or anything else, but he could not run far enough or fast enough to escape what Gus Scholle and the AFL-CIO were going to do to him.[51]

Though Scholle did try to persuade Sander Levin, just completing his first term in the state senate, to run against Ferency, a race which Levin was led to believe would have the full backing of organized labor, the anger that had been unleashed on the state chairman was soon diverted, if not abandoned. Scholle detested Ferency, but he is said to have loved Williams, and the immediate danger to the former governor was now not Ferency's campaign for governor, but Cavanagh's for senator. Moreover, once it was certain that

Ferency was not to be denied the nomination, antipathy toward the Democratic candidate was more than counterbalanced by Scholle's genuine and complete abhorrence of George Romney. Scholle even began to express a certain admiration for Ferency's willingness to attack the Republican governor directly. That, however, was as far as he was prepared to go.[52]

In the primary election, Ferency faced no challenge. Williams was not so fortunate. Though he defeated Cavanagh by a respectable margin, 437,438 to 290,465,[53] the drain on his energy and on the campaign's resources was considerable. The general election campaign now seemed a more difficult undertaking than it had half a year earlier for yet another reason. Senator McNamara died in office and Governor Romney appointed the Republican candidate, Congressman Robert Griffin, to fill the unexpired term. Williams found himself faced with an opponent whose claim of incumbency, no matter how brief, was an advantage.

With everyone's attention fastened on the Williams-Cavanagh primary, there was little time and even less inclination to think about the composition of the part of the ticket that would be selected at the party convention. There was no doubt that both Frank Kelley and James Hare would be renominated as a matter of course for attorney general and secretary of state, respectively. Who would become the party nominee for lieutenant governor, on the other hand, was far from settled. Beyond the requirement that Ferency's running mate be a resident of the Detroit area suburbs, nothing had been done to narrow the field of possible choices when the convention opened. The selection of a candidate for lieutenant governor was not a matter that could be approached as an isolated issue. It was one aspect of a broader process by which the ticket as a whole would be made representative of the various groups and interests the party leadership believed needed to be included in order to attract their electoral support. The nomination of a candidate for one office was bound up with the nomination of every other candidate.

Trustees of the state's three major universities, the University of Michigan, Michigan State University, and Wayne State University, were directly elected by the voters after being nominated in the party convention. These offices, despite the responsibilities they carried, were seldom eagerly sought. The party did little to recruit candidates, and their selection in convention became largely a means by which it provided representation for its major elements. For some time Ferency had believed that greater care should be taken to select candidates for the university boards, and as a means to that end had endeavored to interest Democratic faculty groups in the selection of trustees. The faculty groups at Michigan State University had been told to recruit candidates for the board of trustees, and had been advised that their recommendations would be viewed by the chairman as the main, if not the sole, criterion that the party would use in making its nominations.[54] But while the MSU Democratic Advisory Research Committee (DARC) was working directly with the party chairman, an alumnus of MSU was actively lobbying the county and district party organizations for nomination to the board.

After several years as a member of the senate staff in Washington, John Bruff had decided to return home to Mt. Clemens and practice law. His interest in politics, however, had not diminished, and he concluded that as a graduate of Michigan State University with a great number of party contacts, he might reasonably expect to be nominated for MSU's board of trustees.[55] However, Bruff was not the candidate the MSU DARC recommended. Its candidate was Nate Conyers, brother of Congressman John Conyers. Failure to nominate Conyers would make it impossible for Ferency to keep his commitment to DARC; it would also mean that the party's statewide ticket would not include a single black. Ferency's solution was to enable Conyers to replace Bruff as a candidate for the MSU board of trustees by having Bruff, who lived in Macomb County and thus met the suburban residency requirement, nominated for lieutenant governor. This decision was not universally approved; some felt that Ferency would be helped more by someone whose name was more widely known. The UAW, however, was not opposed, and the tradition that the gubernatorial nominee select his own running mate was honored by the convention. John Bruff had come to the convention to seek nomination as a university trustee; he left it in possession of the nomination for lieutenant governor. Both proved to be equally worthless.

Ferency now had a running mate, but he had yet to obtain a full-time campaign manager. From his own resources it is doubtful the Democratic gubernatorial nominee could have secured the services of anyone, much less someone worth having. Until the primary, the Ferency campaign had been little more than Zolton Ferency himself. After the primary there was still no indication that he would be able to attract the resources necessary to mount a serious challenge to George Romney. But Ferency was rescued from possible embarrassment when the UAW agreed to loan the gubernatorial campaign a union officer to manage his campaign.[56] Though barely forty, Ferency's new campaign manager, Sam Fishman, had almost a quarter century of experience in labor politics. As a teenager in New York, he had been involved in the faction-ridden politics of the radical movement in the late thirties and early forties. One of his first forays into Michigan politics had been with the short-lived Michigan Commonwealth Federation, which, it will be remembered, seemed to demonstrate the practical impossibility of an independent labor party. In the latter years of the fifties, Fishman, then a member of UAW Local 36 in Wixom, began to take an active part in Oakland County politics and was instrumental in fashioning an alliance between the UAW and the liberal contingent of the county party in order to remove the party's conservative old guard. In 1960, after he had become president of the Wixom Local,

Fishman joined with Russ Leach and other local union presidents in the successful campaign to attract UAW votes to John Swainson in the gubernatorial primary.

Fishman's reputation as an adroit political manager was already established and would extend beyond Oakland County to the state as a whole when he became the UAW's Michigan Community Action Program (CAP) director in 1967. In 1966, however, more than a highly talented campaign manager was needed to enable Zolton Ferency to defeat George Romney. On the surface, it appeared that Ferency would receive considerable assistance from G. Mennen Williams's presence on the ticket. But for the same reason that some believed Williams a help to Ferency, others, for the most part members of the Williams campaign, concluded that Ferency's campaign would be a serious hindrance to Williams's senatorial bid. Ferency's interest lay in a close association with Williams; Williams's interest lay in the greatest possible separation of the two campaigns. Self-interest was not the only motive that tended to drive the Williams campaign away from Ferency. Many of those involved in the gubernatorial campaign had been publicly sympathetic to Cavanagh in the primary and had not felt any particular compulsion to provide proof of their loyalty to Williams afterward. No one, however, was more guilty of indiscretion than the candidate himself. Within weeks of the primary, Williams became ill and underwent surgery for the removal of kidney stones. Ferency—holding forth in what he thought, but had no reason to expect, was the privacy of his campaign headquarters—was quoted by Roger Lane of the *Detroit Free Press*, who was there, as saying that the six kidney stones were the only new thing to come out of Williams in two months.[57] Relations between the Ferency and Williams campaigns had never been good; they now became nonexistent. With only a few weeks remaining before the election, the Ferency campaign found itself without funds to cover the postage costs for a last-minute mailing. They appealed to the Williams campaign for assistance. No answer was received.[58]

Ferency was beaten as no Democratic gubernatorial candidate had been beaten in decades. Romney's margin of victory was nearly three-to-two, and was at least partially responsible not only for the election of Republican majorities in the legislature, but for the first defeat ever administered to G. Mennen Williams by the voters of Michigan.

Ferency was not governor, but he was still chairman of the state Democratic party. At first, still smarting from the sting of defeat, he had little if any interest in continuing in the chairmanship. Most of the party leadership, angered at what they chose to believe was Ferency's responsibility for the defeat of G. Mennen Williams and the general destruction of the Democratic party, were eager to see him go. Had he been left alone, Ferency might have decided not to seek another term. But whether because of an instinctive refusal to avoid a fight or an aversion to being seen as having yielded to others, when the leadership demanded he not run, he knew he had to. However, he did not immediately disclose his plans. Instead, while Staebler and Scholle were searching for a candidate who could obtain broad support within the party and who would be less idiosyncratic than Ferency, the chairman's press secretary, James Harrison, initiated a movement to draft Ferency for a third two-year term.[59]

As president of the state AFL-CIO, Gus Scholle was labor's spokesman in the state Democratic party. He represented all of labor, however, only to the extent that the UAW, which constituted well over half the membership of the state AFL-CIO, acquiesced in his judgment. That Scholle normally received UAW support resulted not only from their common belief that labor should be involved in the Democratic party, but from the opinion that Scholle's constant participation in the day-to-day workings of the party provided him with experience and knowledge not available to many other union officials. The presumption, therefore, was that Scholle's judgment was the best informed judgment and should not lightly be ignored. On the question of Ferency's bid for reelection, the UAW's immediate inclination was to support Scholle and Staebler in their opposition to the party chairman.

It will be remembered that in 1963, when Ferency wrested the chairmanship from John Collins, Scholle and Staebler had supported Collins and the UAW membership had backed Ferency. The rationale for the UAW's position had then been that the party leadership should be allowed to choose the chairman it wished. At that time, however, the party leadership was identified with the governor—after fourteen years of party control of the governorship, the fact that Swainson had just been defeated was not seen as a distinction sufficient to alter the definition of leadership within the party. Defeated or not, Swainson had been the party's gubernatorial candidate, and thus was still, in the UAW's judgment, the party's titular head. However, by 1967 it was no longer possible to identify the gubernatorial candidate with the leadership of the Democratic party. Ferency had not been governor, had not come even close to becoming governor, and was generally regarded as having no chance whatever of ever being governor. With a Republican beginning his third term in the governor's office, the leadership of the Democratic party was to be sought in those people who held office in the party or who had established influence in it.

There was nothing clearly inconsistent in the UAW's support for Ferency in 1963 and opposition to him in 1967. Both could be based on the principle that the party leadership should be allowed to select the chairman it wanted. At a meeting of the UAW leadership which included both Emil Mazey and Walter Reuther that principle was invoked. Reuther, who rarely involved himself in Michigan politics, and who knew very little of the practical day-to-day activities of the Democratic party, stated the general principle of going along with the position of the party leadership on the basis that those were the people who were best informed about the situation. That statement would have decided the UAW position had it not been for the presence of Sam Fishman, who, it will be recalled, had served as Ferency's campaign manager. Fishman observed that Reuther's statement of principle was correct and was obviously supported. But having just returned from full-time involvement with the party, he was of the opinion that the struggle over the chairmanship was an ideological one. The UAW, he continued, should therefore be on the liberal side of the dispute and that meant supporting Ferency.[60] Fishman's argument was persuasive. Reuther, whose support of the leadership was based on their supposed possession of information he lacked, had no hesitation about abandoning that leadership when another source of information, a source he trusted, advised him that the leadership was not on the liberal side of a political battle.

With the UAW supporting Ferency, Scholle was unable to find a candidate willing to run against him. Even if he had, Ferency was unbeatable when the Democratic state convention met in February for the election of a chairman. He had little support among party officials but was a great favorite among convention delegates. Whatever elation Ferency may have felt in victory must have been tempered, however, by the knowledge that by their own statement those who could not defeat him in convention would not work with him afterwards.[61] The threat was soon a fact. Once the regular meetings of the party officers began, it was clear that the chairman was faced with a majority bloc that would oppose him at every turn.[62] The chairman could not win a vote. Nor could the UAW provide assistance; labor, including the UAW, was still represented in the party by Gus Scholle.

A working arrangement of controlled hostility seemed likely to continue throughout Ferency's two-year term. The situation became completely untenable, however, when on September 17, 1967 Ferency gave a speech that attacked American participation in the Vietnam War and advocated a Democratic alternative to the candidacy of Lyndon Johnson. Although the chairman had spoken to both Eugene McCarthy and George McGovern before giving the speech, he had not consulted any of the party officers. The officers considered this especially reprehensible in light of the fact that a party meeting had taken place on the evening of September 16, and Ferency had not mentioned even a possibility that he might denounce the incumbent Democratic president. Ferency's only defense was that he knew they would not agree to the statement and he had decided that he simply had to make it.[63]

What followed Ferency's "dump Johnson" speech, as it came to be known, made his prior problems with the party leadership look like a political honeymoon. His office was inundated with telegrams from Democrats all over the state demanding his resignation. The UAW, not yet willing to do open battle with the president, decided the party could not survive under Ferency. The party officers began to apply drastic economic pressure. Over Ferency's protest they voted to cut salaries, eliminate two secretaries and half of the staff. Ferency, who had voluntarily reduced his own salary to $18,500 as an economy measure, had it reduced to less than $14,000 by the officers. The secretary of state, James Hare, who had begun reducing the amount of money coming to the party from his branch managers, reduced it even further.[64] Ferency was confronted with the need to resign or face the continuing reduction of financial support and the consequent economic hardship on those who worked for him. He chose resignation.

Dissatisfaction with Zolton Ferency did not begin with his public denunciation of Lyndon Johnson. It did not even begin with his gubernatorial candidacy in 1966. It began with his insistence in 1965 that the Democratic party, which for the first time in the history of the liberal-labor alliance had come to occupy a majority position in both houses of the state legislature, put principle above expendiency and work for passage of a state income tax. The question of taxation was scarcely novel in 1965. Devising an equitable system by which to produce state revenues had occupied the thoughts, and exhausted the patience, of both G. Mennen Williams and John B. Swainson during the fourteen years the Democratic party controlled the executive branch of government. Beginning in Williams's first term and continuing for almost two decades, taxation was the central issue not only between the parties but within the Democratic party. Debate in the liberal-labor coalition on the issue of taxation, and especially on the specific question of a state income tax, led eventually to one of the most disruptive disagreements between liberals and labor since the beginning of their alliance. Perhaps even more importantly, taxation became the issue on which division opened and widened between the UAW on the one hand and the state AFL-CIO on the other.

Notes

1. Robert D. Novak, *Wall Street Journal*, December 24, 1959.
2. Boyd Benedict (administrative assistant to Governor John B. Swainson), interview with author, October 10, 1971.
3. Neil Staebler, personal communication with author, February, 1982.
4. August Scholle, interview with author, September 12, 1971.
5. Russ Leach, interview with author, December 15, 1971.
6. Ed Purdy, interview with author, April 12, 1973.
7. Russ Leach, interview with author, December 15,1971.
8. Mildred Jeffries, interview with author, September 1, 1971.

9. Sam Fishman, interview with author, March 12, 1973; Russ Leach, interview with author, December 15, 1971; Harold Julian, interview with author, February 23, 1973.

10. Joseph Kowalski, personal conversation with author, 1965.

11. Boyd Benedict, interview with author, October 10, 1971; John Swainson, interview with author, April 19, 1973; August Scholle, interview with author, September 12, 1971.

12. Neil Staebler, interview with author, May 1, 1971.

13. State of Michigan, *Official Canvass of Votes 1960,* pp. 3–4.

14. Ibid., p. 4.

15. Ibid.

16. Ibid.

17. State of Michigan, *Official Canvass of Votes 1958,* p. 36.

18. State of Michigan, *Official Canvass of Votes 1956,* p. 34.

19. State of Michigan, *Official Canvass of Votes 1960,* p. 36.

20. Alfred Meyer, interview with author, November 6, 1971.

21. Zolton Ferency, interview with author, April 23, 1972.

22. Boyd Benedict, interview with author, October 10, 1971.

23. Zolton Ferency, interview with author, April 23, 1972.

24. Boyd Benedict, interview with author, October 10, 1971.

25. Zolton Ferency, interview with author, April 23, 1972; Boyd Benedict, interview with author, October 10, 1971.

26. Zolton Ferency, interview with author, April 23, 1972.

27. Ibid.

28. Ibid.; John Swainson, interview with author, May 12, 1973.

29. Boyd Benedict, interview with author, October 10, 1971.

30. Zolton Ferency, interview with author, April 23, 1972.

31. Zolton Ferency, interview with author, April 23, 1972; Boyd Benedict, interview with author, October 10, 1971.

32. Russ Leach, interview with author, December 15, 1971; Zolton Ferency, interview with author, April 23, 1972.

33. Russ Leach, interview with author, December 15, 1971.

34. August Scholle, interview with author, September 12, 1971.

35. Ibid.

36. Sam Fishman, interview with author, March 12, 1973.

37. Ibid.; Russ Leach, interview with author, December 15, 1971.

38. Zolton Ferency, interview with author, April 23, 1972.

39. Boyd Benedict, interview with author, October 10, 1971.

40. Ibid.

41. Harold Julian, interview with author, February 23, 1973.

42. Zolton Ferency, interview with author, April 23, 1972.

43. Russ Leach, interview with author, December 15, 1971.

44. Ibid.

45. Zolton Ferency, interview with author, April 23, 1972.

46. Theodore H. White, *The Making of the President 1964* (New York: Atheneum, 1965), pp. 277–80.

47. Ibid.

48. Zolton Ferency, interview with author, April 23, 1972.

49. August Scholle, interview with author, September 12, 1971; Zolton Ferency, interview with author, April 23, 1972.

50. For Riegle's version of Mackie's defeat see Donald Riegle, *O Congress* (New York: Doubleday and Co., 1972).

51. James Harrison, interview with author, June 12, 1973.

52. August Scholle, personal communication with author, August 26, 1966.

53. State of Michigan, *Official Canvass of Votes 1966*, p. 6.

54. Zolton Ferency, interview with author, April 23, 1972.

55. John Bruff, interview with author, June 6, 1973.

56. Sam Fishman, interview with author, March 12, 1973.

57. *Detroit Free Press*, October 23, 1966.

58. James Harrison, interview with author, June 12, 1973.

59. Ibid.

60. Sam Fishman, interview with author, March 12, 1973.

61. Zolton Ferency, interview with author, April 23, 1972; Neil Staebler, personal communication with author, February, 1982.

62. Ibid.

63. James Harrison, interview with author, June 12, 1973.

64. Ibid.

PART 2
Labor and the Legislature

CHAPTER 4

The Question of Taxation

Throughout the tenure of Governor G. Mennen Williams, one that began in 1949 and extended until 1961, Republicans dominated both houses of the legislature. Nevertheless, the legislature abstained from passing measures harmful to labor, not only because Williams could be expected to veto it, but because of the Republicans' growing respect for labor's political power in the electorate. Republican members willingly introduced antilabor legislation that would maintain their credentials with business—and carefully contrived to keep it in committee so that no recorded vote that labor might use against them would exist. Williams, for his part, repeatedly requested legislation that would improve the condition of labor. At the beginning of the 1952 legislative session, for example, the governor sent the legislature a message asking that the period of payments for unemployment compensation be increased from twenty to twenty-six weeks. The message recommended increases in both job insurance and workmen's compensation and requested that the benefits of both programs be extended to an additional quarter million workers. The message was ignored.[1] Williams, acting in concert with the leadership of organized labor, called for such legislation knowing full well that little, if anything, would come of it.[2] Republicans introduced legislation designed to jeopardize what the unions had accomplished and then made certain nothing was done about it. However, this tacit understanding that the status quo would be preserved did not extend across the board. It most emphatically did not extend to the question of taxation. And it was on the question of the proper means by which to raise the revenue necessary to support state services that the battleground between the two parties, and eventually within the Democratic party as well, was most clearly determined.

In a March 9, 1951, message to the legislature, Williams predicted that the state would face a deficit of $40 million by the end of the fiscal year. He asserted that the "state's entire financial problem could be solved in one 'package' by enactment of a four percent tax on corporate profits." Each percent of such a tax would yield, according to the governor's estimate, $23 million in state revenue. In January of the following year, Williams repeated his demand for a corporation profits tax to avert a deficit.[3] In June, in a speech to the annual Michigan CIO council convention in Grand Rapids, Williams again argued for adoption of a corporate profits tax. The Michigan legislature, according to the governor, was "dominated by Republican advocates of the 'trickle down' school of thought. They will tax anybody except big business. . . ." Because of this, the legislature "ignored for five years the state's acute need for new revenues to pay the increased costs of state which had grown by more than one-fifth in the last ten years."[4] It was the legislature's expectation that when the situation became desperate, revenue could be "extracted, under the pressure of emergency, from your pockets and the pockets of other common people of this state." Williams provided two examples of attempts to procure revenue at the expense of the "common people." The first was legislation which, by changing the name of certain segments of the sales tax, would withdraw the proceeds from local government and bring them into the state treasury. This would necessarily bring about an increase in local property taxes. The second example is more interesting, for it was in principle precisely the tax program that labor and the Democratic party came to support in the middle sixties. The passage in which Williams takes up this second example deserves to be quoted in its entirety.

> Senator Higgins, Chairman of the Senate Taxation Committee, was quoted today as denying that the Republican leadership was contemplating a personal income tax. He was quoted as saying that no income tax bill has been introduced in the Legislature.
>
> Senator Higgins has got so many bills in his committee to impose new taxes that he apparently has forgotten some of them.
>
> Here, my friends, is the answer. Here is a copy of a bill, Senate Bill No. 339, introduced by Senator Cloon of Wakefield, and sent to Senator Higgins' Committee. The title of the bill is, and I quote: "A bill to provide for the raising of additional public revenue by imposing a specific tax on individuals, corporations and other business organizations, for the privilege of receiving and earning income from any source whatsoever. . . ."
>
> Senate Bill No. 339 is a level-rate income tax bill. It would tax the income of the individual citizen and the income of the huge corporation at the same rate. General Motors and Ford would pay 3 percent of their earnings and the individual citizen would pay 3 percent. Oh, yes, as bait in the hope that the people will be fooled, this bill exempts incomes under ten thousand dollars a year, and is coupled with a plan to take the sales tax off food. But you know how long it would be before that ten thousand dollar level was junked and the new state income tax extended right down into your pocketbook. Then for the first time you would be equal to your boss—you'd both pay the same rate of taxes.[5]

It is difficult to find any explanation for Williams's angry rejection of the Republican proposal other than a belief in the inherent superiority of corporate taxation. An income tax that applied only to individuals making more than $10,000 per year would have effectively removed from its application every member of a Michigan trade union. Moreover, beyond protecting the "common people" from additional taxation, it would have decreased their taxes by removing the sales tax on food. Williams seems to have conceded all this by falling back on the argument that the $10,000 exemption would quickly be removed. That argument, however, was wholly inadequate. If public sentiment made the exemption necessary to the passage of the bill, it is difficult to see the basis for expecting that the public would later have tolerated the imposition of that which they had initially opposed. That Williams could take such a position, and do so in the presence of the assembled leadership of the state CIO, is nothing so much as a clear demonstration of the extent to which labor and the Democratic party perceived the Republican party as the public spokesman of the large corporations, and politics as an extension of class hostility between labor and business. There was, however, another consideration, one that might have induced Williams to attack a proposed income tax, and the CIO leadership to acquiesce in that attack, even without any vigorous hostility to corporate wealth.

The basis of Williams's electoral strength, and the largest single voting bloc in the new Democratic coalition, was the membership of organized labor. That membership was not completely convinced that the unions should be directly involved in politics. On issues of direct benefit to labor—such as workmen's compensation legislation—the membership could be convinced that political involvement was required. On broader issues, however, organized labor found it almost impossible to convince its members that the union leadership had any business entering the political arena. On mental health legislation, to take one example, labor "was not able to give Williams any real help. Our members simply did not see any direct connection between that kind of legislation and what they thought was the real business of their union."[6] The union membership did not favor active participation in the broader social legislation Williams was constantly putting forward, and their acceptance of that legislation depended upon their continued exemption from the additional costs of those programs. The price for the electoral support of union members—the price paid, in other words, for the continuation and the strengthening of the liberal-labor coalition—was the practical necessity to fund new state services through taxation that did not directly affect the "common people."

By the middle of Williams's third term in office, the question of taxation seemed to have become a matter of less than pressing importance. On January 14, 1954 the governor sent a message to the legislature in which he asserted, with some pride of accomplishment, that the "budget for the first time since 1945 is balanced." This had the fortunate consequence of permitting both the governor and the legislature "to assure our people that we will not ask them to pay any additional taxes."[7] The same message, however, requested legislation raising both unemployment compensation and the maximum workmen's compensation benefits to two-thirds of the average weekly wage. Though the request was rejected by the Republican legislature, it indicated the governor's continuing intention to apply pressure for more extensive, and more costly, programs to improve the general social welfare. Nor was he unsuccessful. Each year larger appropriations were wrested from the legislature for, among other things, mental health and education. Williams himself believed considerable progress was being made in convincing Republican legislators to move in the direction, if not at the pace, he wanted. In the spring of 1954 he commented: "During these past five years we have pushed, pulled, hauled and dragged these reluctant Old Guard Rip Van Winkles into the second half of the 20th century."[8] He had every intention of dragging them even further.

At the beginning of his campaign for a fourth term, Williams listed several objectives he would pursue if reelected, among them a massive road-building program and preparation for the state's part in the construction of the St. Lawrence Seaway. Nothing was mentioned about additional taxation or an alteration of the existing tax structure.[9] What had been ignored during the campaign was ignored during the fourth term. By the second year of the fifth term, however, taxation was fast becoming the central subject of political debate. Republicans, without whose support Williams could not have increased the state budget by a single dollar, began to adopt the rhetoric of earlier years on the question of state spending. State Senator Edward Hutchinson claimed that Williams "is leading us down the road to socialism and I'm no socialist." According to Hutchinson: "All Williams knows how to do is spend more and more and spend us into socialism."[10] Although spending levels were very far from constituting even an approximation of the socialism Hutchinson purported to fear, they were by now much beyond what could be supported by the available sources of revenue.

The disparity between expense and revenue was clearly set out in the finance message the governor transmitted to the legislature on February 22, 1957. Taken together, agency requests amounted to $525 million, a figure which exceeded the current expenditure level by 50 percent. Existing sources of revenue were expected to yield $336 million. By reducing the agency requests, Williams had managed to produce a general fund budget of $411 million. To meet even this reduced budget, however, an additional $75 million would obviously have to be raised. As he had in the past, Williams repeated his insistence that individuals not be the source from which the additional money was to be extracted: "The Michigan consumer continued to bear too heavy a portion of this state tax load and . . . he should not be compelled to assume the burden of additional taxes." Nevertheless, Williams mentioned among "possible additional tax sources" a flat-rate income tax. This would produce anywhere from $25 million to $80 million for each percent levied, depending on the size of the exemptions. In parentheses the governor added, "A graduated income tax has also been suggested, but its constitutionality is open to the greatest doubt."[11]

After noting the revenue a flat-rate income tax would produce, the governor directed his attention to other possible sources. Nuisance taxes were unsatisfactory in principle and insufficiently productive in practice. An increase in the sales tax, on the other hand, would easily procure the revenue necessary to cover the higher level of spending. An additional 1 percent on the sales tax would generate "slightly more than $100 million." This or any other increase in the sales tax, however, was "out of the question." The sales tax "is our most regressive tax and to increase it would further weight the tax structure against consumers." Even if this were not the case, a 1954 amendment to the state constitution set the sales tax rate at 3 percent. A ballot proposal to change it would take more time than was available and the prospects of passage were at best doubtful. Rejection of both nuisance taxes and an increased sales tax compelled reconsideration of an income tax: "This source of revenue has been suggested at almost every session and at least one bill to that effect is already pending at this session." But an income tax, when added to the existing sales tax, would be for most individuals "a severe additional burden."[12]

Several years earlier, in the speech to the state CIO cited above, Williams had rejected any income tax, even when accompanied by the repeal of the sales tax on food. Now, however, the objection to an income tax, in addition to a sales tax, "progressively loses force as we go up the scale of income." Thus, "there may well be an argument made for an income tax in the upper brackets." What Williams meant by the upper brackets is clarified by the level of exemptions he insisted would have to be present for an income tax to have "any semblance of equity." They would have to be "high enough to absolve the great majority of the people from paying anything." There would have to be at least a $2,000-per-person exemption. This would "of course, reduce the actual number of taxpayers to a small minority of the population." As we have seen, Williams had earlier rejected out of hand the prospect of an income tax that exempted incomes of $10,000 or less. Now he was at least suggesting that an argument could be made for an income tax which, with a $2,000-per-person exemption, would tax incomes above $8,000 for a family of four. Moreover, this income tax, in support of which "there may well be an argument," did not carry with it a repeal of the sales tax on food. Though there may have been "sound arguments" for it, Williams did not actually recommend the adoption of an income tax. It was not because there were sounder arguments on the other side, but because the governor did "not believe the legislature is prepared to enact such a measure at this time, and under existing circumstances, I have no intention of recommending it." A better, and a more equitable, way to "meet our problem" was the "remaining possibility," a tax on the net income of corporations. This corporate profits tax would be set at a rate of six percent.[13]

Later the same year, Williams tried a different tactic to bring about a resolution of the state's growing problem with the forms of taxation. The governor proposed "the setting up of an independent, blue ribbon citizens tax study commission, the recommendations of which might very well be so persuasive as to win the acceptance of taxpayers generally, the legislature and myself."[14] In conjunction with a tax study carried out by a special legislative committee on taxation, a citizens' committee of the sort requested by Williams was established. On January 6, 1959, the "Citizens Advisory Committee of the Michigan Tax Study" issued its report. The first recommendation made in the fifty-seven page report was also the most important and the most likely to generate controversy. The committee proposed that "a tax, with a graduated rate structure ranging from 3 percent to 8 percent, be introduced and imposed on the personal income of residents."[15]

Among the twenty-five members of the committee were Jack Conway, Walter Reuther's administrative assistant, and Leonard Woodcock, then one of the UAW's most influential and widely respected regional directors. Both Conway and Woodcock supported the report, including the proposal for the graduated income tax. Not everyone on the committee, however, was as satisfied. In a minority report two of the members set forth their opposition "to a program, or part of a program which has the objective of redistribution of wealth, earnings and income." One part of the program which had this objective clearly in view was the graduated income tax; moreover, this had been recognized explicitly by the committee as its intended objective. According to a staff paper prepared on the question of a state income tax: "The progressive (or graduated) income tax is an instrument for leveling inequalities in the distribution of wealth and income. The advantage of redistribution of income is that it checks the tendency toward cumulative economic inequality, and so assures more nearly equal opportunity."[16] For the authors of the minority report, the actual consequence of implementing a graduated income tax would be a diminution of the "incentive to compete, struggle, and succeed," combined with an encouragement of "political irresponsibility" in the form of demands for "additional state services by those who will bear no part of the burden."[17] In place of a graduated tax, the minority report called for a flat-rate income tax as the "most equitable way to tax income."[18] A dissenting opinion, supported by only two of the twenty-five committee members, would normally not be a cause of concern or even notice. In this instance, however, the opinion represented by the two-member minority was nearly identical to the opinion of the Republican majority in the state legislature. If anything, it failed to represent the latter opinion only in implying that there should be an income tax of any sort. Precisely how reluctant the state legislature was to enact an income tax or to make any other kind of major alteration in the tax structure was about to be demonstrated with a vengeance.

The basic recommendations of the citizens' advisory committee were adopted by Governor Williams, and in February, 1959 he proposed a tax reform program based on them.[19] In place of the nearly two dozen specific recommendations suggested by the committee, Williams asked for five major changes, including a corporate income tax and a graduated tax on personal income. The governor's program would generate something in excess of $140 million in new revenue. Without new revenue, the state could expect to have the general fund deficit rise to almost $100 million. This consideration, however, was not sufficient to induce the legislature to adopt a program that included a graduated income tax. Williams's program died in the house. An alternative program containing a flat-rate income tax was introduced by Representative Rollo G. Conlin, chairman of the house Taxation Committee, and was passed by the house. The senate, however, found even a flat-rate income tax obnoxious and refused to ratify what the house had done. But even the senate could not find a way to avoid the need for greater revenue.

> After more than eight months of sometimes heated and bitter debate the Legislature, on August 29, 1959, reached agreement on a tax program that bore no resemblance to those advocated by the Citizens Advisory Committee, Governor Williams or Representative Conlin, neither did it reflect in any way the analysis and conclusions that had been offered in the intensive tax studies conducted for the Citizens Advisory Committee and Special Committee on Taxation of the House of Representatives.[20]

What the tax program did do was to add nearly $130 million in new revenue to the state's general fund. Of this $130 million, fully $112 million was to be procured by raising the state sales tax from 3 to 4 percent. That the state constitution specifically placed a 3-percent limit on the sales tax served only to inspire the ingenuity of the legislature. Instead of stating that the sales tax was to be raised to 4 percent, the legislation stipulated a new 1 percent tax on all retail sales already subject to the 3 percent tax. With this remarkable contrivance, the legislature avoided an income tax, evaded the clear intent of the state constitution, and, complacent in their craft, adjourned. Seven weeks later the state supreme court held the additional 1 percent tax on retail sales unconstitutional. The legislature "reconvened and enacted a so-called 'nuisance tax' package which was to expire at the end of fiscal 1961 in anticipation of a favorable vote in 1960 on amending the Constitution to permit a 4 percent sales tax."[21] In November, 1960, an amendment to the constitution permitting an increase of the sales tax to 4 percent was passed. Acting almost immediately, the legislature raised the rate to 4 percent effective January 1, 1961.[22]

At the same time the voters were approving a higher ceiling for the sales tax, they elected John B. Swainson as G. Mennen Williams's successor in the governor's office. What Williams had not accomplished, Swainson was not about to attempt. In January, 1961, instead of proposing a graduated income tax he asked the legislature to approve as part of a five-point tax reform proposal a 3 percent flat-rate tax on personal income. This, in combination with a 3 percent tax on corporation profits, was expected to yield $306 million annually.[23] Though it would have preferred a higher tax on corporations and a lower tax on individuals, labor supported the Swainson plan. More surprising was the endorsement of an influential segment of the business community. Led by the president of American Motors, George Romney, a group called Citizens for Michigan had been created with the professed intention of restructuring state government along more rational lines. In April, 1961, it released a report in which a comprehensive reform of the tax structure was cited as an immediate necessity. The tax program suggested in the report included a flat-rate income tax.[24] With labor willing to accept less than what it wanted, and business, or at least some of its major components, willing to agree to more than it had before, the prospects for passage of a flat-rate tax appeared better than at any time in the past.

In 1959, when the house had voted for the flat-rate income tax contained in the Conlin proposal, the membership had been equally divided between Democrats and Republicans. In the winter of 1962 there was a Republican majority. Nevertheless, Swainson's flat-rate income tax was approved by the house and sent to the senate. The senate also gave its approval. Then the senate changed its mind.

The bill was passed on a Friday. During the weekend, lobbyists opposed to an income tax launched a counterattack.

> "Haskell Nichols, a Republican from Jackson, was the first to break. On Monday evening, when the senate came back into session, a vote to reconsider passed. Then so many amendments got tacked on the income tax bill that it wasn't any longer in a passable form. We lost."[25]

The income tax was once again rejected by the legislature in favor of still another series of nuisance taxes. Swainson refused to put his name to this, and the tax program went into effect without his signature.

The conflict between Swainson and the legislature was not exhausted with the effective elimination of a state income tax. State Senator John Bowman, though a Democrat, had far less allegiance to his own party's governor than to his constituency in the Detroit suburbs of Macomb County. He introduced legislation, aimed obviously against Detroit, prohibiting a city from levying a tax on those who lived outside the city but earned their livelihood in it. Against the almost unanimous advice of his political advisors, Swainson vetoed the Bowman bill, and paid dearly for it. It is generally believed that more than any other single factor, the loss of support in the suburban areas of the southeastern portions of the state made the difference between victory and defeat in the gubernatorial election of 1962. On the issue of taxation, Swainson had lost to the legislature in the winter and spring of 1962. On another aspect of the same issue, he lost the governorship to George Romney in the fall.

Far from seeing in Swainson's experience an insurmountable obstacle to even minimal reform, Romney began soon after his inauguration to advocate a comprehensive readjustment of the entire tax system. In September he called the legislature into special session and presented his own tax program for consideration. It included a proposal for a 2 percent flat-rate income tax. "Governor Romney's program for achieving tax reform," according to one economist, bore a "remarkably close resemblance to the proposals that had been offered some twenty months earlier by Governor Swainson."[26] Carl Westman, who represented the UAW in Lansing, also believed the Romney plan was similar to what had been proposed by Democratic governors.

In a memorandum sent to UAW regional directors in Michigan on September 27, 1963, Westman described the state tax structure as "a patch-work of regressive excises, nuisances, levies and a sorely over-worked local property tax." Romney's program, in Westman's judgment, "closely resembles the reform proposals of Governor Williams and Governor Swainson. The personal and corporate income taxes are the principal ingredients on the revenue side of all these programs." Nevertheless, there were "serious shortcomings" in the Romney plan. A major deficiency was the flat-rate form of the proposed income tax. Westman reminded his readers that of the income taxes in the thirty-two states then levying them, all but two were graduated. Still, he did not go on to advocate that the UAW pursue the graduated tax as part of an alternative proposal. He argued instead that by replacing the business activities tax with a 3.5 percent corporate income tax the Romney plan would reduce the taxes on business by an amount equal to what individuals would be charged. In Westman's opinion, instead of reducing the amount paid by business it was more reasonable to redistribute the burden within business by shifting "from fixed costs taxes to income related business taxes." That this redistribution would be more equitable was supported by reference to the "well-known fact that Chrysler Corporation during one of its most unprofitable years paid more taxes than did the highly profitable General Motors Corporation." If the corporate income tax were raised from the 3.5 percent suggested by Romney to 5.5 percent, taxation on business would be reduced by a total of $4 million from what it already paid, and, in combination with the 2 percent flat-rate income tax requested by the governor, would generate an additional $50 million in new revenue for the state.[27]

Despite Romney's advocacy and Westman's argument, the legislature failed to adopt an income tax or any other rational revision of the tax structure. Senate Republicans, who had a 23–11 majority, "refused to vote two income tax bills out of committee."[28] Harvey Brazer's comment was appropriate: "The Legislature, perhaps characteristically now, did nothing in response to Governor Romney's proposals."[29] The rejection of the Romney program seemed to prove that the past reluctance of Republican majorities to pass an income tax had not been based on a partisan unwillingness to cooperate with Democratic governors. Indeed, both Williams in his last term and Swainson in his only term had been able to move the income tax through the house, though not the senate. Romney could not get even that far. It began to appear that the prospects for tax reform depended on the possibility of replacing a Republican with a Democratic Majority in both the house and senate. That possibility, however, depended in turn on bringing about something like a revolution, not in the voting habits of Michigan citizens, but in the structural arrangements under which legislative elections took place.

The procedures used to reapportion Michigan's legislative districts had been a matter of concern and contention for the president of the state AFL-CIO from the time he first brought labor into active participation in the Democratic party.

> Since the 1940's Gus Scholle and other union leaders in the state had been pointing out that despite the fact that the 1908 Michigan constitution specifically called for districting on the basis of population, very little had been done to correct inequities resulting from population shifts over time.[30]

Indeed, in 1952 a step was taken not to correct the inequities but to make them permanent. That year an amendment to the state constitution was adopted that wrote the district boundaries of the state senate into the state's fundamental law. What had not been based on population before would now, with the passage of time, become an even more perfect gerrymander. Although those who were behind passage of the amendment paid a price by giving Governor Williams an opportunity to campaign on the record of the malapportioned senate, it remained a malapportioned senate, and it remained Republican.

Seven years later, Gus Scholle, alleging that the 1952 amendment constituted an impairment of his civil rights under the equal protection clause of the Fourteenth Amendment to the United States Constitution, brought suit. Scholle's contention, as it emerged in *Scholle v. Hare,* was based on the fact that because he was a resident of Royal Oak his vote was equal to but one-thirteenth of the vote of a resident of the state's most overrepresented senatorial district. He argued that by 1970 this large disparity would be larger still—his vote then would be worth only one-twenty-fifth of that other citizen's vote. When the Michigan Supreme Court decided that the issue was not a legal, but a political, question, over which the court could not and should not exercise jurisdiction, Scholle appealed to the Supreme Court of the United States. Before taking up *Scholle v. Hare,* however, the Court held in *Baker v. Carr* that apportionment questions were within the proper purview of the judiciary. *Scholle v. Hare* was then returned to the Michigan Supreme Court where, after reexamination, the state court handed down in July of 1962 the first decision in the nation affirming the one-man, one-vote principle. "The decision was widely regarded as a personal victory for Scholle and a triumph for organized labor in the state . . . it was the AFL-CIO alone that footed the bill for the legal expenses."[31] It should be noted that although *Scholle v. Hare* was disposed of on the basis of *Baker v. Carr,* the latter case was itself assisted by the former. Scholle's "original suit in Michigan provided the legal brief for the Tennessee case on reapportionment that, decided by the Supreme Court first, brought the one-man, one-vote rule to the fifty states."[32]

The court's clarity on the principle of legislative apportionment by population was accompanied by confusion about its practical application. Within six months of the decision in *Scholle v. Hare,* the state's voters adopted the new Michigan Constitution of 1963, which, framed before the decision, retained a method of senatorial apportionment that clearly failed to meet the one-man, one-vote standard. Only after the United States Supreme Court decided *Reynolds v. Sims* in 1964 and decisively established the one-man, one-vote principle did the Michigan Supreme Court instruct the state legislature to redraw senatorial districts in conformity with that principle. Under a provision of the new state constitution, the legislature was to accomplish any reapportionment through the agency of a legislative reapportionment commission. Required to be equally balanced between the parties in its membership, the commission was almost necessarily reduced to a nullity. On a question that more than any other would affect the political fortunes of the parties, their representatives on the commission could be expected to exhibit a most intense partisanship, masked only by a pretense that their opponents were the sole transgressors of the duty to remain impartial. The commission reached a deadlock, and under a second provision of the constitution had the issue removed from them to the state supreme court.

The court was composed of seven justices, each of whom had been nominated in a party convention to run in the general election on the non-partisan ballot. Removing the apportionment issue to the court did not avoid the problem of partisanship, but it did avoid a deadlock. The Democrats had a majority among the justices, and the court ordered the adoption of what had become known as the Austin-Kleiner plan. Named after its ostensible authors, Richard H. Austin of Detroit and Robert Kleiner of Grand Rapids, both long-active members of the Democratic party, the plan was actually drawn up—especially in its details—by other hands. The hands belonged to George Weaver, a UAW staff member, and they were dexterous in the extreme. In his office in the UAW headquarters in Detroit, Weaver designed an apportionment scheme that protected the principle of one-man, one-vote while providing the best possible opportunity for the election of the largest possible number of Democrats to the state legislature. Because the court acted swiftly to adopt the Austin-Kleiner plan, Michigan was the first state to apportion in compliance with *Reynolds v. Sims*. The court's speed also made it possible for the new districts to be created in time for the 1964 election.

Reapportionment based on population alone and designed with an eye to improving the prospects of the Democratic party might by itself have produced Democratic majorities in the state legislature. But with Lyndon Johnson's enormous margin of victory over Barry Goldwater, what might have been bare majorities became extremely large. In the house, 73 of 110 seats were occupied by Democrats. In the senate, Democrats held 23 of the 38 positions. If, after his unsuccessful attempt to convince Republican legislators to enact tax legislation, Governor Romney had considered the possibility of dealing with the Democrats, that option now became a political necessity. And what was necessary did not seem impossible. Two Democratic governors had put themselves and their party on record for an income tax. They had not even insisted that the income tax be graduated. During their years in the minority, Democratic legislators had called repeatedly for an income tax as the sole means by which the state's finances could be placed on a solid foundation. Principles advocated in opposition, however, are not always the principles acted on once those in opposition have acquired the power to rule. What John Randolph learned from Thomas Jefferson, George Romney was about to be taught by the Democratic majority.

Though he never knew it, George Romney had an ally in the last place he might have expected to find one. Less than three months after the Seventy-third Legislature convened, Carl Westman, the UAW's representative in Lansing, was arguing that state expenditures would be likely to exceed revenues, and that the consequent deficit should be avoided by means of an income tax. The deficit, however, would not occur immediately. The legislature was considering a budget of $788 million and anticipated revenues were $756 million, but because the state treasury had a surplus of $105 million what would otherwise be a deficit of $32 million would be a surplus of $73 million. This surplus would not last very long, however. Indeed, Westman observed, "On the basis of obligations already assumed the state will be short some $30.5 million by the 1965–66 budget period." It would more likely be much more. "If more realistic projections are made the deficit will grow to a figure of about 66.3 million." In 1966, an election year, the legislature would be confronted with an actual deficit even if that year's budget was no greater than the previous year's. This would compel a choice between increasing taxes or cutting expenditures, a choice elected officials spend most of their time devising ways and means to avoid. In Westman's opinion, were this to happen, "The chances of tax reform will be next to impossible." It was simply a matter of logic to conclude that what ought to be done was "to take the kind of action in 1965 that a little foresight shows necessary—tax increase and tax reform in the second legislative session."[33]

While Westman was attempting to acquire support within the UAW for immediate legislative action, Gus Scholle was being far more equivocal. The Michigan AFL-CIO president suggested that new state taxes would receive the approval of organized labor if they were indispensable and equitable. "If realistic appropriations for . . . state services will require additional revenue, we will look at every tax proposal before the Legislature and will approve those that will not shift taxes from business and industry onto the individual."[34] This was hardly a vigorous endorsement for a major restructuring of the tax system of the sort envisaged by Westman. Even the allusion to principles of equity seemed designed to mask the absence of any specific policy the AFL-CIO's president was prepared to advocate. Scholle would go no further than to express the willingness of the state labor organization to take "a close look" at a Republican plan to increase the state inheritance tax.[35]

Scholle's reluctance to do more than provide vague assurances that labor would support new taxes when no other alternative remained was apparently a view that few Democratic legislators had any reason to quarrel with. After the expiration of the first six months of the Seventy-third Legislature, Democratic members appeared content "to coast along on estimates of the accumulating general fund surplus more optimistic than Romney and his advisors consider justified."[36] The editorial writers of the *Ann Arbor News* believed they could account for this: "Apparently the lawmakers hope to scrape by until after the 1966 election—when senators will get four-year terms—and then carry out tax reforms including income taxes."[37] This was very close to the truth.

It has been pointed out before that despite the large numerical superiority enjoyed by the UAW within the state AFL-CIO, Gus Scholle, and not Walter Reuther or anyone else in the UAW, directed labor in its day-to-day political activities. For a period of almost twenty years, Scholle was labor's spokesman in the state legislature. Whenever the legislature was in session during those two decades, Scholle hosted a weekly luncheon for the Democratic legislative leadership. He considered it one of his personal triumphs that the press never discovered the existence of this private institution. The luncheons themselves resembled a union meeting. Most of the participants had been connected with the labor movement at some point. In 1965 the speaker of the house, Joseph Kowalski, still listed his occupation as a UAW international representative. Ray Dzendzel, the senate majority leader, had been an official of the Building Trades Union. Scholle, Kowalski, and Dzendzel were all very practical men and had spent most of their political lives associated with Democratic minorities in the legislature. For them it was self-evident that their new majorities would immediately vanish in the wind with the passage of an income tax unless there was a clear and present necessity to obtain new revenue. Even then it would be a risk. But to adopt an income tax when the passage of more social legislation than the state had seen in thirty years had still left a surplus was consciously to commit political suicide, and that they were not inclined to do.

Much less concerned with the electoral fortunes of state legislators than Scholle, Kowalski, or Dzendzel was, of all people, the chairman of the state Democratic party. Zolton Ferency saw nothing very attractive in the reluctance to so much as begin work on a tax reform program. He saw, instead, the betrayal of a long-standing party promise: "We can't be for something for fifteen years and then, when we finally have the power, do nothing about it. This is the major question facing the state and the refusal to act is based purely on politics, on the fear of not getting elected."[38] More than passing judgment on the past performance of the Democratic legislature, Ferency was attempting to exert party and public pressure on Democratic legislators who were to return in September to take up a tax proposal the governor was scheduled to present. At first this tactic seemed to produce some results. The AFL's Committee on Political Education (COPE) and the AFL-CIO executive board agreed to support a temporary flat-rate income tax if additional revenue was necessary to fund improved programs in education and mental health. To this contingency was added another condition. The endorsement would be offered only if the level of personal exemptions was considered sufficient by the AFL-CIO executive committee. Scholle, however, let it be known that he personally favored a $1,500 personal exemption. In Ferency's judgment, all this was little more than deliberate deception; conditional support for an income tax only clouded the issue and was worse than no support at all. In the middle of July he adopted a tactic more direct than public statement.

Democrats at first did not know quite what to make of it when the state chairman proposed convening an extraordinary state party convention on October 2 and 3 in Detroit. The main purpose of the convention, according to Ferency, would be to review and to praise the accomplishments of the first session of the first Democratic legislative majority in thirty years. As the chairman's talents had more often been used for criticism than for congratulatory ceremony, there was some suspicion that his real purpose lay elsewhere. That purpose was not difficult to discover. Ferency announced that because a fall legislative session on taxation was to open on September 14, a tax reform seminar would be included as an important part of the convention proceedings.[39]

Until Ferency called for the special convention, dispute over the question of taxation had for the most part been kept within the confines of the liberal-labor coalition. Now the issue was joined directly and publicly. Responding to Ferency's proposal, Gus Scholle asserted that "since everyone, including Governor Romney, has praised the Legislature, there is no particular reason for the convention."[40] To make certain there was no mistake about the real source of his objection, Scholle was careful to add: "There is little enthusiasm from the rank and file union member for an income tax bite at this time."[41] Scholle's statement had failed to change Ferency's mind about either a fall convention or tax reform, and he was quick to reply. Indirectly dismissing Scholle's opposition by suggesting that the "same people who have always been reluctant about tax reform are still reluctant," Ferency stated his belief that "there has been increased support for tax action this year."[42] As the chairman had only recently berated the Democratic members of the legislature for failing to do what the party had recommended for fifteen years, it is not clear from what quarter this growing support had come. It clearly had not come from Democratic Senator Garland Lane, chairman of the Senate Finance Committee, who, the same week that Ferency and Scholle began their public battle, predicted that an income tax would not be enacted because it would not be needed before 1967.[43]

Senator Lane's prediction was based upon the existence of a $135 million surplus, which was much larger than had been anticipated when the Seventy-third Legislature convened in January. This made the position of those advocating immediate action on tax reform more difficult and seemed to give Scholle's position more authority. Carl Westman, for example, who had earlier argued that without new sources of revenue a fiscal crisis would occur in 1966–67, now had to argue for immediate action, because without it the 1967–68 period would prove calamitous.

Failure to enact new taxes in the face of a growing operational deficit means by the 1967–68 budget period the needs of the state will be neglected to the point of crisis. At that time we can look for actual net deficits approaching the level of at least $122 million, with the very real possibility that a slight economic slump could magnify these problems greatly.[44]

While Westman was pressing his arguments on the UAW leadership, and Gus Scholle and Zolton Ferency were publicly debating the issue with increasing stridency, George Romney was sequestered in the governor's mansion on Mackinac Island. He was not alone.

Among the Democrats elected to the state legislature in 1964 were an unusually large number of freshmen. Unlike most of their more seasoned colleagues, many of these new members believed that reform was not only desirable but a practical possibility. The reluctance of their own leadership to place financial reform above the exigencies of the next election was not for them the full and final answer to the question. Romney seems to have understood that, and he set about to take advantage of it. He had become governor largely because of his ability to convince others that politics should not be allowed to intrude on government. This had proven to be a very powerful device in electoral politics and he now sought to apply it to his battle with the legislature. To replace political debate with rational discussion, the governor organized what he termed a nonpartisan legislative committee. Though every member of it was a Democrat or a Republican, partisanship was removed by the selection of an equal number from the legislative contingents of both parties. The notion seemed to be that partisanship disappeared with the elimination of the possibility of one party or the other winning on a straight party vote.

Romney might have convinced others, and might have even believed, that what he had created was nonpartisan, but the Democratic leaders in the house and senate were not persuaded. They had not been asked to name the Democratic members on the Romney committee; they had not even been consulted. They found it more than curious that the Democrats asked to serve were characterized by both brevity of service in the legislature and intensity of support for an immediate alteration of the state's taxation structure. When this nonpartisan tax committee, working under the direction of the governor in a series of meetings on Mackinac Island, produced a program almost indistinguishable from the one the governor had been proposing on his own, the Democratic leaders were the least surprised people in the state. But though they felt contempt for the transparency with which the governor had attempted to cloak his designs and a certain condescension toward the Democratic members who had allowed themselves to be so easily used, they had now to deal with a program offered publicly by the governor as a result not of his own efforts but of the deliberations of both Republicans and Democrats. The game had become more serious.

One effect of the Romney proposal was to help Carl Westman in his continuing effort to convince the UAW that tax reform should not be postponed. On September 14 the union released an eight-page document written by Westman entitled "A Policy Statement on State Tax Reform." Although the Romney proposal "recognizes the fiscal needs of the state" and could raise nearly $200 million in new revenues, it was deficient because it failed to recommend sufficient reform. The governor, according to the union policy statement, "does advocate imposition of a personal income tax as the keystone of the program, but the income tax he proposes permits exemptions of only $600 per individual." It was the size of the exemption, and not the adoption of an income tax, with which the UAW disagreed. Indeed, the first of eight "mandatory ingredients of tax reform without which any tax revision program would fall far short of success" was a personal income tax. Not only was it the first in order, the personal income tax was viewed as "the keystone of any reasonable reform proposal." A 3 percent tax with a $1,000 exemption would yield something more than $340 million and although it was not graduated would correspond "somewhat to the principle of ability to pay due to the impact of personal exemptions." Along with a 3 percent income tax with a $1,000 personal exemption, the UAW proposed a 5 percent corporate income tax and a 6 percent tax on financial institutions. The remaining five points in the program were directed toward the removal or reduction of some existing taxes.[45] While not in complete accord, neither were Romney and the UAW in fundamental disagreement over either the necessity for tax revision or the central elements required. Perhaps most important was the emphasis both the governor and the union placed on the income tax as the necessary prerequisite for any significant alteration in the tax system. Gus Scholle did not agree.

From the very beginning Scholle had opposed adoption of an income tax before the 1966 election. With Romney conducting a full-fledged public campaign in behalf of the tax, and managing to convince a growing number of people that he had bipartisan support; with the chairman of the Democratic party declaring that failure to fight for tax reform would be a betrayal of party principles; and with the UAW, which comprised a majority of the membership of the state AFL-CIO, sounding more and more like press agents for the governor, Scholle could scarcely rest secure with an argument based solely on the fear of losing the next election. From crass considerations of partisan advantage, Scholle moved to a concern for equitable arrangements. On the same day Romney presented his plan to the legislature, Scholle provided a proposal of his own to the house Democratic caucus. There was no individual income tax in it. Instead, Scholle's plan called for a 5.5 percent corporate tax and a referendum on a graduated income tax.

In its way Scholle's plan was ingenious. It managed to combine the notion that an income tax was not needed with the proposition that only a graduated income tax was fair. A 5.5 percent corporation tax would raise about $180 million. An adjustment in the business activities tax, which taxed business whether or not it made a profit, would reduce state revenue by $104 million. A further reduction of $12 million would result from lowering the tax on beer, a nuance consciously designed to obtain broad support for the program as a whole—for beer and against an income tax seemed unbeatable. The new revenue, therefore, would be $64 million. This, along with the $135 million surplus then in the treasury, would be more than enough until the voters could themselves take up the second provision in Scholle's program, a graduated income tax.

Under the provisions of the 1963 Michigan Constitution, a document for which George Romney, more than any other individual, was responsible, a state income tax was permissible only if it were imposed on everyone at the same rate; a graduated income tax was strictly prohibited. This had been one of the main reasons the Democratic party had argued against ratification, and no one had argued more insistently than Gus Scholle. He was within the bounds of consistency, then, when he argued against the imposition of a flat-rate tax and in favor of a constitutional amendment that would permit the application of a graduated tax. In a speech given only a few days before the unveiling of his tax program, Scholle asserted: "A fair tax plan takes the biggest bite from the fellow making the most money."[46] Scholle's plan proposed putting the constitutional amendment before the voters in the 1966 general election.

What Scholle had devised was almost immediately taken over as the official position of the house Democratic leadership. There was even a certain confusion about the actual origin of the proposal. The Michigan AFL-CIO attributed authorship not to Scholle, but to the speaker of the house. According to the union paper: "House Speaker Joseph Kowalski rejected the governor's proposals and came up with a set of his own."[47] Kowalski, it was reported, "wants the legislature to accomplish fiscal reform in two steps. First, a readjustment of business taxes. Second, elimination of the constitutional ban on a graduated tax . . . on individuals." Moreover, "if a personal income tax comes, Kowalski said it 'should be as equitable as we can make it.'" Not surprisingly, the *AFL-CIO News* added that, in Kowalski's judgment, "because of the state surplus, the need for additional taxes now is most questionable."[48]

With Kowalski, Scholle, and the UAW all opposed in one way or another to the Romney proposal, no one was surprised when the sixty-member executive board of the Michigan AFL-CIO voted to reject it. Less certain was the form any recommended alternative would take. An observer might have assumed that the UAW's predominant power on the executive board would produce a position closer to the union's own policy paper, which had called for a flat-rate tax, than to the Scholle-Kowalski demand for a future referendum on the graduated income tax. That assumption would have been given apparent confirmation by some of Scholle's own remarks to the executive board. Citing the existing budget surplus as an impediment to convincing "anyone that fiscal reform is necessary and that financial chaos is just around the corner," Scholle seemed both to abandon his earlier insistence that the reform could be delayed and to adopt the sense of urgency of not only Carl Westman but Zolton Ferency as well. Members of the executive board were informed that "the cold, hard facts are that the state is in fiscal trouble and the time of crisis is foreseeable and not very far way. The Michigan tax structure is now plagued by regressiveness, inflexibility and inconvenience." Worse still, "in the next two years it will also be plagued by inadequate revenues and rapidly mounting deficits."[49]

Crises were foreseeable, and foresight was clearly required. For Carl Westman foresight had meant taking immediate measures to produce new revenue. For Gus Scholle it meant taking immediate measures to set in motion the processes by which to produce a more equitable tax structure. Scholle, with the executive board following him without division, proposed that labor support the "Kowalski plan" with its twin requirements of a corporation tax and a vote by the people on a graduated income tax. He went further still. As if to ignore the possibility that the constitutional amendment on a graduated tax might fail, through either the inability of the legislature to obtain the two-thirds vote needed to put it on the ballot or rejection by the voters themselves, Scholle persuaded the board to accompany its rejection of the Romney program with the assertion that labor could not accept any plan incorporating a flat-rate income tax.[50] This after the UAW had issued its own policy statement in which a flat-rate tax was described as not only acceptable, but, with proper exemptions, progressive.

Scholle's position had now become the official position of organized labor. Reaction was swift. Ferency displayed his displeasure by insisting that "all the progress we have made in the past few years will be meaningless unless we have tax reform." Expressing what was, perhaps, the beginning of the disenchantment with organized labor and established institutions generally that would eventually drive him out of both the chairmanship and the Democratic party altogether, he argued that fiscal reform could be brought about only through the generation of an informed public opinion: "The real issue is to build the bridge of understanding—nonexistent now—between the taxpayer's needs and the projects for which his tax money will be spent."[51] The editorial writers of the *Detroit News*, though they had as little love for Ferency as they had for Scholle, were infuriated: "A corporate income tax without a

personal income tax along with it is an open invitation to Scholle-type dema-
gogic tax policies which would drive industry and jobs out of the state."[52]
Criticism was also levied against both Scholle's rejection of a flat-rate tax as
inequitable and his complaint that the Romney plan (which the *News* insisted
was not a Romney but a "bipartisan" tax plan) provided a $2 million savings
to industry.

To be attacked in the editorial columns of the *Detroit News* was such a
regular occurrence for anyone with a position of authority in either the Democratic party or the labor movement that it was considered in those circles
almost as a rite of passage. No one was singled out by the *News* for attack
unless he was threatening, and to be considered a threat by what was clearly
an enemy of Democrats and union leaders was not the least effective means
of gaining or increasing influence among them. Scholle, who was nothing if
not animal shrewd, understood this, and had presented the *News* with a direct
opportunity for its attack by writing a lengthy letter to the editor outlining his
objections to the Romney tax plan. This time, however, there was another
result. Within the UAW, the editorial criticism of the Scholle letter, instead
of producing express condolences and implied congratulations, provided the
basis for a devastating critique of the entire Scholle policy, a critique which
even began by suggesting that the criticism offered by the *News*, "aside from
the snide political innuendos, was substantially correct." Substantially correct, but very far from exhausting the legitimate objections that should be
raised. In a memo to Roy Reuther, entitled "The Gus Scholle Case Against
Tax Reform," Carl Westman proceeded to raise them.

Westman wrote with obvious agitation. Scholle had placed labor in a
position that was economically untenable and politically irresponsible.

> O.K., if you have a tax with a certain amount of progressivity and you want
> more, fine! But the issue in Michigan now is between a moderately fair, flat-rate
> tax with exemptions ($600 or $1,000) and an inadequate, harshly regressive
> revenue system that victimizes our most unfortunate citizens.
>
> To obstruct or delay any improvement in the equity of the system simply
> because it does not quite come up to some hypothetical level of perfection is
> making somebody else's misery the price of principle.[53]

Westman's major criticisms were directed at Scholle's irrational attitude toward business and his misunderstanding, if not deliberate distortion, of the
relationship between a flat-rate income tax and progressivity.

Until the last few years of the Williams administration, labor and the
Democratic party had seemed to view the issue of taxation almost from the
perspective of participants in an overt class struggle. An income tax on individuals would be oppression; a tax on corporations would constitute clear
victory for the people. No one seems to have believed this more devotedly
or to have been more reluctant to surrender his belief than Gus Scholle.

According to one UAW official, as late as 1965 Scholle had been against an income tax in any form and only because of pressure from the UAW had he renounced outright opposition.[54] But if he had changed his position, if not his mind, on the advisability of an income tax on individuals, his conviction that business was a source of almost unlimited public revenue remained undiminished.

> Gus does not like facts that tend to diminish the potential importance of his corporate profits tax as the answer to all fiscal ills. He ignores, for example, the fact that the Conlin commission study and most other studies indicate that business is not getting a free ride in Michigan. He forgets, for example, that all three reform plans submitted by the two former Democratic governors included substantial relief for business. He also neglects in his comparison, the impact of business taxes other than taxes on corporate profits. Michigan, for example, now has two taxes on corporations that yield about $100 million.[55]

Insisting on a high rate of taxation on corporate profits may have been a matter of political principle with Scholle, but according to Westman it was incompatible with his professed intention to obtain equity in taxation. Both "business price-administering practices and the pressure of monopolistic competition" would have the effect of transferring the tax Scholle thought should be paid by private concentrations of wealth to "the consumer and the worker." Based on a neat division between the powerful and the rich on the one hand and the impoverished on the other, Scholle's economic analysis assumed as the principle of equity in a tax system the ratio between taxes on business and taxes on individuals. "Implicit in this argument, of course, is his belief that all taxes on individuals are paid by lower income people and all business taxes are paid by fat coupon clippers. Unfortunately the facts do not square with his romantic interpretations." Even the Romney program, a program Scholle had claimed would increase taxes on individuals by "two million dollars while decreasing taxes on business by $152 million, would have given substantial relief to low income people."[56]

Westman believed that Scholle's failure to perceive the absence of a clear class distinction between individuals and business was accompanied by an inability, or at least an unwillingness, to recognize that a flat-rate and a progressive income tax were not necessarily contradictory. Calling Scholle's assertion that a flat-rate tax could not be accommodated to the principle suggested by the phrase *ability to pay* "a plain distortion," Westman argued that

> a flat-rate tax may not provide the kind of progression that you want in certain income classes, but to say flatly that the flat-rate tax advocated by the proponents of tax reform "places a disproportionate burden on low income families and individuals" is not true, especially in view of the kind of tax system we now tolerate in this state.[57]

There was an equal absence of validity in Scholle's contention that adopting a flat-rate tax would make the possibility of securing a graduated income tax almost nonexistent: "Most of the 34 state income taxes we now have are the product of efforts to reform regressive tax structures."[58]

The Westman memo reflected a position that was receiving growing support within the leadership of the UAW. This was not surprising. Although Scholle, who took very little part in union activities other than political matters, continued to believe that most of the world's misfortunes were the direct responsibility of the legendary malefactors of great wealth, the UAW had long since concluded that corporations had not merely a right to exist but a positive obligation to grow; prosperous manufacturers were necessary to the well-being of the union's membership. Because business prosperity was necessary for improvement in the condition of the union's members, a limit was imposed on what labor could, or would, demand. In the judgment of some, this led to the loss of the militancy that had characterized the union in its initial struggle for recognition, but it also provided the basis for an informed appreciation of what was in fact possible to obtain. The notion of class warfare had been supplanted by a sophisticated understanding of mutual need and cooperation. Unlike Scholle, the UAW leadership understood that a tax system adverse to business was not always an advantage to labor, and that some improvement was better than none at all. The UAW agreed with Scholle that a graduated income tax was the most desirable form for a tax on individuals, but knew that it was not within the realm of possibility unless a constitutional amendment was passed, and that amendment might never come. A flat-rate tax was the sole available alternative. The proper level of exemptions could make a flat-rate tax more progressive than the existing tax structure. An immediate, if limited, improvement was possible, and for the UAW leadership that was more desirable than either complaints about the limit on legislative prerogative or fiscal proposals that approached equity only in appearance.

Always reluctant to attempt to persuade their constituents that what hurts momentarily may still be beneficial, legislators in the state house were more resistant than anyone to passage of an income tax, as long as they could avoid it. In the first week of October the Romney plan was put to rest. Joseph Kowalski, speaker of the house, UAW international representative, and close friend of Gus Scholle, presided over the interment.

> When the Romney-backed $150 million tax package gave up the ghost, Democratic House Speaker Joseph H. Kowalski was standing there in the spotlight, smoking pistol in hand. Sighs of relief were breathed from many a lawmaker's chest. But what escaped widespread notice was that many of the sighs came from the lungs of Republicans, barely visible in the shadows at the rear.[59]

Romney's program was voted down, and the plan authored by Scholle and attributed to Kowalski was never voted on at all in its entirety. Only a single element of the program was taken up by the house; the Democratic leadership attempted to obtain legislative approval to put before the voters a constitutional amendment permitting the imposition of a graduated income tax.

According to political scientist E. E. Schattschneider, "Parties are unable to hold their lines in a controversial public issue when the pressure is on." This condition, moreover, "constitutes the most important single fact concerning the American parties. He who knows this fact, and knows nothing else, knows more about American parties than he who knows everything except this fact."[60] Nothing was more controversial in Michigan politics than the issue of the graduated income tax. The prohibition against graduation had been adopted in the constitutional convention with Republican support over Democratic objections. What had divided the parties in 1961 and 1962 had also become, by 1965, a divisive issue within the Democratic party. The state party chairman and the UAW were willing to accept, at least temporarily, a flat-rate tax. The AFL-CIO and the Democratic legislative leadership insisted that a graduated tax was the cornerstone of any fundamental alteration of the tax structure. But now, when the vote was taken in the house on whether to afford the voters an opportunity to decide the question, the issue became once again strictly partisan. Every one of the seventy-three Democratic members voted for it, and every one of the thirty-seven Republican members voted against it. Seventy-four votes were needed to obtain the two-thirds necessary to place a constitutional amendment on the ballot; the measure failed. Republican opposition had been consistent. Democratic preference for the graduated tax had been equally unchanging. Disagreement among Democrats had been over the question of what was immediately possible, not over what was ultimately desirable. On the fundamental issue legislators went with their parties and the proposition that Schattschneider considered the single most important fact of American politics was, in this instance at least, demonstrably false.

With the approach of the 1966 elections, few Democrats believed the numerical advantage they enjoyed during the Seventy-third Legislature could be maintained. Some of the 73 Democrats in the house and 23 in the senate must have been elected more through the electoral annihilation of Barry Goldwater than through the normal result of the new apportionment. Richard L. Miller, executive secretary to the speaker of the house, fully expected to see the Democratic majority diminished by 12 or 15 seats. A reduced majority in the house and a paper thin margin in the senate were the expectations of those most closely concerned and best equipped to know. By 4:00 A.M. on the day following the election, it was clear that even the most conservative predictions had not been cautious enough. Republicans had recaptured control in the senate, and what was more astonishing, had achieved absolute equality in the house, electing 55 of the 110 members. Worse was yet to come. One of the Democrats reelected to the house had become disgruntled when the speaker had rejected his application for extended travel outside the country at state expense, and his revenge took the form of abstention on the vote of the newly assembled house to organize itself. Instead of a 55–55 standoff in the election of a speaker, the vote was 55 Republicans for Robert Waldron and 54 Democrats for Joseph Kowalski, with Representative E. D. O'Brien, a Democrat, abstaining. George Romney had a new legislature with which to work on an old problem.

Under the guidance of Gus Scholle, the Democratic legislative leadership had decided that with a financial surplus accumulating in the state treasury they could postpone a tax increase and thus ensure their continued control of the legislature. Their conclusion had been disproven, but the assumption on which it had been based was valid. By July, 1966 the surplus had reached a height of $167 million. After that it began to decline with decided speed. Romney believed that by July 1, 1967 the surplus would drop below the $50 million level. In his state of the state message, delivered January 12, 1967, the governor insisted that "taxation must be the number one job of this legislative session." As this was not the first time he had demanded that the legislature respond to such a request, Romney announced that he did "not intend to sign any appropriation bills for the next year until I can see where the money is coming from."[61] Where Romney wanted the money to come from was a tax program of his own devising. In a refurbished version of his past proposals, the governor offered a plan that contained a 2.5 percent personal income tax, a 5 percent business income tax, an 8 percent tax on financial institutions, and a seven-cent increase in the cigarette tax.

In the early spring Romney's prospects seemed to improve because of an unexpected chain of events. Joseph Kowalski, having lost the speakership, occupied the position of Democratic leader. (Because of the at least formal equality of the party representation in the house, this title was used rather than the more normal "minority leader.") One day in the latter part of March he suffered a cerebral hemorrhage while working at his desk; he died three days later. In the special election held to fill his seat, James Hoffa, Jr., the son of the president of the International Brotherhood of Teamsters, won the Democratic primary. Like most state legislative districts in Detroit, the Nineteenth District was looked upon as a place where a Republican candidate was the embodiment of a perverse refusal to face facts. In this case, although the Republicans concentrated everything they had on what was after all the only election around, the issue never seemed in doubt. However, when the ballots were tabulated, somehow, unaccountably, the Republican Anthony Licata had won. Perhaps wiser after the event than they had been before, Democrats concluded that the junior Hoffa had lost the general election for the same reason he had won the primary, his name and his name alone. In a contest with half a dozen other Democrats, the Teamster name and Teamster money had been enough. In a race between only two entrants, there were simply too many people who viewed the name Jimmy Hoffa with distrust and aversion. The governor, however, who seemed to find in prayer an astonishingly regular confirmation of his ambitions, proclaimed the Licata victory a "miracle." Whatever the cause, the Republican replacement of Joseph Kowalski dissolved the even division of the house. For the remainder of the Seventy-fourth Legislature, Republicans would have a working majority of fifty-six to fifty-four. The Democrats, moreover, would have to find a new leader.

In a system of automatic succession, Kowalski would have been replaced by the Democratic floor leader, J. Robert Traxler. However, Representative Traxler was in only his third term, and perhaps more importantly, he had failed to demonstrate either the energy or the comprehensive grasp of legislation the Democratic caucus thought necessary. The position instead was awarded to William A. Ryan of Detroit, who like Kowalski before him had come to the legislature from the labor movement—although Kowalski had been a UAW organizer and Ryan the editor of the paper published by the Association of Catholic Trade Unionists. In appearance and manner the new Democratic leader seemed no more awe inspiring than a bookkeeper who had entered upon his middle years and had as his one ambition a quiet retirement from a quiet life. Few realized, and fewer still found it easy to believe, that William Ryan had once been a Marine Corps drill sergeant. What every member of the legislature, Democrat and Republican alike, did know about Ryan was that he was fanatically dedicated to work. A year earlier he had been given the responsibility of merging the Wayne County Department of Social Services with the state Social Services Department. The task required an exhaustive study of what were perhaps the two most complicated administrative structures in the state. When Ryan took the floor of the house to report on what had been done, there were not more than a half dozen people in Michigan who could follow his discourse in detail. Based more on faith in his integrity and respect for his intelligence than on a careful analysis of his report, the legislature approved the proposal. Ryan's attention to detail verged on addiction, and this characteristic, which some viewed as a pronounced personal peculiarity, would perhaps more than anything else prevent George Romney from imposing his own notion of a proper scheme of taxation on the citizens of Michigan.

Romney's January assertion that he would refuse to sign any appropriation bills before he was certain there would be money to pay them might have been dismissed by some as a threat without force. State services obviously had to be continued, and the governor could scarcely afford to permit at least the most essential among them to expire for want of a signature. No one could doubt the governor's intention, however, when on April 14 he submitted to the legislature a budget for fiscal year 1967–68 for consideration in the event it failed to adopt a tax reform program. This budget was considerably more austere than the one submitted in January; from the original $1.153 billion request, $185 million had been removed. The 16 percent reduction was effected not by an equal diminution in all government expenditures, but through a very large decrease in the budgetary allowances for mental health, state employment, education, and building construction at colleges and universities—programs to which Democrats more than Republicans assigned a high priority.

Economics alone required that tax reform of some sort be adopted before the next fiscal year. Democratic leaders in the house and senate were as aware of this as the governor was. They were also aware that the governor had a very powerful incentive to get tax reform through the legislature without delay; Romney's presidential ambitions had begun to encounter difficulty. Public opinion polls "indicated his political fortunes were lagging, and he could not afford the luxury of a loss before the Michigan legislature."[62] With Republican majorities of fifty-six–fifty-four in the house and twenty–eighteen in the senate, Romney's ability to lead his party would be seriously suspect if the legislature refused to follow him on what he called the most important issue facing the state. As if to prove his political power and his unwillingness to compromise on principle he decided to try to obtain passage of his program with the support of Republican votes alone. The governor's perception of the public interest, however, was not shared by every Republican legislator. Six Republican house members had campaigned in 1966 on a pledge not to support any state income tax. They kept their promise, and fifty instead of fifty-six Republicans in the house voted for the governor's program. Several Democrats who doubted that needed revenues could be obtained any other way were disposed to follow the fifty Republicans. But, flouting the usual assumption that lobbyists call on legislators, William Ryan asked the unions to exercise what influence they could to discover and prevent defection. Pressure generated by a combination of legislative and labor leaders succeeded; not one Democrat joined the fifty Republican members, and the governor's program failed by six votes. With the beginning of the next fiscal year less than two weeks away, George Romney's political life seemed to be hanging by a rope held by the party that opposed him.

When Ryan first ran for the state legislature in a special election to fill a vacated seat, the campaign manager for his Republican opponent circulated literature suggesting the contest was one between a candidate who was not bossed and was not a socialist and a candidate who was both. The voters chose to disregard the questionable description and elected Ryan by a margin of almost two-to-one. A decade later that Republican campaign director was speaker of the house, but his attitude toward Ryan had not changed. Robert Waldron warned the governor that under no circumstances should he trust anything Bill Ryan might say or agree to. Romney, who now had no alternative but to negotiate with the Democratic minority, suggested to Ryan that they meet together to resolve the differences that existed between them. He asked Ryan whether there would be any objection to permitting the news media, including television, to cover the negotiating session. The governor believed that in addition to providing public attention, this would prevent Ryan from retreating from any commitments given or concessions granted. Ryan, persuaded that Romney was the one most likely to bargain in bad faith, agreed to the unprecedented request. With more members of the press and television present than legislators, negotiations opened in the governor's office on June 23.

Romney began with a proposal that had as its major elements a 2.5 percent personal income tax with a $600 per person exemption, and a 5.5 percent business profits tax. Under this proposal, 10.4 percent of the new taxes levied would be on business and the rest on individuals. Ryan and the Democrats argued that business should assume no less a share than the 30 percent it was currently required to pay. In place of the $600 personal exemption, Ryan proposed $1,000; he also asked for the elimination of the sales tax on food in the form of a $15 per capita tax credit.

The exemption and per capita tax credits would both benefit individuals. They would also reduce the tax paid by unincorporated business, which took the form of taxes on the individuals engaged in the particular enterprise. This was understood by Ryan and the Democrats but was only comprehended in part by the governor's taxation specialist, Gerald Miller, who was present throughout the negotiations and was called upon frequently for technical information. Ryan was aware that even before the negotiations began Miller had been treating a tax credit differently from a tax exemption when computing business income. Miller recognized that an exemption, by reducing the tax on the income of unincorporated business, meant that the percentage of taxes paid by business altogether was less than it otherwise would be. With an exemption, then, both individuals and business would pay less than they would without it, and that fact was an essential element in determining the actual tax ratio between business and individuals. This much was understood. What was not understood was that a tax credit would also reduce the tax paid by unincorporated business. It was not at all clear why Miller was making this mistake, but it was clear that each time he computed the tax ratio between business and individuals, the amount business paid with a tax exemption was less than it would pay with a tax credit, even though each should have had the same net effect.

By the fourth day of negotiations even the pretense of patience had disappeared. At one point Romney rose from his chair at the head of the table, ready to leave the room. At another point Ryan somehow managed to scream louder than the governor, something it was thought impossible for anyone, least of all the placid William Ryan, to accomplish. At the end of the day Romney made what he considered a major concession; he offered to accept a $12 tax credit. Ryan responded by complimenting the governor for this evidence of a willingness to compromise, and promised an answer the next day. When the answer came, the governor was appalled. Rejecting the proffered $12 credit, the Democrats instead insisted on a $1,200-per-person tax exemption. With not a little anger, Romney replied that were this to be done business would be driven out of the state. Ryan had been waiting for this moment for five days. Denying that he or any other Democrat had the slightest desire to drive business away, Ryan suggested that it was his understanding that the business ratio would be less with the $1,200 exemption than with the $12 credit the governor had offered. Romney immediately denied the truth of this statement and turned toward Miller for confirmation. Ryan, as if in deference to the governor's own tax authority, said, "Gerry will figure it out." Miller's answer to the governor's inquiry was, "Yes, Governor, it is true." George Romney was dumbfounded. Surrounded by television cameras, Romney was compelled to accept the $1,200 personal exemption. Everything else fell quickly into place. The income tax rate was raised from 2.5 percent to 2.6 percent, and in exchange the business profits tax was increased from 5.5 to 5.6 percent. Negotiations ended at 3:30 P.M. on June 28, nearly a week after they had begun, with an agreement on a tax program which would net $270 million in new revenue. Several years later, Bill Ryan, who was the only one who really understood what had happened, looked back on this encounter with George Romney as "the craziest thing I've ever seen!"[63]

Ryan had managed to extract greater concessions from Romney than the governor had ever intended. Nevertheless, Democrats remained adamant in their insistence that the agreed-upon tax program was one for which Republicans would have to take major responsibility. From the outset there had been an understanding that if an agreement were reached, twenty Democrats in the house could be counted upon to vote in favor of passage. In exchange, the "Democrats demanded that key Republicans, including William P. Hampton, Republican floor leader from Bloomfield Hills, go on record for the bill."[64] At 1:30 A.M. on the day after agreement had been reached in the governor's office, forty-two Republicans and exactly twenty Democrats approved the compromise tax program.[65] Senate approval followed within days, and Michigan, after more than a decade of struggle between and within the parties, had a state income tax and some measure of reform.

Notes

1. *Detroit Free Press,* January 11, 1952.

2. Doris B. McLaughlin, *Michigan Labor: A Brief History from 1818 to the Present* (Ann Arbor: Institute of Labor and Industrial Relations, 1970), p. 130.

3. *Detroit Free Press,* January 11, 1952.

4. Address of G. Mennen Williams to Annual Michigan CIO Council Convention, Grand Rapids, Michigan, June 3, 1952, UAW Archives, Solidarity House, Detroit, Michigan.

5. Ibid.

6. Robert Dingwell, interview with author, 1971.

7. Message to the Sixty-seventh Michigan Legislature from Governor G. Mennen Williams, January 14, 1954, p. 2.

8. *Detroit Free Press,* April 21, 1954.

9. "Williams Kicks Off Democratic Election Drive," radio script, Michigan CIO Weekly Labor News Commentary, September 26, 1954, UAW Archives, Solidarity House, Detroit, Michigan.

10. *Detroit Free Press,* January 12, 1957.

11. Finance Message to the Sixty-ninth Michigan Legislature from Governor G. Mennen Williams, February 22, 1957.

12. Ibid.

13. Ibid.

14. *Detroit Times,* July 19, 1957.

15. Report of the Citizens Advisory Committee of the Michigan Tax Study, 1958 to the Special Legislative Committee on Taxation, Michigan House of Representatives, January 6, 1959, p. 8.

16. Ibid.

17. Ibid., p. 45.

18. Ibid.

19. Denzel C. Cline and Milton C. Taylor, *Michigan Tax Reform* (East Lansing: Michigan State University Press, 1966), p. 10.

20. Harvey E. Brazer, "Michigan's Fiscal Outlook," *Wayne Law Review* 11, no.2 (Winter, 1965): 439.

21. Ibid.

22. Ibid.

23. Ibid.

24. "A Suggested Program for Michigan Tax Reform," Report of the Subcommittee of the Taxation Committee of Citizens for Michigan (April, 1961), p. 2.

25. Boyd Benedict (administrative assistant to Governor John B. Swainson), interview with author, July 20, 1971.

26. Brazer, "Fiscal Outlook," p. 443.

27. Carl Westman to Michigan UAW Regional Directors, Inter-Office Communications, RE: Romney Tax Program, September 27, 1963, UAW Citizenship Department files.

28. C. R. Mollenhoff, *George Romney: Mormon in Politics* (Des Moines: Meredith Corp., 1968), p. 197.

29. Brazer, "Fiscal Outlook," p. 444.

30. McLaughlin, *Michigan Labor: A Brief History,* p. 139.

31. Ibid., p. 141.

32. T. G. Harris, *Romney's Way* (Englewood Cliffs, N.J.: Prentice-Hall, 1968), p. 217.

33. Carl Westman, Memo to Leonard Woodcock RE: Fiscal Situation in Michigan, April 6, 1965, UAW Citizenship Department files.

34. *Michigan AFL-CIO News,* May 19,1965.

35. Ibid.

36. *Ann Arbor News,* June 10, 1965.

37. Ibid.

38. Ibid.

39. *Lansing State Journal,* July 18, 1965.

40. Ibid.

41. Ibid.

42. Ibid.

43. Ibid.

44. Westman, Memo RE: Fiscal Situation in Michigan.

45. UAW, *A Policy Statement on State Tax Reform,* September 14, 1965.

46. *Port Huron Times Herald,* September 16, 1965.

47. *Michigan AFL-CIO News,* September 22, 1965.

48. Ibid.

49. *Detroit Labor News,* September 23, 1965.

50. Ibid.

51. *Detroit News,* September 29, 1965.

52. Ibid.

53. Memo from Carl Westman to Roy Reuther, n.d., UAW Archives.

54. Russell Leach, interview with author, December 15, 1971.

55. Memo from Carl Westman to Roy Reuther, n.d., UAW Archives.

56. Ibid.

57. Ibid.

58. Ibid.

59. Roger Lane, *Detroit Free Press,* October 4, 1965.

60. E. E. Schattschneider, *Party Government* (New York: Holt, Rinehart and Winston, 1942), pp. 131–32.

61. Mollenhoff, *Romney,* p. 270.

62. Ibid.

63. William Ryan, interview with author, June 18, 1973.

64. Mollenhoff, *Romney,* p. 270.

65. *Detroit News,* June 29, 1967.

CHAPTER 5
Methods of Influence

Passage of a state income tax was almost coincidental with what was one of the most important but least noticed transfers of political power from one institution to another in Michigan history. For two decades, Gus Scholle, president of the state AFL-CIO, had been the spokesman for organized labor in both its political and legislative affairs. His view of politics as the battle-ground between business and wage earners had been consistent. More and more, however, this belief was rejected by many within the UAW leadership. A widening division of opinion had developed over the years in which the question of taxation had been the major subject of debate. Where Scholle saw a simple conflict between industry and individuals, the UAW discovered mutual dependence, in which injury to either business or wage earner might harm, but could never help, the other. The UAW had been able to induce the AFL-CIO president to change from opposition to an individual income tax to acceptance of a graduated tax, if and when the costs of government permitted no alternative. The UAW was never able to convince him that a flat-rate tax with a proper scale of exemptions should not only be accepted but advocated. Neither the UAW nor events would heed the interests or the opinions of Gus Scholle very much longer. Within six months of the adoption of a state income tax, the UAW broke away from the AFL-CIO, and Scholle found himself at the head of an organization so reduced in both membership and financial resources that only his reputation gave him even the appearance of significant political power.

As the 1968 election approached, Gus Scholle no longer spoke for organized labor in Michigan. Nor was this the only change worthy of notice. The only major figure in the Democratic party who could rival Scholle for abrasive independence was Zolton Ferency. His temperament, along with his gubernatorial ambitions in 1966, had led him into an independent course as party chairman, heedless of the advice and indifferent to the warnings of party regulars and union leaders. As a result, Ferency, with a really remarkable variety of talents, had proceeded in the year of the locust to run for governor, ignore party organization, antagonize labor, alienate most of the members of the state legislature, repel independent voters, and, generally, make an astonishing and perhaps unsurpassed contribution to the greatest Democratic defeat in over twenty years. Antagonism between Ferency and the leadership of organized labor, which in some measure had been suspended during the course of electoral hostilities with the Republicans, resumed with even greater intensity. The mutual recriminations that invariably follow defeat were added to all the hostility that had existed before. In 1967, after a series of public denunciations of the incumbent Democratic president had resulted in open warfare between Ferency and many of the party regulars, the chairman simultaneously resigned and began a "spontaneous" grass roots demand for his return. The former was accepted while the latter was accorded a quiet and a decent burial.

With Ferency's resignation the party's executive committee had the responsibility to appoint an acting chairman to serve until January, 1969, when the party would meet in convention. In a de facto recognition of political realities the executive committee had been broadened to include the voices, if not the votes, of Democrats holding statewide office, the mayor of Detroit, the Democratic leaders of the state house and senate, and representatives of the UAW and the AFL-CIO. Labor's point of view was by no means restricted to its designated representatives. The two Democrats holding statewide office, the attorney general and the secretary of state, were both longtime members of the liberal-labor coalition. And although more than a few called into question their liberalism, there were not many who doubted the sincerity of their loyalty to labor, or at least to labor's leadership. Equally loyal were the two legislative leaders, both of whom had been union officials. In addition, most of the elected party officers were either founders of the original coalition or employed by labor. It is safe to say that all the officer's viewed a party that did not include labor's active collaboration as little more than an unmitigated disaster. This body, especially after its experience with Zolton Ferency, was not likely to give the chairmanship to someone whom labor did not know or found unacceptable. In fact they selected someone who seemed created to appeal to the two groups Ferency had most antagonized, labor and the state legislature.

The 1964 election brought to Lansing the first legislature in which more than half its members had college degrees. Among the new bright young men, no one was brighter, and certainly no one had more ambition, than state senator Sander M. Levin. Educated at Chicago, Columbia, and Harvard Law School, Levin had not become a state legislator because of the position's financial attractions. Appointed chairman of the Senate Labor Committee, Levin quickly established a reputation for exhaustive preparation in committee and shrewd performance on the floor. Prudently declining Scholle's suggestion that he contest the gubernatorial nomination in 1966, Levin was reelected without difficulty to the state senate. After Ferency's inglorious defeat few doubted Levin's design. To become governor, however, he had first to become known outside his own district. In almost every other state, chairmanship of a political party is a certain prelude to political oblivion, but Levin knew that Michigan Democrats had nominated as their last two gubernatorial candidates men who had achieved their reputations as the elected leaders of their party. While Ferency was trying to generate local sentiment for his own return, Levin wrote letters to Democrats of every description for advice on what he should do if offered a position for which, it may be assumed, not all of them had considered him a candidate.

Levin had worked well with labor in the legislature; he was respected by other legislators; he had served as chairman of the Oakland County party and had done much to improve its fortunes. He was ambitious for higher office, but that ambition was a guarantee that he would do everything he could to lead the party through a successful campaign in 1968. He was acceptable to labor, liked by liberals, respected by party regulars, and considered more likely than anyone else available to repair the divisions that had set factionalism in motion and brought the party to its lowest point since the formation of the liberal-labor coalition in 1948. Not everyone was yet convinced that this second-term legislator would be the best possible gubernatorial candidate in 1970, but few had reservations (and fewer still expressed them) about Levin's ability to work well with the divergent elements within the Democratic party. With a new chairman, with the UAW independent of and far superior in strength to the AFL-CIO, and with very little time for decent preparation, a reorganized Michigan Democratic party entered the 1968 election campaign.

Under provisions of the constitution adopted in 1962, the governor and members of the state senate were given four-year terms. In 1968 only the seats in the state house of representatives were up for election and those 110 seats became the central concern of the state campaign. During the years in which Gus Scholle exercised undisputed leadership of labor's political activities, the state Democratic party had very little to do with legislative campaigns. Under both Neil Staebler and Zolton Ferency, the state central committee supplied legislative candidates with information on public issues and handbooks on campaign organization but little else. Advice was plentiful but financial assistance was almost never available. Apart from what they were able to raise within their own districts, Democratic candidates might hope for, but not always receive, contributions from the state AFL-CIO. What the AFL-CIO gave was largely what Gus Scholle decided to give and his decision was often based not so much on where assistance would most improve the prospects of victory, as upon a calculation of the effect a contribution was likely to have upon the attitude of the recipient. It made no sense, for example, to give the incumbent of a safe Democratic district any assistance at all, if the aim was to use resources to increase the electoral prospects of Democratic candidates generally. It was eminently reasonable, however, if the intention was to secure or to maintain influence with incumbents.

Scholle's method did a great deal more to preserve and promote his own influence than it did to convince legislators that the Democratic party was a force to be reckoned with. The UAW, on the other hand, was less concerned with building individual relationships than with creating institutions that would have the proper purpose, and would function in the required way, regardless of the individuals involved. Far from viewing the party as a threat to its own independent power, the UAW gave it every encouragement and every possible form of assistance. This was demonstrated early in the 1968 campaign, when a plan was devised for what was a necessary condition for Democratic success in both the state and federal election: a comprehensive and effective voter registration program.

Of the eighteen house seats that had been won by Democrats in 1964 and lost in 1966, there was only one district in which the Republican vote had increased by more than a few hundred between the two elections. With that one exception, the Republican vote had stayed almost constant and the Democratic vote had decreased by as much as 7,000.[1] It had always been assumed that Democratic candidates fared better when the turnout was higher, and it had always been known that the highest turnout took place in presidential elections; seldom, however, had there been such direct confirmation that those who voted only in the quadrennial presidential elections supported Democratic candidates. Even though 1964 had been an unusually good year for Democratic candidates, and not all of those who voted against Goldwater could be expected to remain opposed to the Republican party, Democratic strategists assumed that of those who voted in 1964 but not in 1966, the greater number would cast Democratic ballots. All of those people, however, had been stricken from the rolls of eligible voters after the 1966 election—in Michigan, as in many other states, eligibility was retained only by voting every two years. Everyone who had voted in 1964 but failed to do so in 1966, along with an undetermined number of those newly eligible, had to be registered.

Though the results of registration often have a great deal to do with the outcome of partisan contests, registration itself is not considered a partisan activity. Limitations on union activity in federal elections do not apply to expenditures made by labor on programs designed to increase the number of voters. The distinction between good government and good politics, however, has never been as clear as some would suggest. In 1968 labor and the Democratic party spent a quarter of a million dollars on a registration program in

Michigan. The state Democratic party contributed less than one-fifth of this amount. The UAW, on the other hand, supplied almost $100,000. The remainder was obtained from the AFL, the Teamsters, and the Humphrey presidential campaign.

Registration for the 1968 campaign was the first organized political campaign undertaking in which the UAW acted independently of the AFL-CIO. As the single largest financial contributor, the UAW might have attempted to lay down a registration plan for all the other participants. It might even have decided to run its own separate registration campaign. The latter alternative was by no means incompatible with the narrow self-interest of the union. An intensive registration drive among its own membership and in blue-collar areas generally might have increased the political strength directly attributable to the UAW itself and thus increased its ability to manuever between groups competing for its support. Instead, the UAW adopted a longer view, in which alliance with the Democratic party was essential. The union's substantial financial contribution to the registration program was used to bring the AFL, the Teamsters, and the Humphrey campaign into a working relationship with the state Democratic party. In the meetings convened to coordinate the registration campaign, the UAW used its position as the major donor to establish a common acceptance of the state party as the institution within which and for which everyone was working.[2]

Because a voter registration program affects all political campaigns in the area it covers, it might seem that no single campaign and no single candidate would feel especially indebted to those who provide the means to accomplish registration. It would follow that the UAW was not really giving up any influence on candidates by merging its own contribution to a registration effort with a cooperative venture under the formal leadership of the state Democratic party. It is also true, however, that the UAW not only agreed, but insisted, that financial assistance to specific legislative campaigns be treated in precisely the same manner as the registration campaign.

Democratic legislative candidates traditionally received money to run their campaigns from three sources: labor, lobbyists, and individuals within their own districts. What they were able to raise seldom bore any relation to what they needed to spend. Incumbent legislators with considerable seniority often had money literally pushed on them by all those who wanted to establish or to maintain good relations, but nonincumbents, whose need for assistance was far greater, had a much more difficult time. From the point of view of the state party, it had always been sensible to distribute available resources in a way that would elect the greatest number of Democratic legislators. However, that required coordination among the organizations that most frequently contributed to Democratic campaigns.

In 1968 a working committee composed of the state party chairman, the director of the party's legislative campaign, the director of the UAW citizenship department, and the house Democratic leader was established for the first time. The committee agreed on general guidelines for contributions and determined the specific amounts to be given individual candidates in the general election. At the outset three important and somewhat unprecedented principles were laid down. The first, which was almost implicit in the composition of the committee, was an understanding that the party, which had collected $25,000 from a fund-raising event for the legislative campaign,[3] would contribute to a particular candidate only in coordination with labor and other funding sources that could be identified; there was really no point in giving more assistance to a candidate than what was actually needed. The second principle followed directly from the first. No candidate was to receive any assistance whatever until he had submitted a budget that specified how much he expected to raise, the sources from which it would be obtained, and the way in which it would be spent. This requirement provided a means for determining the candidate's actual financial need. It also permitted the committee to gain some information about the candidate's understanding of what was involved in a legislative campaign. The third principle imposed some control on the kind of campaign that would be run. No candidate would receive direct financial assistance. Instead, the party would contribute by providing campaign materials or paying bills invoiced by the candidate, with the prior approval of the committee. In other words, coordination characterized more than the registration program; it was adopted as the common campaign policy of the state party and the UAW. The party provided the formal framework for agreement, but the union supplied the power that made coordination possible.

In the 1968 legislative campaign the UAW sought to do everything it could to increase the power and influence of the state Democratic party. But, as James MacGregor Burns observed of Congress, the party in the legislature is jealous of its independence.[4] Legislators are always more concerned with the opinions and attitudes of their constituents than they are with the policy pronouncements of a political party; allegiance to the latter rarely helps, and may often jeopardize, their prospects for reelection. In the case of Michigan's Democrats, what would be an uneasy relationship in the best of circumstances had deteriorated into open animosity during the last years of Zolton Ferency's chairmanship of the state party. By making repeated attacks upon the legislature, Ferency succeeded not in persuading the Democratic membership to follow his lead, but in making them almost openly hostile to the party. Some of this tension was reduced (though it was never completely removed) when Sander Levin, himself a state senator, became the acting party chairman. Still, neither the UAW nor anyone else ever expected that the party as such could soon or easily exercise any real influence within the legislature. Within a month of the 1968 election, the UAW established its own office in Lansing from which to lobby the legislature.

At first Harold Julian, who was entrusted with the task of representing the UAW in Lansing, adopted what had been Gus Scholle's favorite device, the weekly legislative luncheon. After several months, however, he discarded it, for reasons that may be discerned from the comment of a legislator who was a regular participant.

> Nothing ever got done at those things. Most of the legislators who attended saw it mainly as an opportunity to get free booze. Harold would be talking about some damn bill and most of the guys were all half-looped. When Harold stopped and they started they talked about everything except what was really important about the bill. I don't think Harold quite understood that when Gus had those luncheons what he really wanted was to get those guys blitzed. They loved Gus for it and he knew it.

The provision of liquor in plentiful supply was one lobbying technique that the UAW had little interest in pursuing. Only in the last few years of his life did Walter Reuther permit alcoholic beverages to be served at official UAW functions, although his prohibition policy had not been followed with great fidelity when he was not personally in attendance. The union, however, used nearly every other lobbying technique with effect. Indeed, when the UAW found itself faced with the organized opposition of the Teamsters on an issue of fundamental importance to the state, it called on nearly every technique and tactic known to man.

The lobbying techniques of the nation's two largest unions could not have been more different. Whatever effectiveness the Teamsters had in the Michigan legislature was the result of intimidation. Over the years the legislative agent of the Teamsters, Otto Wendell, used without compunction what one legislator called "the sledge hammer technique." Although according to one source, "a lot of legislators resented it, being political animals they bent." They bent because, directly or indirectly, they had been bought. Wendell was never without large financial resources, and he was never reluctant to expend them lavishly. When an election drew near, Wendell would approach certain legislators before they filed an official declaration of candidacy and tell them how much they should bill him before filing. Because money received before filing did not have to be reported as a campaign contribution, no record of the transaction would be available, and the money could be spent in whatever way the legislator desired. Legislators with safe districts who accepted money from Wendell had little inducement to expend it on a campaign. The money was easy and the terms were good. Unlike the UAW, which developed very broad legislative interests, the Teamsters were interested solely in legislation that directly affected them. As Frank Fitzsimmons once put it, "The Teamsters do not believe in causes." But the Teamsters do believe, and believe devoutly, in the Teamsters. One of the more veteran members of the legislature said of Wendell and his union: "They don't bother you much, but when they do, and they have helped you, you better be there."

In the late sixties and early seventies the Teamsters owned eight Democratic members of the house. They constituted what was openly referred to as the Teamster caucus. All eight were from heavily Democratic areas in Wayne, Oakland, and Macomb counties. All eight districts had essentially blue-collar constituencies. Each member believed that continued strong support from the Teamsters would be sufficient to protect them from the UAW. It was not chance alone that caused each of the eight districts to undergo substantial alteration in the legislative reapportionment plan before the 1972 election. Nor was it chance alone that caused three of the eight to be defeated in the primary election of that year. But while they existed as a bloc, they formed the center of a wide circle of Teamster influence. Other Democrats were amenable, at least on occasion, to Teamster persuasion; and Wendell would negotiate with any Republican who would listen, and more than a few did.

That Wendell's influence often extended beyond the eight house members he had paid for was largely due to his professed willingness to spend money against those who proved reluctant or unwilling to do his bidding. He once became sufficiently angry with Joseph Kowalski to threaten an expenditure of $50,000 to defeat the then speaker of the house in the next election. Kowalski replied that it would take at least that much to pay for the bodyguards Wendell would need if he were ever stupid enough to come into the district. Kowalski, who was at least as tough as Wendell, and a good deal more powerful, added political revenge to verbal retaliation. For the remainder of his tenure as speaker, his staff had standing orders to report on any legislation that Wendell and the Teamsters were trying to get out of committee.[5] Any such legislation was killed. If it was good legislation—for example, a needed change in truck safety requirements—a new sponsor would reintroduce it and carry it through. It is doubtful, however, that Wendell thought this tactic very impressive. Even the buying and selling of legislators was probably too tame for his instincts. He once remarked to a group of young legislative interns that years earlier Jimmy Hoffa had become so enraged that he had hit Wendell over the head with a telephone. He seemed to remember it as a mark of affection.

There was little enough affection, however, when the UAW and the Teamsters lined up on opposing sides on a bill to provide Michigan with a system of transportation not utterly dependent on the truck and the automobile. Detroit is the home of the automobile. The country's three leading automobile producers, the UAW, and the Teamsters derive their well-being from and depend for their existence on the manufacture of motor vehicles and on the continued commitment of state and federal governments to the construction and maintenance of roads to drive them on. Even before it was suspected that energy was not an inexhaustible resource, some attention began to focus on development of a transportation plan that included alternative methods of moving people and goods from place to place. A first, faltering step was attempted in 1966 when the house democratic caucus approved a measure commissioning a study of the need for a comprehensive transportation plan and the governmental reorganization that might be required to undertake it. The bill never emerged from committee, and the only executive department directly concerned with transportation remained the state highway department which was dedicated to maintaining and extending the highway system.

In 1971 Governor William Milliken proposed a transportation bill of his own devising. Although this was the governor's program, and the governor was a Republican, the UAW decided to support it. More than that, the UAW put everything it had behind the program. The floor manager of the bill in the house, Representative Philip Mastin, "worked closer with labor on that bill than on any other even though it was a bill that had no direct effect on labor."[6] The Democratic floor leader, Representative Marvin Stempien, confirmed Mastin's impression. According to Stempien, "The UAW operated just like it was a labor bill. They pulled out all the stops. They had dinner meetings. They cajoled. They pled."[7] The UAW did everything that could be done, and they very nearly failed.

One group that was not especially excited about the transportation program was the black legislators. In 1971 every one of them was from Detroit. More specifically, every black legislator was from either the First or the Thirteenth Congressional district in Detroit. The First and the Thirteenth understood clearly that in Detroit victory in the democratic legislative primary election was equivalent to victory in the general; they also understood that the power of the district committee was a direct result of its willingness to endorse and elect candidates. Their success was impressive, especially to those legislators who had been elected with the aid and assistance of the district committee.

The transportation program presented black legislators with two major problems. First, they could not afford to have the proposed transportation board established without a guarantee that it would contain black representation. This problem was resolved by an agreement that two of the positions would be given to blacks. The second difficulty was more complicated. Hubert Holley, chairman of the First District democratic committee, was much opposed, at least outwardly, to a move that would make it easier for people to work in Detroit and live in the suburbs. The erosion of the tax base that was accompanying the departure of the white middle class to the outlying suburbs might easily be intensified by any important improvement in public transportation. The counterargument, however, was obvious. A really efficient transportation system would go far toward returning the suburban shopper to Detroit. It might also encourage business to expand within the city rather than escape from it. Holley's basic objection, however, was caused less by the effect of the proposed transportation system on demographic patterns than by its possible implications for transportation workers. In addition to being chairman of the First District committee, Hubert Holley was also president of the Detroit Bus Drivers' Union. Assurances from the UAW that his union could only benefit from the plan eventually eliminated the district chairman's objections, and the attitude of several First District black legislators changed with remarkable speed.

Black objections were met without too much difficulty. Neither compromise nor conciliation could be employed to meet the objections of the Teamsters. The only thing that would work was the only thing the Teamsters understood and respected, the naked exercise of power. For the Teamsters, the transportation bill had both an immediate and a long-range effect, and both were seen as direct threats. The immediate threat was, of course, the additional taxation the plan would require; part of the needed revenue would come from an increase in the gasoline tax from seven to nine cents per gallon. A more distant but very real concern was the eventual diminution in the amount of shipping done by truck that would occur once alternative methods of transportation were actually employed on a large scale. Both concerns were fully shared by that group which, on the basis of any orthodox economic class analysis, should have been most opposed to any position the Teamsters might take, the Trucking Association. The Teamsters and the Trucking Association were very formidable when they acted individually; together, according to many legislators, on legislation that affected them directly they could not be broken. They were even more difficult to break on the transportation issue because, as the speaker of the house described it, "This was a measure that increased taxation so the Teamsters and the Truckers were in fact on the popular side."[8]

The transportation bill was a matter of crucial importance to the Teamsters; it was not an issue that directly affected the wages, hours, or working conditions of the membership of the UAW. However, insofar as encouraging alternatives to motor vehicle transportation threatens a decrease in the volume of motor vehicles produced, the direct impact on automobile workers must be economically adverse. In this sense, the UAW could be said to have fought against its own narrow self-interest on the transportation bill. Nor was the fight restricted to mere pronouncements about the need to do what was in the general interest. As already noted, the UAW treated the transportation measure as if it were a labor bill. Anything less would have meant certain defeat; the Teamsters and the truckers working together in opposition to a measure that would inflict an additional tax burden on the citizens of Michigan were a very formidable combination. The Teamsters very nearly won. With fifty-six votes needed for passage, the UAW and the governor managed to get fifty-eight votes for the enacting legislation. On the bill to finance the program, only fifty-seven legislators could be found who were willing to ignore the blandishments and withstand the threats of the Teamsters and the truckers. It was a dangerously small margin of victory.

The willingness and the ability of the UAW, which was heavily involved with the Democratic party, to work closely and successfully with the Republican governor contradicts the view that an interest group is compelled to choose between association with a political party and the exercise of influence with members of both major parties. On the transportation package, the governor exerted pressure on Republican legislators and the UAW concentrated on Democrats; there were occasions, however, when the UAW managed to exercise direct influence on Republicans. Some Republican legislators considered it unpatriotic to so much as acknowledge the existence of the UAW or the Democratic party, but there were others who in the judgment of labor (a judgment made almost as an apology for suggesting that a Republican could have any worth at all) really "ought to be a Democrat." Carl Pursell in the state senate and Charles Varnum in the house were both in this category. The UAW considered Pursell someone who had generally been "quite helpful." Varnum, it was said, would give the UAW a vote on anything "unless it would kill him in his district."

For practical purposes Republicans like Pursell and Varnum were as good as Democratic legislators from the UAW's perspective. In fact, their voting records on the issues of greatest concern to the UAW were considerably better than those of some declared Democrats. Despite their records, however, in their election campaigns neither Pursell nor Varnum received an endorsement or any other form of assistance from the UAW.[9] The UAW occasionally talked about supporting some Republicans, but largely in order to threaten Democrats. Still, Varnum and Pursell and others like them did not go unrewarded. As there were different kinds of Republicans, so were there different kinds of endorsements. Varnum and Pursell did not receive the endorsement of the UAW, but their Democratic opponents did not end up with very much either. Partly because they were very difficult to defeat, but also because a Democratic replacement would not have been much of an improvement, the UAW's opposition to Varnum and Pursell in the general election was little more than a formal gesture. An endorsement of the Democratic candidate was made and then largely forgotten. Neither the UAW nor the Republican legislators ever spoke about this; there was no need to.

Republicans who really ought to be Democrats were not the only Republicans the UAW was sometimes able to influence. No member of the Michigan legislature was more Republican than Charles Zollar. A self-made man of great wealth, State Senator Zollar seemed on first impression to embody all of the more outrageous characteristics of the stereotype, rural Republican. Senator Zollar was so large that had he become plump he would have thought himself thin. He was in his mid-fifties; his wavy hair was silver and seemed to signal an unyielding belief in the virtue of hard currency. Always wearing boots, and never without a string tie, the senator appeared bent on the eradication of cities and all their ineradicable vices. In fact, Charles Zollar was an extremely competent and industrious man, fanatical in his attention to detail, and more familiar with the details of state government than most governors. In his first term in the senate he attended almost every meeting of the Senate Appropriations Committee, though he was not a member of it. In his next term he became a member of the committee and in 1971 became its chairman. As chairman, in the judgment of some observers, he was perhaps more powerful than the governor. With great power and ample competence, and with a district that had been solidly Republican even in the depression and gave no indication of ever repenting of its decision, Zollar had no use whatever for the UAW. But there was something he was interested in, and he came to believe that the UAW might be useful helping him get it.

A candidate tends to view the office he seeks as an eminently worthy position, a position which, if ever attained, would satisfy his most intense ambitions. Election, however, very frequently serves not to quiet but to quicken the desire for greater power and larger fame. During only four years in the state legislature, Charles Zollar had risen from relative obscurity to become one of the two or three most formidable men in state government, but in 1972 he was not only willing but eager to exchange his power for the comparative impotence of a freshman congressman. Advancement from the state to the federal level of government was scarcely something Zollar could expect as a matter of course. His congressional district was heavily Republican, but the incumbent, Republican Congressman Edward Hutchinson, had what appeared to be a stranglehold on it. Despite the odds against victory, Zollar, whose state senate term did not expire until 1974, had really nothing to lose by running in the Republican primary against Hutchinson in 1972.

Zollar's ambition was not entirely inconsistent with the interests of the UAW. In its judgment, Charles Zollar was very bad, but Edward Hutchinson was considerably worse. Hutchinson occupied one of the safest Republican congressional districts in the state; only a major miracle would permit a

Democratic candidate to beat him. Replacing Hutchinson with Zollar would be an improvement, if only a minor one. There was, however, an additional consequence that would follow were Zollar successful, a consequence that held out prospects far more interesting and far more important. Zollar in the congress would not be in the state senate. His replacement as chairman of the Senate Appropriations Committee would be Senator Harry DeMaso of Battle Creek. DeMaso, though a Republican, possessed the supreme virtue of entertaining a radical dislike for the governor. Moreover, unlike Zollar, he was willing to at least grant the UAW an audience. A certain mutual contempt prevented the UAW and Senator Zollar from entering into explicit discussions of their common desire to remove the Senator to Congress, but it did not preclude the implicit recognition of their mutual interest.

While Zollar was contemplating the attractions of life in Washington, the UAW found itself faced with a very serious problem. A shutdown of a Muskegon foundry had thrown six hundred UAW members out of work. Almost three quarters of them were black and over fifty; it was feared that most had silicosis. No employer would consider hiring any of them unless a determination had been made that they were free of the disease. The UAW wanted to obtain medical examinations for each of them, but the cost would be nearly $30,000 if the examinations were done by private physicians, and only $10,000 was available from the local union. The examinations had to be made: if a worker did not have silicosis he was eligible for employment, if he had it he was eligible for workmen's compensation. The UAW asked the State Department of Health if it would conduct the examinations. Although the department said it was willing to comply with the request, it indicated that it could do so only if the legislature appropriated enough money to cover the cost. Harold Julian immediately talked with William Copeland, the Democratic chairman of the House Appropriations Committee.[10] Copeland assured Julian that he would insert a line item in the department's budget to take care of the matter. He also suggested that a meeting be arranged with the governor's office, the health department, and the chairman of the Senate Appropriations Committee, Charles Zollar. At the meeting, Zollar agreed that something ought to be done and asked the health department if they would do it. When he received an affirmative reply Zollar asked John Dempsey, who was representing the governor, if the governor would go along. Dempsey said he would. Zollar then closed the meeting with a promise that it would be taken care of. He kept his promise and a short while later asked the UAW for a favor.

Zollar wanted information. He asked Harold Julian whether it would be possible for him to know when and where union meetings were to be held in the Fourth Congressional district. He also was interested in finding out when shifts changed at plants in the district. Zollar did not ask that the UAW invite him to speak at union meetings, nor did he request any other form of assistance. He simply wanted the information. Julian told Zollar the UAW would be happy to help, and put him in contact with Art Vega, the UAW political coordinator in Benton Harbor, the largest city in the Fourth District. Several days later it was the UAW's turn to try to gain an advantage from what it suspected was likely to be only a brief interlude in the normal hostility that prevailed between the union and the senator.

Doug Fraser, then vice-president of the UAW and chairman of the union's political arm, UAW-CAP, strongly supported a half-billion-dollar housing program being considered in the state legislature. It had passed the Democratic-controlled house, but was languishing in the Senate Appropriations Committee. The UAW did not know precisely how intense Zollar's congressional ambitions were at the moment, nor did they have any idea whether Zollar attached any importance to the fact that they had agreed to furnish him with information about union meetings and shift changes, information which he could easily have acquired on his own. Believing there was nothing to lose and perhaps a great deal to gain, Harold Julian called Zollar. He first asked the senator if he had gotten in touch with Vega. Zollar replied that he had not wanted to bother Vega on the weekend but would be calling him soon. Julian then said that if the senator encountered any difficulties he should let him know right away. Having demonstrated his concern for Zollar's interests, Julian proceeded to ask about the housing bill. The chairman explained that his committee had to take up the budget bills before anything else could be considered. Then he asked what position the UAW had taken on the bill. Julian told him, what Zollar must already have known, that the UAW was very much in support of it. As if to suggest that he had not known this before and that the union's position was conclusive for his own judgment, Zollar replied simply that the bill would be reported out during the next week. It was, and the UAW, by doing nothing to discourage the amibitions of a usually hostile opponent, had obtained more from Senator Zollar than he would ever receive from the union.

If it was sometimes possible for the UAW to work with Republican legislators, even some who were generally their most irreconcilable critics, they did not always find it easy to work with Democratic legislators, even some who had spent their working lives in the union and whose political existence was inseparable from continued union support. Few legislators owed more to the UAW than State Representative Jelt Sietsema, and few occasioned more irritation. Seitsema represented the Ninety-fourth District in the eastern portion of Grand Rapids and its adjoining suburbs. In 1964 his older brother, George, was elected from the district but was defeated in the general election in 1966. Two years later no one could be found who was willing to run against the

Republican incumbent—on the last day for filing there was still no one to represent the Democratic party. Finally, at 3:30 in the afternoon, the UAW took Jelt Sietsema out of the plant where he worked, drove him to the clerk's office, and paid the required $100 filing fee. The UAW and the Democratic party had gotten themselves a candidate, but there was soon some doubt whether it had been worth the trouble. Sietsema (who, it must be admitted, had not shown much initiative up to this point) let it be known that he was a working man and that campaigning was a luxury that he could not frequently afford. What little time he did devote to campaigning led some to believe that it was a luxury the UAW and the Democratic party could not afford either. Proving that victory does not always go to those who work the hardest and want it the most, Jelt Sietsema was elected to the state legislature. It is a tribute to the organizational abilities and political skills of the UAW, and especially to its regional coordinator, John Annulis, that Sietsema was not only elected in 1968 but reelected in 1970. Sietsema, however, seemed convinced that what he had become was owing to nothing but his own understanding of the real desires of the wage-earners in his district.

In the 1972 session of the Michigan legislature, Republicans introduced a bill in the house to alter the method by which state supreme court justices were selected. The existing method stipulated in the state constitution had little to commend it. Every two years each political party meeting in convention nominated two candidates for the court, and though nominated in this way the candidates ran on the nonpartisan portion of the ballot. The Republican bill, however, did not attempt a departure from either the election of judges or the involvement of the political parties in the selection of candidates. Instead, the bill sought to replace the statewide election of justices with an arrangement in which each of the seven judges would be elected from separate judicial districts. The proposed districts were included in the bill. It was no surprise that the seven districts to be created contained four that were clearly Republican, one that was marginal, and only two that would be safely Democratic.

After the bill was introduced the Democratic speaker of the house sent it to the Committee on Elections, where it would presumably receive its just reward. The chairman of the committee, Al Sheridan, was one of the most politically astute members of the legislature. Since his committee was responsible for legislation concerning nearly every aspect of elections, and since Sheridan exercised considerable control over his committee, getting along with Mr. Sheridan was considered by most legislators, especially Democratic ones, as the first principle of political prudence. With a Democratic majority on the committee, Sheridan could foresee no obstacle in the way of providing the supreme court bill an early death, and he allowed it to come before the committee for consideration. Jelt Sietsema, either caring nothing for political prudence or more likely knowing nothing about it, voted with the Republicans, and Al Sheridan found himself on the losing end of a vote in his own committee. He was mortified.[11] The UAW was incensed.

A day after Sietsema's vote, Harold Julian was on the phone to John Annulis in Grand Rapids. Whenever Sietsema differed with the UAW on a particular piece of legislation, his favorite and often only argument was that his opinion was shared in full by his local. After numerous repetitions of this position, Julian's patience had vanished. He finally told Sietsema that he had no objection to a legitimate disagreement on the merits of legislation, but under no circumstances could Sietsema argue that he knew the actual sentiment of the UAW better than Julian. The position of the UAW on legislative matters was determined by a process that included every local union in the state and not just Sietsema's own local in Grand Rapids. Moreover, there was some doubt that Sietsema even knew what the attitude of that single local really was. Just how true this was, Sietsema was about to discover. After hearing from Julian, John Annulis went to work. A meeting was arranged in Grand Rapids with Sietsema and a number of UAW representatives, including the president of Sietsema's local. The state representative was told in no uncertain terms that his vote on the supreme court bill did not have the support of anyone in the room or anyone else in the UAW. In the days following the meeting, Sietsema was inundated with telephone calls from angry UAW members, many of them from his own local. Thoroughly shaken, Sietsema went to the speaker of the house, Bill Ryan, and, "white-faced and trembling," promised to do whatever Ryan wanted him to do to help defeat the bill on the floor of the house.[12]

The UAW's ability to convince Sietsema that the union membership in his district was opposed to the position he had taken on the supreme court bill was clearly both the necessary and the sufficient cause of his change of heart. That fact points to the essential source of the UAW's power. More than the money or the manpower it could contribute to a legislative campaign, the union membership in a legislative district constituted the cornerstone of UAW influence. To prevent legislators from claiming that their election to office demonstrated that the union membership in their district supported them even if the UAW leadership did not, the union adopted its own independent endorsement procedure. Any candidate who desired the endorsement had first to request it; then and only then was the candidate invited to appear before the executive board of the CAP council of the congressional district in which his legislative district was located. The executive board's recommendation was then passed on by the full membership of the district CAP council. It was then brought before the full county CAP delegate body for final decision.

The endorsement procedure of the UAW was very democratic, and it had another characteristic as well. The district committees, at least in Wayne County, almost unfailingly exhibited a bias against incumbents. According to one UAW staff member, "The intolerance toward incumbents has been based for the most part on the activity or non-activity of incumbents in the district."[13] The willingness of the district organization to refuse to endorse incumbent state legislators led to a biennial ritual. Gus Scholle, Joe Kowalski, and then Bill Ryan would come to the county delegate body to reverse endorsements against incumbents, and a substantial number would be reinstated.[14] There were, however, occasions on which the county body went along with the district committee and withheld endorsements from large numbers of Democratic incumbents. One year, fifteen incumbents in Wayne County were denied union endorsements. However, they were not denied election. This raises the question (a question that every legislator had on his mind) whether the union endorsement made much, if any, difference.

The UAW record in opposition to incumbent legislators in Democratic primaries was not terribly impressive. One explanation for this lack of success centers on the relative importance of the office. In most election years the union's attention, like the public's, was fastened on a presidential or gubernatorial campaign. The energies and the resources of the union were directed into the campaign of Democratic candidates for the most powerful political offices; little remained for attempts to unseat Democratic incumbents in any of the 110 house or 38 senate districts. Indeed, after defeating an incumbent Democrat with a nonincumbent in 1954, the union waited sixteen years before it could repeat the achievement. The achievement, however, was notable. In 1970 the UAW decided to oppose the Democratic leader in the senate.

Raymond Dzendzel, the senate Democratic leader, and State Representative Jack Faxon had the same ambition. Both wanted the senate seat occupied by Dzendzel. That was the beginning and the end of what they had in common. Dzendzel had some of the virtues and all of the vices of a representative of the building trades, the union with which he had long been associated before coming to the legislature. He was comfortable and reasonably competent when dealing with legislation that had a direct and immediate effect on wage-earners. He was generally opposed to legislation that sought to effect broader purposes. Legislation that appeared to benefit blacks and other minorities at the expense of the predominantly white membership of the building trades evoked his raging opposition. As his voting record was less than liberal, his manner was less than charming. He was generally gruff, often crude, and never forgiving. Jealous of what he considered his rightful prerogatives, and insistent on the enforcement of his own opinions, the senate Democratic leader was loved by few and despised by many. Dzendzel cared nothing for that. He believed politics was like any other business; success depended on power, and power depended on favors granted and promises received. Dzendzel, in short, was the archetypal "pol."

If Dzendzel bore a close resemblance to a character from Damon Runyon, Faxon was the creation of comic opera. He was simply outrageous— and he knew it, loved it, and did everything he could to promote it. In the spring of 1966, Faxon induced the speaker of the house, Joseph Kowalski, whose interest in art was limited to the pictures on highway billboards, to have the legislature authorize and sponsor an exhibition of Faxon's paintings. When the pictures, most of which bore a striking resemblance to the designs of Persian rugs, were being assembled in the rotunda of the capitol building, a reporter asked Kowalski what in the world was going on. Faxon had prepared the speaker for this eventuality. With a look of great profundity, Kowalski replied, "Haven't you heard? Faxon is the new DaVinci and I am the new Medici." Kowalski's enthusiasm for the arts ended abruptly when Faxon was discovered lecturing on his paintings in the rotunda while Democrats in the house were attempting to override a gubernatorial veto. For Faxon, politics, like life in general, was a performance in which the main object was to capture center stage. The stage was better lit and there were fewer competing players in the senate.

The UAW's dissatisfaction with Dzendzel had been increasing for some time, but endorsing Faxon in a senate primary would constitute a considerable risk for the union. If Faxon got the endorsement and Dzendzel won, relations between the UAW and the senate Democratic leader would be even worse than they already were. The difficulty was compounded by the fact that no matter what the UAW did, the AFL-CIO would certainly endorse Dzendzel, who was still a member of the Building Trades Union. Nevertheless, the UAW gave every indication that if Faxon decided to enter the primary, the risk would be taken. Faxon, who would be giving up his house seat by running for the senate, decided to do it, and the UAW knew it had to go all out. Several union coordinators were brought into the campaign full-time. These coordinators, in turn, brought a large number of volunteers into the campaign and organized their efforts. Among the volunteers, the largest single group was made up of UAW retirees. Made up for the most part of men and women who not only remembered but had participated in the early struggles of the union for recognition, they retained much of the commitment and even militance that characterized the UAW in the 1930s and 1940s. Having decided to lend its support to Faxon, the UAW was going to be, in Faxon's words, "damn sure he didn't lose it."[15]

Formal endorsement by the UAW was a foregone conclusion. Endorsement by the Seventeenth Congressional District Democratic committee was an altogether different matter. In the state as a whole, county and congressional district committees did not generally endorse candidates in party primaries. It was felt that a candidate who could not win a primary on his own was not likely to have much prospect of success in the general election. In much of Wayne County, however, the Democratic primary *was* the election. If the congressional district organization failed to endorse in the primary, there was no way for it to influence the outcome of an election. The decision to endorse a particular candidate in the primary was the single most important decision made by the district committee, and in the Seventeenth district in 1970, the decision on which of the two state senate candidates to endorse was not only important to the district but indispensable to the candidates.

The UAW was at once separate from the Democratic party and an integral part of it. The union endorsed Faxon without any influence from the district Democratic committee. The district committee's endorsement, however, was not made independently of the UAW. In 1972, approximately half of the membership of the Seventeenth District Democratic committee was made up of UAW members and those who, for a variety of reasons, invariably supported whatever position the UAW adopted. All these members of the district committee voted to endorse Faxon; most of the others voted to endorse Dzendzel. Faxon received the committee's official endorsement by a small margin; without the UAW's involvement in the district party organization, it is doubtful, to say the least, that he would have had any chance at all of getting it.

The primary election did not end with the district endorsement; Dzendzel was not without friends or finances. During the campaign Faxon and the UAW divided responsibility. Faxon's own people did much of the work involved in voter registration; they were especially effective at identifying, registering, and influencing those who had moved into the senate district since the preceding election. The UAW almost by itself manned the polls on election day, and directed the get-out-the-vote program. Faxon's personal campaign, the effort of the UAW, and the contributions of the Seventeenth district organization combined to deal the incumbent senator a crushing defeat. Dzendzel lost by a vote of 15,739 to 8,848. The UAW had demonstrated that where it was fully determined to unseat an incumbent legislator in a Democratic primary, it had the skill and the power to carry it off.

Faxon's victory proved what the UAW could do; it also demonstrated the very real limitation on its power. The effort and resources expended to defeat an incumbent state senator in a party primary could not be repeated in a large number of legislative districts at the same time. Legislators were aware of this; most would have shared the opinion, voiced by a state representative from Detroit, that "it is difficult for an incumbent not to get the union endorsement if he has supported labor legislation."[16] Another was more emphatic: "Unless you really make a point of demonstrating hostility to them, labor will stick to the incumbents."[17] Still, those are general political rules, and candidates have a pronounced tendency to view themselves as exceptions. Those who have no prospect of victory will seize on any pretext to convince themselves the impossible has become a certainty. Those who have little if any chance of defeat find a harbinger of things to come in an unfriendly remark from a single constituent. Legislators saw what the UAW did against Ray Dzendzel as something that could not often be repeated, but might very well happen to them.

Even Democratic legislators who believed themselves invulnerable in their districts had reason to fear. State Representative Jim Tierney, who had incurred the displeasure of the UAW by his opposition to open housing legislation, managed to overcome an attempt by the union to defeat him in 1970. Instead of proving that the UAW could be ignored, this seemed to confirm in the minds of a number of Democratic legislators the union's willingness to oppose an incumbent even where that opposition could not be successful. The prospect of campaigning more vigorously and spending more profusely than they were in the habit of doing, in order to withstand a challenge by the UAW, was not one that most could entertain with equanimity. But there was a deeper and more direct cause for concern.

The greatest political advantage possessed by most incumbents is the fact of incumbency. For some it is the only advantage. It permits a legislator who has managed to keep his voting record largely hidden from public view or interest to avoid the obscurity that surrounds other candidates for his job. It permits him to send his constituents the widest possible variety of inoffensive materials at public expense. Under the Michigan election law, he can even be designated as the incumbent officeholder on the ballot if another candidate has the same or a similar last name. To obtain that advantage some incumbents have paid the filing fees for identically named candidates to run against them. Friends, wives, even total strangers have been employed in this high calling. Incumbency also carries with it easier access to sources of support. The incumbent is generally better acquainted than the challenger with the lobbyists for special interests, and the special interests are better acquainted with the incumbent—and are also aware that with or without their support the incumbent will usually be reelected. To defeat an incumbent requires either a great concentration of resources on a single campaign, as in the Faxon-Dzendzel race, or the candidacy of another incumbent.

Since the Supreme Court's decision in *Baker v. Carr* apportionment has been viewed as a constitutional question. In some interesting respects it remains very much a political question, and it is precisely because of two provisions of the state constitution that apportionment in Michigan is eminently political. To avoid partisanship (or so at least was the argument) the drafters of the constitution provided for a commission made up of an equal number of Democrats and Republicans to draw up an apportionment plan after each census. Since the adoption of the state constitution in 1962, the commission has had two opportunities to demonstrate its impartiality. On both occasions it has deadlocked. On each occasion two plans have been proposed, one by the Republicans and one by the Democrats. The constitution provides that in the event of a deadlock the state supreme court will resolve the conflict. The seven justices on the court are each elected to eight-year terms on a nonpartisan ballot. To get on the ballot, however, a candidate must be nominated by a political party meeting in state convention. Both times the apportionment commission deadlocked and the issue was transferred to the court a majority of the justices were Democrats. In each case the issue was resolved by adopting the plan proposed by the Democratic commissioners. In both instances it was difficult to find anyone who was astonished at this result.

After the census of 1970, a coalition of interested groups was formed to fashion a legislative reapportionment plan. The three major groups in the coalition were the Democratic state central committee, the UAW, and the Michigan AFL-CIO. Before the coalition was formed, the unions had decided among themselves to work with the state central committee on reapportionment, and thus did not devise a plan of their own. Instead, the Democratic party's own technicians were given the job of actually drawing specific district lines. It is a fair assumption that the UAW's technicians were consulted with some frequency. A group that was neither included in the working coalition nor regularly consulted was the Democratic membership in the state house and senate. Some legislators believed they had been deliberately frozen out of any participation in a decision that meant more to them than to anyone else. Their complaint was not unfounded. The two ranking Democrats in both the house and the senate were invited to several meetings, but they were not included as regular members. Other legislators were consulted, but only for the purpose of gaining information about the political composition of specific areas, and never for the purpose of asking advice about what should and should not be done.

There is an obvious conflict between a Democratic legislator's desire to increase the number of Democratic voters in his district and the ambition of the party and labor to diminish the size of Democratic majorities in some districts in order to increase the total number of winnable legislative seats. There were, however, two additional reasons for drawing a reapportionment plan without the active involvement of Democratic legislators. In the first place, to the extent to which legislators were not involved, the apparent power of the party and labor to decide what kind of district a legislator would have was enhanced. That would in turn serve to increase the influence labor and the party could exercise on Democratic legislators. In the second place, there were some legislators the UAW could defeat only if their districts were altered significantly. Eight house members in particular had incurred the union's displeasure: Arthur Law, James Del Rio, E. D. O'Brien, Joyce Symons, Russell Hellman, Harold Clark, Bill Huffman, and Jelt Sietsema. The reapportionment plan designed by labor and the party, proposed by the Democratic members of the apportionment commission, and ultimately adopted by the Democratic majority on the supreme court, directly destroyed the political careers of Law, O'Brien, and Clark. (Law, for example, who had strenuously resisted open housing legislation, found himself in the 1972 primary election with a district that was changed to include almost every black voter in Pontiac.) The other five were reelected, though by diminished margins. There were limits to what could be done through reapportionment, even when it was done with a free hand.

Through its influence over reapportionment, its endorsement of candidates, and its able use of lobbying techniques, by 1972 the UAW had become a very influential interest in the state legislature. In the judgment of Democratic legislators, it was the single most influential interest. In response to a survey conducted among them,[18] 73.9 percent of house Democrats identified the UAW as the most influential organization in the legislature. The Michigan Catholic Conference was a distant second, with 17.3 percent of the respondents designating it as the most influential organization. Among senate Democrats, 85.7 percent selected the UAW, and only 14.2 percent the Michigan Catholic Conference. Republicans in the house, though not the senate, agreed that the UAW was the predominant power in the legislature. Thirty-three percent of the house Republicans ranked the UAW first among the lobbies, with General Motors and the Michigan Catholic Conference tied for second with 26.6 percent each.

Democratic members of the state legislature not only saw the UAW as exercising the most influence within the legislature, but perceived the union to have the broadest possible interests. Every senate Democrat who responded stated that the UAW was interested in "every type" of legislation. In the house, 68 percent of the Democratic respondents agreed with their colleagues in the senate; 32 percent saw the UAW's interest as limited to legislation that had a "direct economic consequence for members of organized labor."

Every Democratic senate respondent, and 92.3 percent of the Democratic house respondents, described the UAW as "progressive." The remaining 7.6 percent of Democratic house respondents was equally divided between describing it as "reactionary" and "conservative." While there was near unanimity that the UAW was politically "progressive," there was almost as much agreement that the UAW was not always in harmony with the views of its membership. No Democratic respondent in the senate, and only 20 percent in the house, agreed that the union's legislative position was always "an accurate reflection of the desires of its membership in your district." All the Democratic senate respondents, and 76 percent of the house respondents, stated that the union accurately represented its members in their districts "most of the time."

It is not difficult to identify the kind of issue on which Democratic legislators perceived a divergence between the positions of the union and the opinion of the membership. Legislators were asked to identify from a list of eight those issues they thought the UAW should take an interest in. The eight issues were: housing, abortion, hours and wages, taxation, consumer protection, civil rights, transportation, and education. Among senate Democrats, every respondent thought the UAW should be interested in seven of the eight. Among house Democrats, at least four out of five respondents believed the UAW should be interested in seven of the eight. Only 57.1 percent of the senate Democrats, and less than half of the house Democrats, thought the UAW should involve itself with the abortion issue. As one Democratic state representative put it: "It doesn't matter what the UAW's postion is on abortion. Seventy percent of my constituents are Catholic and all of them want me to vote against it. I'm sure as hell not going to fight that."[19]

For all of its power and influence, the UAW discovered in the early 1970s that on social issues like abortion and busing its ability to give direction to Democratic legislators was seriously limited. As these issues came to occupy a more prominent place in the public mind than the economic issues that had formed the basis for the liberal-labor coalition, and the coalition that made up the UAW itself, the UAW and the Michigan Democratic party would be confronted with the most serious and the most perilous situation they had ever faced. In 1972 the intrusion of these new social issues would combine with the emergence of a new group of political intellectuals to bring to an end the willingness of the UAW to use its power to support rather than to direct the Michigan Democratic party. How this came to pass and the consequences that followed from it are questions that must be addressed later. It is necessary first to examine the way the UAW came to occupy the predominant position in the state party.

Notes

1. State of Michigan, *Official Canvass of Votes 1966*.

2. During the 1968 campaign the author served as director of the Michigan Democratic party legislative campaign and in that capacity participated in the meetings mentioned in the text.

3. In the same year the Connecticut Democratic state central committee contributed a total of $2,940 to state legislative campaigns. David W. Adamany, *Campaign Finance in America* (North Scituate, Mass.: Duxbury Press, 1972).

4. James MacGregor Burns, *The Deadlock of Democracy: Four-Party Politics in America* (Englewood Cliffs, N.J.: Prentice-Hall, 1963).

5. From 1965 to 1967 the author served as administrative assistant to the speaker of the house.

6. Philip Mastin, interview with author, June 21, 1972.

7. Marvin Stempien, interview with author, June 24, 1972.

8. William Ryan, interview with author, June 18, 1973.

9. This policy was not followed in 1974, when Pursell did receive some support from several UAW locals.

10. Harold Julian, interview with author, February 23, 1973.

11. Alfred Sheridan, interview with author, February 9, 1973.

12. William Ryan, interview with author, June 18, 1973.

13. Michael Kirwin, interview with author, October 21, 1972.

14. Ibid.

15. Jack Faxon, interview with author, June 21, 1972.

16. Raymond Hood, interview with author, June 29, 1972.

17. Jack Faxon, interview with author, June 21, 1972.

18. The survey was conducted by the author during the spring of 1972.

19. Casmir Oganowski, interview with author, June 21, 1972.

PART 3

Labor and the Party Organization

CHAPTER 6

Detroit and the Politics of Race

It is sometimes assumed that the UAW's entrance into politics was inspired by ideological concerns rather than by the close attention to organizational imperatives which, according to much of the political science literature, characterized the political ventures of the AFL under Samuel Gompers.[1]

The UAW's first attempt to enter city politics in Detroit seems to supply evidence for this understanding of the union's motivation. In 1937 one of the candidates for the Common Council was a young union organizer who was quickly making a name for himself. Having survived a field of sixty-six to become one of the eighteen council candidates in the general election, Walter Reuther began the second part of his campaign with a statement that lacked little in militancy.

> As an automobile worker, as a union official, as a member of the Socialist party, as a patriotic citizen of Detroit, I pledge myself to the service of all the people of the city. I shall try to make Detroit a healthful and hopeful community to live and work in, not just a happy hunting ground for Wall Street profiteers.[2]

Reuther's candidacy was part of a UAW slate. In addition to the future president of the union, Richard Frankensteen, R. J. Thomas, and Maurice Sugar were backed by the UAW. All four, it should be noted, were among the front rank of union leaders. Thomas would soon be president of the union; Frankensteen, with the support of the communist faction, would one day be a serious contender for that office; and Maurice Sugar was at the time "the UAW attorney closely linked with the union's communist faction."[3]

All four survived the October primary. According to an estimate by the *New York Times*, the UAW spent $60,000 in the campaign. In addition, it had classified the 125,000 union members in the city by ward and precinct. Though a tedious undertaking, this was seen as a "permanent investment because the union is in politics to stay."[4] Nor did union efforts stop at the provision of money and manpower. Governor Frank Murphy, a former Detroit mayor, yielded to union pressure and allowed himself to be photographed with both Frankensteen and Sugar, "wishing them well."[5] However, he "refused to endorse UAW candidates in the Detroit elections."[6] Both Frankensteen and Sugar, according to the *New York Times*, seemed certain winners, and Walter Reuther "appeared to have an even chance to win."[7] But even though the slate had done extremely well in the primary, none of its members was elected. With a record vote of 425,000, Walter Reuther received only 126,323 votes and finished fourteenth in a field of eighteen. The UAW-endorsed candidate for mayor lost by a full 100,000 votes. Both an unprecedented turnout and the poor showing of the union slate were in part attributable to "a concerted effort on the part of the city newspapers to equate its [the UAW slate] election with a John L. Lewis 'takeover' that would turn Detroit into an experimental laboratory to test out communist doctrine."[8]

Reuther's campaign rhetoric; the association of some members of the union slate with the socialist or communist party; and the interpretation given labor's intentions by the Detroit newspapers all helped give credence to the opinion that this first attempt to participate in Detroit city government sprang solely from an ideological commitment unrelated to any realistic appraisal of organizational needs. In fact, however, the UAW was largely motivated in the election by a desire to eliminate the antiunion activities of the city government, personified in Police Commissioner Heinrich Pickert's thinly veiled hostility toward organized labor, as well as an assessment that a labor slate had a reasonable prospect of success. That the UAW failed rather badly is to be ascribed not to an indifference to political realities, but to an inability, caused by nothing so much as inexperience, to interpret the actual political situation correctly.

The union and its eager leadership had been inspired by two facts. First, Roosevelt had carried Detroit by 200,000 votes the year before. Second, early in 1937 the union had succeeded, with the acquiescence if not the positive assistance of public authorities, in securing recognition from the immensely powerful General Motors Corporation. The conclusion seemed self-evident. Union organization could be thwarted only by an adverse government, and the adverse government of Detroit was plainly within the grasp of the union and those sympathetic to it. Those were serious miscalculations. A large plurality for a Democratic presidential candidate in Detroit was both a recent phenomenon and an irrelevancy for city politics. As recently as 1928, when Al Smith had received at least a bare majority of the nation's urban vote,[9] Detroit had given Hoover 63 percent of its vote. Moreover, the working class of the city had voted in precisely the same way as the city as a whole: 63 percent for Hoover and 37 percent for Smith.[10]

Even on the assumption that the Democratic majorities in 1932 and 1936 had become a constant, and therefore reliable, political fact, it was not at all clear that they had any meaning for city elections. Although the city charter that had been in force since 1918 provided Detroit with probably the strongest mayor's office in the country, it also provided for the least amount of partisanship possible. Both the mayor and the nine members of the Common Council were elected at large on a nonpartisan ballot in the year following presidential elections. The nonpartisan ballot and the off-year elections combined to remove partisanship from city politics in Detroit. Moreover, the electorate had become decidedly hostile to any appeal to party sentiment— or even, for that matter, to the notion that city government had anything to do with politics at all. Indeed, when Frank Murphy, perhaps the most famous Democrat ever to be mayor of Detroit, first ran for that office, he campaigned on a platform of "reform and relief. By reform he meant getting politics out of government and putting civil service into government."[11] Nor was this mere campaign rhetoric. Elected by over 13,000 votes, Murphy "conceived his government as a unified, nonpartisan effort in the spirit of the city charter . . . his appointments calmed the opposition, demonstrated his sincerity of purpose, and set what some consider to be a peak of competence in Detroit civic life."[12]

Murphy as mayor had supported nonpartisanship but as governor his refusal to order the involvement of the National Guard during the 1937 sit-down strikes convinced the citizenry that an alliance between labor and government was a certain precursor of illegality and disorder. In "the popular mind Murphy had opened the dike and thus bore the responsibility for a national crisis."[13] The UAW slate in the Detroit city elections of 1937, then, had been put forward to improve the relationship between labor and city government at a time when precisely that kind of relation was viewed as inimical to public order. The slate, moreover, depended for its success on an electorate whose partisan preferences in presidential politics were more than offset by the nonpartisan institutions and traditions of city government.

The suggestion that the UAW's involvement in Detroit politics arose from ideological propensities separate from organizational concerns has been accompanied by an assertion that throughout the 1940s and 1950s, the union failed to elect a mayor, or even to back "a winning candidate."[14]

Yet just four years after its first entrance into city politics, the UAW demonstrated its ability to comply with the exigencies of electoral politics. It had become clear that Detroit voters were not overly enthusiastic about electing labor leaders to city office. The union, however, was less interested in electing its own than in obtaining a city administration that would not be hostile to the legitimate activities of the union organization. For this reason, labor threw its support to Edward J. Jeffries. With the support of labor, Jeffries, who had once served with Frank Murphy on the Recorders Court, became mayor of Detroit in 1941, a fact that has been strangely overlooked by those who characterize the union as having been both doctrinaire and unsuccessful in city campaigns.[15] Though Richard T. Frankensteen ran against Mayor Jeffries in 1945 while still a UAW official, that was not an attempt by the union to elect one of its "own left-wing candidates."[16] Frankensteen was not labor's candidate, not simply because he failed to receive support of either the Building Trades or the Teamsters, but because he was the candidate of only a portion of the UAW. What is generally forgotten in the analyses of the UAW's activities in politics during this period is the great struggle within the union between the Reuther faction on the one hand and a communist faction on the other. Frankensteen, though never himself a communist, was sufficiently opportunistic to ally himself with the union's left wing in the hope of using its support to gain the presidency of the union. Once a close personal friend of Walter Reuther, with whom he shared the distinction of having been thoroughly beaten at the famous "Battle of the Overpass," by the mid-1940s Frankensteen had become Reuther's most formidable adversary. From this perspective it is not difficult to see that, at best, Frankensteen was keenly supported by only one of the two union factions, and that by no means the largest. One observer has suggested that "the split in the 'labor vote' partially accounted for his defeat."[17] The Reuther faction scarcely viewed Frankensteen's loss as an unmitigated disaster.

In 1947, the UAW, and the CIO as a whole, endorsed Jeffries against the challenge of a conservative member of the city council, Eugene Van Antwerp.[18] Jeffries failed in his bid for reelection to a fourth term, and Van Antwerp became Detroit's new mayor. However, much of the power of the mayor's office would be exercised by George Edwards, president of the Common Council, close friend of Walter Reuther, and a former UAW organizer. In 1947 Edwards was in his seventh year of service in Detroit government. A law school graduate, Edwards, along with Walter Reuther, had taken an active part in the Kelsey-Hayes sit-down strike and had become one of the union's most able organizers. He was still an organizer in 1942 when newly elected Mayor Edward Jeffries asked him to serve in the city administration. Edwards, the only member of the administration from organized labor, quickly became an integral part of the mayor's inner cabinet. When two council seats opened up, the mayor urged Edwards to run. With the help of both Jeffries and the UAW, Edwards became a member of the council.

After a tour of duty with the army Edwards returned, and, in November 1945, receiving the highest vote of any candidate, became president of the Common Council.[19] Few doubted that Edwards, who was barely thirty, would go on to higher office. "Edwards, it was conceded at the city hall, will be hard to beat in a future mayoral election . . . in all three of his council races he has had support of both the Detroit Citizens League and the daily newspapers."[20] With the election of Van Antwerp, described by someone close to city hall at the time as "barely competent," much of the substantive work of city government, including preparation of the entire city budget, was simply delegated to Edwards. By the end of his two-year term, Edwards had become not only the most knowledgeable and most experienced man in Detroit government, but also one of the best known Democratic politicians in Michigan.

No one was more qualified to become mayor of Detroit than George Edwards, and when Van Antwerp decided not to seek reelection, no one appeared more likely to do so. Indeed, in the early months of the mayoral campaign of 1949, Edwards seemed well on his way to an easy victory. Six months before the election, polls showed him a certain winner. Described as "the most attractive candidate to appear on the Detroit scene since Mayor Frank Murphy in the 1930s,"[21] Edwards seemed more than a match for Albert Cobo, who, though elected seven times as city treasurer, had the image more of an accountant than of a city leader. But Cobo did have one thing that Edwards did not: the full support of the city newspapers.

As Edward Banfield and James Q. Wilson have pointed out, "newspapers are particularly important to the election of candidates in nonpartisan cities—especially the larger ones."[22] Of the larger cities with nonpartisan electoral systems, perhaps none has been more susceptible to the influence of the daily press than Detroit. "In Detroit, newspaper-backed candidates for city council have usually won, sometimes against labor-backed opponents."[23] In 1949 George Edwards knew well in advance that the newspapers would not endorse him in a contest for mayor. He had been told, however, that he would have their support if instead of running for mayor in 1949 he decided to run for the U.S. Senate in 1950. The papers obviously failed to endorse Edwards in the mayoral contest more because of their desire to have a conservative city administration than because they vigorously opposed the man himself. No one then was more astonished than George Edwards when, in the last months of the campaign, the Detroit papers unleashed on him a flood of editorial vindictiveness without parallel in the city's history. The theme that had been used in 1937, that the victory of the labor-supported candidate would be the prelude to the radicalization of city government, was elaborated and intensified. Edwards was characterized as the embodiment of every left-wing impulse that had ever inspired any portion of the American labor movement. That he had been a close associate of the same Walter Reuther who was at that moment leading the battle to rid the UAW of its communist element was less interesting to editorial writers than the fact that Edwards had been an organizer in a union that contained communists.

The papers' efforts were at least indirectly assisted by the campaign activities of the UAW itself, which were, as one participant described them, "not sophisticated in their application." The attempts to convince the union membership to support Edwards and encourage them to take an active part in the campaign were "done in a crude fashion." That may be something of an understatement. Those active on Edward's behalf in the union often used the language of class warfare, and that, when the newspapers got hold of it, lent credence if not factual support to the charges of radicalism.

The question of radicalism was not the only significant issue in the 1949 election. Race relations clearly had an important place in the minds of many voters. While a member of the Common Council Edwards had very early supported open housing legislation in the city. For many white homeowners, the unfounded charge of political radicalism had less importance than Edwards's stated position on the rights of blacks. "At dozens of property owners' meetings Edwards was denounced as pro-Negro."[24] Nor was this sentiment confined to the white middle class. "To the astonishment of secondary UAW leaders, the new homeowners in Detroit among the auto workers spoke openly in the shops against 'labor's man.' "[25] So pervasive was this racial feeling that the AFL withheld its support from Edwards and endorsed Cobo.[26] Whether or not this was, as the *Detroit News* characterized it twenty years later, the CIO's "bitterest political defeat in the motor city," it was without question a decisive one.[27] Cobo, the conservative businessman, received three out of every five votes cast.[28]

It has been said that after Cobo's victory the UAW's efforts on the local scene have been half-hearted and ineffective.[29] Indeed, the same writer claims that "the left gave up trying to take control and the city has been governed ever since by conservative businessmen and moderate politicians.[30] This, like the analyses noted above, is based on a rather questionable assumption. It has been pointed out that the UAW slate in 1937 was entered for the purpose of protecting the union organization; that the UAW was not at all averse to supporting Edward Jeffries, the "greatest vote-getter in Detroit's history";[31] and that the 1945 candidacy of Richard Frankensteen was something less than a full-fledged UAW undertaking. It should now be reiterated that Edwards, who eventually became a distinguished jurist on the U.S. Court of Appeals, was a left-winger only in the eyes of those who read and believed what was written in the newspapers. The writers themselves, even if they were not aware that the Van Antwerp budgets they applauded had been designed by Edwards, had certainly not forgotten the editorial support promised Edwards should he decide to run for a seat in the U.S. Senate.

The union's political activity in Detroit had in fact never really been an ideologically inspired movement to seize control of the government, and so its effort after 1949 may be viewed as less a retreat from radicalism than a continuation of a policy that took account not only of a candidate's political opinions but of his potential electability. That is not to imply that the UAW was essentially opportunistic. The UAW, along with the CIO as a whole, continued to back even "inconsequential candidates" rather than support Cobo, who in each of his successful bids for reelection "ran as an avowed conservative,"[32] and whose principal accomplishments while in office were "keeping the city's books balanced and . . . holding off increases in the city's tax rate."[33] What the UAW policy entailed can perhaps best be understood by examining the relationship it developed with Louis Miriani, who upon the death of Albert Cobo in 1957 left the city council to take up the duties of mayor.

Less than a year after taking office, Miriani sought election in his own right. One observer has asserted that in 1957 "the influence of labor in Detroit elections was so weak that almost all unions joined with business and the press to endorse Miriani."[34] For the UAW, however, it might not have been simply a question of lending support to a candidate it could not defeat. Presented with the same tactical situation during Cobo's tenure, it had not flinched at the prospect of endorsing his opponents, though defeat was certain. Opposition to Cobo was replaced by support of Miriani for another reason, one that is not difficult to discern. Although Miriani was not a liberal in the eyes of labor, he was clearly more flexible politically than Albert Cobo. He was hardly labor's man, but he did give labor access to city government; and labor (particularly Al Barbour, president of the Wayne County AFL-CIO council) used that access to advantage, especially on the question of race relations. Through the continual exertion of pressure and persuasion, UAW leaders were able to bring about a notable difference in the mayor's racial policy. One of the UAW leaders most involved described this transformation: "In the very beginning we had some very serious disagreements with Miriani over race relations. Gradually, however, we began to bring him around and on a number of issues very important to race relations at the time he adopted our position."[35]

There was scarcely any great astonishment when the UAW decided to endorse Miriani for reelection in 1961. In the judgment of the union, the mayor had significantly improved his record. It was also generally conceded that Miriani was as certain of reelection as any mortal man could be. His opposition was a brash young man of thirty-three whom "no one in the establishment took . . . seriously."[36] At the outset of the 1961 mayoral campaign, Jerome P. Cavanagh appeared to have as much chance of being elected mayor as he had of being designated heir apparent to the Crown of England. Miriani was "the unanimous choice of the entire power structure in Detroit: the UAW, the Teamsters, the AFL-CIO council, the Chamber of Commerce, the auto companies, the newspapers."[37] He had, in addition, the support of Detroit's most prominent black leaders, and of the principal businessmen. Henry Ford II endorsed him.[38] Despite all this, Miriani fell victim to "the biggest political upset in Michigan politics in 32 years," losing to Cavanagh by more than 40,000 votes.[39]

Cavanagh's victory has generally been attributed to a great outpouring of support from Detroit's black community, which was aggrieved by Miriani's apparent "support of discriminatory police practices" and his failure to assist in the strengthening of the city's commission on human relations.[40] Indeed, the Trade Union Leadership Council (TULC), a predominantly black organization within the trade union movement, endorsed Cavanagh and did much to mobilize the black electorate. Black disfavor combined with the resentment of "many white workers" who considered Miriani "too inactive in the face of the city's massive unemployment."[41] That assessment is the basis for the conclusion that in the 1961 mayoral compaign the UAW "moved well to the right of their rank and file . . . by endorsing incumbent Louis Miriani."[42] The union endorsed Miriani, according to this analysis, because the Wayne County AFL-CIO had been successfully co-opted during his terms as mayor.[43] In brief, then, the theory is that the UAW, co-opted by Miriani, moved to the right of its membership and endorsed the more conservative of the two mayoral contenders.

There are several things wrong with this interpretation. In the first place, while much of the black UAW membership did indeed support Cavanagh based on the belief that although Miriani's civil rights attitude had improved it had not improved enough, the race was lost not in the black community, but in the northeast section of Detroit. Here, the homeowners' association, which included large numbers of white union members, opposed Miriani out of a firm conviction that he had become altogether too disposed to support black demands.[44] If it can be said that the UAW moved to the right of its membership by endorsing Miriani, that same endorsement, from the perspective of the white home-owning rank and file, would have to indicate a move to the left. Indeed, what these facts show is that it is not, after all, adequate to define a candidate's political attitudes solely on the basis of the opinions of those who cast ballots on his behalf.

Even the narrower argument that the union's endorsement of Miriani indicated a movement to the right of the most liberal component of its rank and file is problematic. For while the UAW was supporting Miriani, not only in 1961 but in 1957 as well, it was working in the closest cooperation with blacks to elect "liberal civil-rights candidates in local election campaigns for councilman."[45] Indeed, in 1957 the "UAW enthusiastically supported William Patrick, Jr., who became the council's first black member,"[46] an accomplishment, it should be noted, that the 29.2 percent of the population who were nonwhite could not have achieved on their own in the at-large elections to the council. Thus, the UAW is alleged to have moved to the right of the union's black membership at the same time it was assisting the black community to do what it had never before been able to do politically.

If it is not clear that the union leadership moved to the right of its membership, it is equally doubtful that the union endorsed Miriani because he "successfully wooed individual union leaders, made them advisors and personal confidants and gave then some of the perquisites of power."[47] The choice at the time was between an incumbent with whom labor had obtained some advantage and a more liberal challenger who had the distinct disadvantage of being certain to lose. The choice was neither difficult, nor, in the light of all the circumstances, imprudent. The decision to support Miriani was not different in kind from the decision made the year before to withhold support from Hubert Humphrey in his quest for the Democratic presidential nomination. According to Joseph Rauh, Reuther "did not go for Hubert because he felt that was kind of a useless gesture and the kind of thing you let idealists do . . . you don't go for the guy who is not going to win."[48] That the UAW's endorsement of Miriani was based upon rather broader considerations than the narrow self-interest of individual union leaders receives further support from the fact that the endorsement was passed upon by the elected union delegates in the Wayne County AFL-CIO council. This is not to suggest that the leadership exercised no influence over the proceedings of the delegate body, but it would have been difficult to effect as wide a departure from rank and file sentiment as has been alleged merely because of such narrow and personal ambitions.

There is a certain irony in the attribution of narrow self-interest to the union leadership in the 1961 mayoral contest: the reasons for much of the organized black support of Cavanagh are closely connected with the desire of the black union leadership to advance themselves within the union. A great deal of credit has been given to the black population of Detroit and to the Trade Union Leadership Council for mobilizing black voters for Jerome Cavanagh in 1961. Even though the black vote was not by itself sufficient to defeat Miriani, it was quite clear that the black community had become a power to be reckoned with politically. That power was derived from the very large increase in the city's black population. From 300,500, or 16.2 percent of the total population, in 1950, it had grown to 482,223, or 28.9 percent, by 1960. With blacks comprising close to a third of the population, any leader or group of leaders who could deliver the black vote would inevitably assume a major role in affairs. In 1961, this leadership seemed to be coming from the Trade Union Leadership Council (TULC), a group of predominantly black trade unionists organized to express black concerns in the ranks of organized labor. Since much of what would take place throughout the sixties and into the seventies in Detroit and in the state Democratic party as a whole centered on the black community, the relationship between it and the UAW merits examination.

In 1910, when the population of Detroit was slightly under half a million, blacks comprised little more than 1 percent of the total, but with the announcement by Henry Ford of the then unprecedented five-dollar day on

January 5, 1914, the black trek to Detroit began in earnest. Three years later there were 2,874 black workers in the city. Within two years this figure had jumped to nearly 11,000, more than half of whom were employed by Ford at the River Rouge plant. By 1929 the 450,000-man work force was almost 10 percent black. That same year, with the population of Detroit one-and-one-half million, triple what it had been twenty years before, 120,000 blacks made their homes and their living within the city limits.[49]

During the twenties, many blacks who had improved their economic condition by emigrating to Detroit and its industrial opportunities found their societal situation little different from what it had been in the South. Indeed, racial antipathy may have been even more pronounced. In the 1924 mayoral primary, Charles Bowles, the candidate of the Ku Klux Klan, received the largest vote of any candidate, 123,679 out of approximately 323,000 cast. (Bowles's votes, it should be added, were all write-ins.) He was only denied nomination because 17,000 votes were invalidated on technicalities. If blacks found the political climate hostile, private peace was no more easily obtained. When Dr. Ossian H. Sweet, a black, moved into an all-white neighborhood, his house was immediately put under a state of seige. After an exchange of gunfire left a white man dead, Sweet was accused and arraigned on a charge of first-degree murder. However, he had a good lawyer and a fair judge. The trial came to a close when the defense attorney, Clarence Darrow, delivered an eight-hour summation that Frank Murphy, the presiding judge, later said was the most emotional experience of his life.[50] Sweet was acquitted. He was fortunate: in Detroit between 1924 and 1926 over forty blacks were shot down by police, many of whom had been recruited in the South.[51]

Despised by many of their white fellow citizens and apparently denied even minimal consideration by city government, blacks received no better welcome from trade unions. In 1921, the Detroit Urban League was providing black workers to break a strike in the metal trades, a craft union open only to whites.[52] In 1933, blacks made an attempt to organize their own trade union, the Federation of Negro Labor.[53] Only with the coming of the CIO did blacks obtain the opportunity to enter trade unions in Detroit on an equal basis with whites. For the UAW, the inclusion of blacks was indispensable to its ability to organize the auto industry. In the late thirties and early forties, both Chrysler and Ford sought to weaken the union by employing black strikebreakers and instigating racial animosity among workers. The union, however, managed to secure strong support within the black community as a whole. In November, 1939, when Chrysler hired sixty blacks as strikebreakers "to walk through UAW picket lines at the Dodge plant in Hamtramck," dozens of black unionists and community leaders urged them to refuse.[54]

During the early forties the UAW demonstrated precisely how serious it was about racial equality. Between 1940 and 1942, war contracts, along with the loss of thousands of white workers to the armed forces, brought more than 60,000 new blacks into Detroit. Despite the critical labor shortage, many employers were reluctant to hire them. A. Philip Randolph, however, induced President Roosevelt to issue Executive Order 1098, which prohibited racial discrimination in hiring by employers engaged in defense work. The order was of critical importance; it enabled the UAW and the NAACP to pressure employers into hiring over 75,000 blacks in Detroit war plants.[55] This success, however, was not accompanied by any improvement in the racial attitudes of white citizens. Indeed, a large influx of southern whites, who were also drawn by the prospect of employment in the new defense industry, added to the intensity of antiblack sentiment. The UAW quickly moved to make sure that within the union any such prejudice would not be allowed overt expression. At a rally in Cadillac Square cosponsored by the UAW and the NAACP, Walter Reuther informed his listeners that any white who refused to work alongside a black should leave the plant and not return, for that worker had no place in the union.[56] Despite these efforts, in June, 1943, Detroit was the scene of one of the nation's worst race riots. Walter White of the NAACP found one hopeful sign in that turbulent time: "There were two areas in Detoit during the riots where peace was maintained—in the plants which had been organized by the UAW-CIO and in the nonsegregated residential areas."[57]

The UAW commitment to racial equality demonstrated to blacks that the union (and the CIO, of which it was a part) was one of the only institutions that would provide them a channel into the mainstream of American life. In a report issued in 1943, the NAACP, after commenting on what the CIO had done for black workers, described the relation between blacks and the industrial unions: "Every attack on labor is an attack on the negro, for the negro is largely a worker. . . . Organized labor is now our national ally. The CIO has proved that it stands for our people within the unions and outside the unions. . . . If labor loses a battle, the negro loses also."[58] Blacks saw the CIO unions as their natural allies in the quest for economic improvement, and soon came to view them as political allies as well. In 1944, the CIO's Political Action Committee "enjoyed great credibility among blacks for its work in defeating some of the most rabid antiblack congressmen of the day: Joe Starnes, Cotton Ed Smith, and Martin Dies."[59]

In the 1940s blacks saw the CIO unions as economic and political allies who supported their demands for equal treatment; they did not believe that the unions were institutions in which blacks would be able to acquire leadership positions. Unions, in other words, were viewed as white institutions in which blacks belonged—and belonged on an equal basis with white workers—but did not lead. Blacks depended on others for an improvement of their condition. They could use their votes to reward their friends politically, and they could join those labor organizations that helped them economically, but they could not supply leadership in either field. Nor was this point of view without foundation, either then or later. Indeed, as late as 1960, James Q. Wilson could argue that in Chicago, at least, effective black political leadership was noticeably absent.[60] In Detroit, however, the UAW played a larger role for blacks. It became not just a means of improving their condition, but an institution that developed black leaders and then, to an increasing extent, provided them with places of power within the union—and through the union, within the community as a whole.

As early as the 1920s the Ford plant at River Rouge was the single largest place of employment for Detroit blacks. Local 600, which represents UAW workers in the Rouge, gave many blacks who would later assume important leadership positions their first training in union affairs. In 1940 and 1941, Robert "Buddy" Battle, Horace Sheffield, Nelson "Jack" Edwards, Marcellius Ivory, and James "Jimmy" Watts began careers as local union officers. Though B. J. Widick describes Local 600 in the early forties as a training ground for a new breed of black militants in the trade union movement, black leadership in Local 600 and the union as a whole rather quickly acquired a highly developed sense of self-preservation. The case of John Luster is instructive.

In 1946 Luster decided to run for the PAC committee from his branch of Local 600. Once his decision was known, the black caucus that had developed within Local 600 attempted to countermand it. Their reasons were not difficult to discern: only a small number of black positions were available, and the caucus was determined to dispense them as it saw fit. Moreover, there seems to have been a tacit understanding that blacks selected by the black leadership caucus would be those who were acceptable to the white leadership. Despite Luster's protestations, the black caucus would not agree that he had a right even to seek election. The leadership of the caucus claimed that the consequence of his candidacy would be the animosity of white union officials. That was something to be avoided at all costs, as any increase in conflict between blacks and whites would threaten the loss of whatever power blacks then possessed. In short, the status quo may not have been the best, but at least to those blacks who occupied leadership positions in the union it was clearly superior to what might follow from any attempt to get more.

Luster, nevertheless, made the race, and the predicted hostility proved not to have been imaginary. Both blacks and whites devoted time and energy to "cut up" Luster and his campaign. Though he somehow managed to win, his troubles did not end. The president of the union, who had been paying the required per capita tax on nine delegates to the PAC committee, decided to certify only eight. Since Luster had finished ninth in the balloting, he would be trimmed from the delegate list. Thoroughly aroused, and far from intimidated, Luster complained to Al Barbour, the president of the Wayne County CIO. Barbour, however, was reluctant to involve himself in local union politics and sent Luster back to fight his case within the confines of Local 600. After months of hearing promises to certify his election, Luster returned to Barbour and in a manner of speaking informed him that he had come to perceive certain defects in Barbour's character and background. This produced an angry exchange and gave Luster no grounds to expect Barbour's intervention on his behalf. Barbour did intervene, however, and Luster's election was finally certified.

If at the local union level blacks who had ambitions for union careers encountered white reaction and black reserve, the highest echelons of the UAW seemed to offer encouragement to black aspirations. When, for example, Walter Reuther was elected president of the UAW, he stipulated that Jimmy Watts, a black, be one of the three speakers who would place his name in nomination before the convention. It is interesting to note that when Watts asked him what he would like him to say, Reuther informed him that he ought to say whatever he wanted. Once Reuther was elected president, Watts was appointed his administrative assistant.

By 1959 black membership in the UAW had reached an estimated 15 percent of the total. Moreover, there were probably more blacks in staff positions than in all the other major unions combined.[61] Nonetheless, no black had yet been elected to a UAW policy-making position. That this was a source of some irritation among the black membership became obvious at the UAW's 1959 convention, when Horace Sheffield addressed the assembled delegates and, after reminding them of the UAW's insistence that blacks be represented on all levels of government, asked the difficult question that "the negro people are asking . . . 'What about the UAW?' " Nor was Sheffield content to raise the issue for discussion alone. He proceeded to put it to the test by placing the name of a black, Willoughby Abner, in nomination for the union's vice-presidency.[62] Abner declined the nomination, but it was clear that the black leadership in the UAW no longer felt constrained to refrain from criticizing the absence of black membership on the UAW executive board. Black unanimity on the desirability of black representation, however, by no means extended to choosing precisely which black should be selected. This is not to imply that there were not obvious claimants to the position. In fact, it was generally believed that either Horace Sheffield or Nelson "Jack" Edwards would become the first black to serve on the union's highest policy-making body.

Both Sheffield and Edwards, along with "a number of prominent black unionists in auto, steel and other unions," had "formed the Trade Union Leadership Council in Detroit."[63] The TULC, a forerunner of the National American Labor Council organized in 1960 by A. Philip Randolph over the protest of George Meany, was designed to be a vehicle for black advancement within trade unions. The TULC, it should be noted, was not an all-black organization; it quickly opened its doors to such white unionists as Brendon Sexton, Leonard Woodcock, and Sam Fishman. In the 1961 mayoral campaign the TULC supported Cavanagh while the UAW as a whole endorsed Miriani. This was bound to achieve a certain popularity in the black community, where Miriani was generally detested, and was certain to gain its leadership, especially Horace Sheffield, TULC president, considerable prestige. This would provide Sheffield with a base of power in the black community that would apparently increase his claim to the first black position on the UAW executive board. There were, however, certain risks. Miriani, it must be remembered, was seen as a certain victor in the general election. Indeed, on the day before the primary the *Detroit Free Press* stated matter-of-factly, "Regardless of who wins the second nomination, he is not expected to give Miriani even a close race in the November run-off."[64] Although its endorsement of Cavanagh seemed unlikely to do Miriani any real harm, the TULC's deviation from the UAW position was not taken lightly. According to one member of the TULC, "the labor hierarchy threatened some of their people for going for Cavanagh."[65] There even seems to have been a "campaign to fire Horace Sheffield, the head of TULC," for having led black unionists astray.[66] Placed in perspective, however, these risks were not great dangers. Sheffield, for example, was not experiencing efforts to have him ejected from the union for the first time. After he nominated Willoughby Abner for a seat on the executive board in 1959, Emil Mazey had demanded that Reuther fire him.[67] He had survived then and no doubt would survive again.

Sheffield, then, had little to lose, but a very great deal to win. Cavanagh would either win or lose, but Sheffield would win either way. Apart from the election result, the endorsement was sufficient to increase his prestige in the black community, prestige which could perhaps be used to advantage in the impending contest for the much-coveted executive board position. With Cavanagh's victory, Sheffield was able to gather even greater fruits from the endorsement. Six weeks after the election it was reported in the daily press that Sheffield was "among Cavanagh's closest advisors in the negro community."[68] In fact, Sheffield had built up so much credit with Cavanagh that the new mayor "would check everything with Horace that affected blacks."[69] Sheffield's attempt to secure a strong base in Detroit's black community seemed to have succeeded beyond what anyone could reasonably have imagined. To those outside the union, it seemed that the TULC head now occupied a position of power that must elevate him to the union's executive board. What they did not appreciate was that although Sheffield had apparently moved without a false step in city politics, in the internal affairs of the union he had made a fatal miscalculation.

The incumbent president of Local 600, in which Sheffield and a great many other active members of the TULC had their base, was Carl Stelleto. In 1961, Stelleto was seeking reelection to another term of office. Sheffield and Buddy Battle, head of the foundry workers in the local, decided to back the challenger, Harry Philo. Sheffield, it should be noted at the outset, had always been a Reutherite; that is, he had been a firm adherent of Walter Reuther during the struggles against the communist party faction for control of the union. Philo, on the other hand, had not taken the same position. As one UAW official put it, "the CP had colonized Philo very early." In the judgment of at least some members of the Reuther group, electing Philo to the presidency of Local 600 would enable the communists, even as late as 1961, to reestablish themselves within the union, and in the union's largest local. Though Stelleto withstood Philo's challenge and retained the presidency of the local, his margin of victory was narrow; only a few thousand votes separated the two candidates in the final tally. Sheffield's participation in the Philo campaign cost him dearly. Not only did it arouse the ire of the Reutherites, who were fervent anticommunists, but it enabled Reuther to suggest to Sheffield that it was difficult to see how someone who could not even carry his own local could aspire to a seat on the executive board. A year later, in 1962, Nelson "Jack" Edwards, a staff representative, was elected as a member-at-large of the UAW executive board, becoming the first black to serve on the board in its history.

The position of the black man in America is and has been somewhat anomalous. At the same time that blacks have criticized the disparity between the pretense of equality and the practice of discrimination, they have striven, sometimes desperately, to be included in the white society they condemn and the racist institutions they castigate. Many whites, especially those most genuinely sympathetic to black aspirations, have seen both those impulses as deriving from the principle of equality. Such great attention has been devoted to the quest of black people for equality of opportunity that the battles within the black community for more than equal power have largely gone unnoticed. It is only a seeming paradox that some of the most vicious struggles for power have taken place within a group that has made equality its watchword and battle cry. It is precisely because the policies to be pursued are largely not at issue that the struggle for place and position can become so intense. One leading political figure in the Detroit black community put it this way: "I don't really think you could say that blacks in Detroit are divided between liberals and conservatives. We don't really have any conservatives that I know of. It isn't issues that cause the fights. The name of the game here is power. The fights are between those who have it and those who want it."

In 1962 Nelson "Jack" Edwards had power, but as Thomas Hobbes pointed out, power is a commodity that has only a relative value. Edwards was now the first black member of the UAW executive board, but Horace Sheffield retained his hold on the TULC, and through it his influence in the black community as a whole. Those who did not view this as an inequitable distribution would have been better equipped to anticipate events by recalling that, for Hobbes at least, the relativity of power requires the constant acquisition of more power to protect what has already been accumulated. The search for power after power which "ceaseth only in death" had not come to an end for Nelson "Jack" Edwards. Sheffield's influence in the black community had somehow to be at least counterbalanced and even superseded. The opportunity to accomplish this arose in 1964, when it became clear that a second black congressional district had been created.

For a number of years Michigan was represented in the Congress by a single black member, Charles Diggs, Jr. By 1956 Diggs was one of three blacks "sitting in the House of Representatives" who "were wielding their seniority effectively," the other two being the venerable William Dawson of Chicago and the flamboyant Adam Clayton Powell of New York.[70] In the latter part of 1963, the state legislature was compelled by the U.S. Supreme Court's apportionment decisions to redraw the boundaries of congressional district lines. Before the new district boundaries were drawn, however, the firm of George Crockett and Maurice Sugar encouraged a young black lawyer to enter a primary contest against an incumbent congressman, Lucien Nedzi. The district had not yet been drawn, but it was expected to contain if not a majority of blacks, at least a sufficient number to make the candidacy worth the effort. Thus, a year before the election, John Conyers, Jr., began a campaign to unseat an incumbent white congressman in a congressional district not yet created. The situation was further complicated by the fact that Nedzi was not without support in the black community. In the congressional primary of 1962, when Nedzi ran for the first time, a number of black union members had helped defeat the recommendation of Gus Scholle and Al Barbour that labor take a hands-off position. Nedzi had not forgotten.

The choice between a white incumbent and a black challenger in a biracial district was removed when four blacks in the state legislature opposed the UAW's position on congressional reapportionment. Organized labor, in conjunction with the state Democratic party, sought to create as many Democratic districts as possible. Their plan was calculated to do precisely that. State Senator Basil Brown, the only black in the state senate and a man of considerable ability, had a somewhat different objective. Persuading three black members of the house to hold firm, he struck a bargain with Republicans in which the four votes at his disposal would be cast in favor of the Republican plan if that plan provided for two predominantly black congressional districts in Detroit. A plan containing this provision, was introduced in January, 1964, and the four black Democrats joined with the Republicans to make Michigan the first state in the union to have more than one black congressional district.

John Conyers, Jr., now faced not the opposition of an incumbent congressman but another kind of difficulty. Before the new black district was created, while Conyers was already compaigning, another potential black candidate was making a cautious calculation of the possibilities. Richard Austin, who years earlier had become Michigan's first black certified public accountant, was one of the best known and most highly respected members of Detroit's black community. Once the district lines were drawn, Austin was persuaded by his friends, including a number of labor leaders, to enter the race for Congress in the new First District. Had Austin begun his campaign as early as Conyers, there is little doubt that he would have received the endorsement and the support of almost every important black leader in Detroit. As it was, by the time he did declare his candidacy, Conyers had already accumulated commitments from several of the most influential black leaders, the most important of whom was Nelson "Jack" Edwards. However, Austin was far from being preempted. The two most important endorsements were yet to be made: neither the UAW nor the TULC had yet taken a position.

The contest for the Democratic congressional nomination from the First District, a nomination that was equivalent to election, very quickly became entangled in the struggle for leadership of both the black membership of the UAW and the black community as a whole. In 1964, the TULC "controlled" the First District,[71] and the fight for its endorsement was to have repercussions for both the UAW and the First District for years to come. Conyers was not without strength in the TULC. Indeed, he was himself the TULC's legal counsel. His father, John Conyers, Sr., who was "a long-time UAW activist and staff member, argued in the TULC for an endorsement" of his son. He was supported by Nelson "Jack" Edwards, who now sought to use Conyers's candidacy, as Horace Sheffield had used Jerome Cavanagh's three years earlier, to "broaden his base in the black community." Sheffield, however, now threw his support to Austin. Edwards had obtained the UAW executive board seat, but Sheffield had retained his strength in the TULC, and he used it to full advantage. Austin got the endorsement. Incensed, Edwards led his followers out of the TULC, quickly formed an organization of their own, and endorsed John Conyers, Jr., for Congress.[72]

Conyers had the support of one member of the UAW executive board in Edwards, but another member, Emil Mazey, was pushing hard for a union endorsement of his boyhood friend Richard Austin. It is at this point necessary to recall that the UAW was still a part, although the strongest part, of the AFL-CIO. Until 1964, the normal endorsement procedure for congressional races in Wayne County began with the district COPE's interviewing committee. This body interviewed the candidates for each of the positions for which an election was being held in the district. Endorsements would then be made for the congressional seat, as well as, for example, state house or state senate districts located within the congressional district. The endorsement was then subject to approval by the full district COPE committee. That approval, in turn, was offered for ratification to the Wayne County AFL-CIO executive board. The last step in the endorsement procedure was a vote on each proposed endorsement by the Wayne County COPE delegate body elected by the membership. In 1964 all this went by the boards. One of those most involved in the Conyers-Austin struggle never was able to understand quite how it all happened, but

> the machinery completely broke down. The district committee never made any decision about it. It somehow went directly to the Wayne County AFL-CIO, probably because there was so much politicking involved. Everybody was at each other's throat. All the labor groups were spending all their time trying to line up support for Conyers or for Austin.

The Wayne County AFL-CIO executive board endorsed Conyers and "things weren't complicated any more, they were confused." The UAW, for the most part, was less than pleased. Indeed, though Conyers would later downplay Edwards's assistance, only Edwards prevented the UAW from at least trying to take the endorsement away from Conyers in order to give it to Austin. Instead, many of the union's political operatives joined forces with other Austin supporters to persuade the Wayne County AFL-CIO delegate body to reject the executive board's endorsement of Conyers and replace it with what one UAW official has referred to as a "negotiated truce." In effect, the resolution endorsing Conyers was amended to give labor's formal endorsement to both Conyers and Austin. This, of course, meant no endorsement at all—and that, of course, meant that everyone who was sympathetic to one of the candidates and was in a position to do something about it, did. The ensuing hostilities continued to affect political relations in both the state Democratic party and the First Congressional District for years.

Despite the dual endorsement, Nelson "Jack" Edwards, who was leading Conyers's campaign, had a decided advantage over Horace Sheffield, who was giving assistance to Austin. Sheffield, explained one black union activist, "was functioning as a representative from the TULC rather than from the UAW and for that reason didn't have the clout that Edwards had who was seen as sort of the embodiment of the UAW." An example of the power differential derived from the difference in positions occurred when a UAW staff member managed to have a number of deputy sheriffs released from their normal responsibilities to work in the Austin campaign. Discovering what had happened, Edwards talked with County Sheriff Peter Bruback, who not only returned the deputies to their respective law enforcement duties but released a number of other deputies to work full-time in Conyers's campaign.

Conyers won the primary, but only by the smallest of margins. Indeed, the result was so close that a formal request for a recount was filed. Even though the recount gave Conyers the election by thirty-eight votes, the request for it increased his antagonism toward the UAW. Conyers believed that people within the union had provided Austin with both the money and the encouragement to request the recount. After the recount, when it was apparent that the intensity of feeling between the candidates and their partisans was likely to jeopardize even the possibility of decent relations within the district, a number of labor and community leaders sought to bring about some kind of political reconciliation. A series of meetings led finally to a meeting of nearly all the important figures in the First District. Conyers, Buddy Battle, Austin, John Luster, and Horace Sheffield, among others, met in Austin's office and reached what seemed to be an agreement satisfactory to everyone concerned. There would be an end to fighting; a mutually acceptable list of officers would be worked out for the district party organization; and there would be no attempt to attack Conyers while he was serving in Washington. At this point Conyers was asked what he would need to feel assured that his recent opponents would live up to the agreement. Conyers ignored the question and, addressing himself to Austin, proceeded to raise a series of other questions. Austin's response was to say that if Conyers could not answer the question he had been asked, there was very little point in continuing the discussion. Conyers then asked that the question be repeated. He answered finally that he needed no additional assurances. Agreement was reached and everyone in the room shook hands. Immediately after the meeting broke up, one of Austin's lieutenants cornered Conyers in the hall and, after stating he was authorized by Austin to act in his name, offered to give Conyers any additional assurances of good faith he might require. Conyers replied simply that he had enough and would be back in touch after he had talked things over with his own people. Austin and his friends waited for a call from Conyers. It never came.

Conyers did discuss the situation with his own people, but this group was no longer an undivided camp. Even before the campaign was over a very serious split had begun to develop between Conyers and Nelson "Jack" Edwards. It had now grown into a dispute of great proportions. One of those directly involved described the situation in the following way:

> Edwards and the other labor people who had backed Conyers had an interest in certain positions within the district. Conyers though wasn't much interested in giving any influence to labor. He really wanted to control things with people who were loyal to him instead of to the union. A lot of trouble started. At one meeting the top really blew off. Conyers blasted both Edwards and Walter

Reuther. For the labor guys in the room it was demeaning. Here was the guy they had gone all the way for, he couldn't have won without them, and he is attacking Edwards and Reuther in a very personal way.

Indeed, the attack was so vicious that Edwards walked out.

The district was split, not simply between the supporters of Austin and Conyers, but between Conyers and the UAW. The new congressman now faced the task of electing a slate of candidates for party office in the district without much of the support he had depended on for his own election. At the district convention in January, Conyers proceeded to demonstrate that victory does not always require the support of a voting majority. As the newly elected congressman, he assumed the role of district convention chairman and put his own most loyal followers in charge of counting the votes cast for district offices. According to one of the UAW representatives present,

> when our people saw what was going on a number of them decided there wasn't any point staying around and left. A number of others remained but didn't bother to vote. Conyers didn't have to steal the district leadership election, it was enough that he gave every indication of intending to do it.

Despite provocation, the UAW did not run anyone against Conyers in any of the ensuing congressional elections. Much of this must be attributed to Conyers's very close attention to his record on labor legislation. It would have been impossible for the UAW to persuade its members in the district that there was anything wrong with his voting record. Moreover, some of his pronouncements that were completely at odds with union preferences also strengthened his position with his constituents. Thus, for example, in 1968, when the UAW was doing everything it could to elect Hubert Humphrey, Conyers kept postponing his own endorsement of the nominee. In the district, the late endorsement created the impression that Conyers was an independent black who would not simply obey a predominantly white institution.

Though Conyers's position in Congress appeared unassailable, the political situation in the district was not one that inspired equal confidence. And Conyers was not satisfied with a district that was safe electorally; he wanted to be able to intervene in party politics in the district. Every two years following his election, both the UAW and Conyers actively sought the election of precinct delegates who could be counted on in the struggle for control of the district's executive board. In the latter part of 1968 tension in the district, though it had been somewhat abated through the conciliatory efforts of many of the leading parties, was high enough to warrant one of the very few direct intrusions into Michigan politics that Walter Reuther ever made.

On the day after Christmas in 1968, John Conyers met privately with

Douglas Fraser, then a UAW board member, and Walter Reuther. The union was displeased with Conyers's late endorsement of Hubert Humphrey in the presidential campaign, and Conyers had intimated on a number of occasions that Reuther was directly responsible for some of the difficulties that existed between the congressman and the union leadership. In an effort to smooth out relations, Reuther promised Conyers that the UAW would not oppose Conyers in the operation of the First District. Conyers "got a pledge from Reuther that he could be a congressman without having to watch his flank in the District."[73] The UAW, however, was not going to abdicate its political interests in the district. There would be no opposition to Conyers himself, but there might very well be disagreement "on issues if they arise." Conyers, for his part, promised "to work more closely with the UAW on political issues in Michigan and Washington."[74]

This exchange of nebulous guarantees fell short of providing improved relations between Conyers and the UAW. In the judgment of Saul Friedman, the political commentator of the *Detroit Free Press,* two things barred the way to any real accommodations. One was "the continued power struggle among some Negroes who are UAW leaders." The second was "Conyers' continued suspicion of those who have been his rivals in the past."[75] Friedman also noted another more fundamental cause for continued tension: the growing hostility between Conyers and Detroit Mayor Cavanagh, "who may have opposition this year from the Congressman or some other Negro."[76] For the first time, the election of a black mayor in Detroit had become a real possibility. That possibility opened up the prospect of enormous complications in the relations between black and white in the city and in the union. But nowhere would the impact be as great as within the black community itself. Election of a black mayor would bring about a major alteration of power relationships, because Detroit's first black mayor, whoever he was, would immediately become a national figure, recognized as the spokesman not only for the city but for the black community as a whole. As the opportunities for political power broadened, the causes of distrust and suspicion deepened.

Notes

1. Edward Banfield and James Q. Wilson, for example, claim the UAW decided to take an active part in Detroit city politics because of the doctrinal position held by at least the younger, more radical UAW leadership. Edward C. Banfield and James Q. Wilson, *City Politics* (Cambridge: Harvard University Press, 1963), ch. 19.

2. Frank Cormier and William J. Eaton, *Reuther* (Englewood Cliffs, N.J.: Prentice-Hall, 1970), p. 123.

3. Ibid.

4. *New York Times,* November 1, 1937.

5. Cormier and Eaton, *Reuther*, p. 124.

6. J. Woodford Howard, *Mr. Justice Murphy* (Princeton: Princeton University Press, 1968), p. 162.

7. *New York Times*, November 1, 4, 1937. See also *Detroit News*, October 6, November 8, 1937; Cormier and Eaton, *Reuther*, p. 124.

8. Cormier and Eaton, *Reuther*, p. 124.

9. B. J. Widick, *Detroit: City of Race and Class Violence* (Chicago: Quadrangle Books, 1972), p. 38.

10. Ibid.

11. Richard D. Lunt, *The High Ministry of Government* (Detroit: Wayne State University Press, 1965), p. 28.

12. Howard, *Murphy*, p. 34.

13. Ibid., p. 158.

14. Banfield and Wilson, *City Politics*, p. 61.

15. Ibid.

16. Ibid.

17. Widick, *Detroit*, p. 153.

18. Ibid.

19. Ibid., p. 154.

20. *Detroit News*, November 11, 1945.

21. Widick, *Detroit*, p. 154.

22. Banfield and Wilson, *City Politics*, p. 157.

23. Ibid.

24. Widick, *Detroit*, p. 154.

25. Ibid.

26. Ibid.

27. *Detroit News*, September 8, 1969.

28. Banfield and Wilson, *City Politics*, p. 324.

29. Edward C. Banfield, *Big City Politics* (New York: Random House, 1965), p. 61.

30. Ibid., p. 51.

31. Banfield and Wilson, *City Politics*, p. 156.

32. Widick, *Detroit*, p. 154.

33. *New York Times*, April 28, 1956.

34. Widick, *Detroit*, p. 154.

35. Edward Purdy, interview with author, September 9, 1971.

36. Widick, *Detroit*, p. 155.

37. Ibid., pp. 154–55.

38. Banfield, *Big City Politics*, p. 57.

39. Widick, *Detroit*, p. 155.

40. Ibid.

41. J. David Greenstone, *Labor in American Politics* (New York: Alfred A. Knopf, 1969), p. 63.

42. Ibid.

43. Ibid.

44. Edward Purdy, interview with author, September 9, 1971.

45. Greenstone, *Labor in Politics*, p. 257.

46. Ibid., p. 256.

47. Ibid., p. 138.

48. Quoted in Cormier and Eaton, *Reuther*, p. 371.

49. Widick, *Detroit*, p. 27.

50. Ibid., p. 6.

51. Ibid., p. 16.

52. Ibid., p. 26.

53. Ibid., p. 57.

54. Ibid., p. 74.

55. Ibid., p. 93.

56. Cormier and Eaton, *Reuther*, pp. 206–7.

57. Quoted ibid., p. 207.

58. "The 1943 Line-up vs. the Negro," *NAACP Bulletin* 3 (February, 1943), quoted in Patricia Cayo Sexton and Brendon Sexton, *Blue Collars and Hard Hats* (New York: Vintage Books, 1972), p. 210.

59. Mark R. Levy and Michael S. Kramer, *The Ethnic Factor: How America's Minorities Decide Elections* (New York: Simon and Schuster, 1972), p. 41.

60. James Q. Wilson, *Negro Politics* (New York: Free Press, 1960).

61. Jack Stieber, *Governing the UAW* (New York: John Wiley and Sons, 1962), p. 41.

62. Ibid., p. 43. See also UAW Convention Proceedings, 1959, pp. 360–61.

63. Widick, *Detroit*, p. 149.

64. *Detroit Free Press*, September 10, 1961.

65. Prince Moon, interview with author, December 20, 1971.

66. Widick, *Detroit*, p. 155.

67. Ibid., p. 150.

68. *Detroit Free Press*, December 24, 1961.

69. Sam Fishman, interview with author, June 6, 1973.

70. Levy and Kramer, *The Ethnic Factor*, p. 43.

71. *Detroit News*, May 7, 1969.

72. Ibid.

73. *New York Post*, January 10, 1969.

74. Ibid.

75. Ibid.

76. Ibid.

CHAPTER 7

The UAW and the Politics of Detroit

The possibility of electing a black mayor and the prospects for black political advancement in general derived from a simple and a rather stark demographic fact. Year by year the black population of Detroit was increasing, both in absolute numbers and as a percentage of the whole. In 1950 Detroit reached a population of 1,849,568. This reflected a slow but steady increase during the preceding twenty years. In each of the next two decades, population decreased by almost 10 percent. By 1970, Detroit had lost over 300,000 people, and was left with a total population of 1,511,482. The numerical decline by itself does not clearly reveal what was taking place. In each of the two decades roughly one quarter of the white population left, 23.5 percent in the 1950s, and 29.1 percent in the 1960s. At the same time, the black population underwent a substantial increase, 60.5 percent between 1950 and 1960, and 37 percent between 1960 and 1970. By 1970, 43.7 percent of the Detroit population was black.

As the black population increased, demands for larger influence began. However, it was one thing to insist on greater participation for black members of the community and quite another to agree on how that objective could best be obtained. In 1967, for example, a number of black state legislators called for the replacement of Detroit's at-large method of electing all nine members of the Common Council with a ward system. State Representative Jackie Vaughn claimed that almost 90 percent of Detroit's black population favored the election of council members by districts. Vaughn felt it to be "shameful that in all this time only two Negroes have been elected to the council and they were handpicked by whites."[1] Nelson "Jack" Edwards found this argument unconvincing. In a telegram to several black legislators, the only black member of the UAW executive board warned that "establishment of the ward system would be a retrogressive step and contrary to the best interests of the people of Detroit." It was also not in the best interest of blacks: "I believe that our interests transcend getting a few more jobs for Negroes. . . ."[2]

Edwards did not say why the ward system was not in blacks' interest, but the explanation is fairly evident. A ward system would have a profound and disturbing effect on the attitudes and opinions of those elected. Instead of council members responsive to the interests of the city as a whole, the ward system would bring into office men and women necessarily devoted to the interests of their own constituencies. In Detroit, that would mean black members from black constituencies, and white members from white constituencies. Even if nonpartisan elections were replaced with partisan contests, there would still be no citywide organization capable of imposing a citywide perspective on council candidates. In Detroit, the congressional district committees are independent party organizations. Without an effective citywide organization race would become the primary, if not the only, basis for electing council members. The opportunities for racial demagoguery would be irresistible.

There was another reason the ward system would not be totally beneficial for blacks. Election by district would no doubt increase the number of black members of the common council; but it would also have the effect of limiting the number of blacks on the council to roughly the same proportion as the black percentage of the city population. In other words, once Detroit had a black majority, the council might or might not have a black majority, depending upon the way district lines were drawn; but an all-black council, or anything close to it, would be out of the question.

The UAW had managed to overcome early attempts to divide it on racial lines by emphasizing the common status of whites and blacks as workers and their common interest in economic improvement. The political coalition between whites and blacks also rested on the belief that the Democratic party was the instrument for the economic advancement of blue-collar workers. For white workers, civil rights might not be all that attractive, but it was a relatively small price to pay for what they believed the union and the Democratic party had done and would continue to do for them. For blacks, the coalition with whites, both in the union and in the Democratic party, had brought about not only economic gains but substantial improvements in civil rights. Where blacks were by themselves a majority, however, the necessity or even the desirability of a coalition with whites seemed less apparent. And in Detroit blacks were becoming majorities in more and more areas. Two congressional districts, the First and the Thirteenth, had black majorities and had elected black congressmen.

In 1968 approximately two-thirds of the Thirteenth District was black. Like the other Wayne County congressional district organizations, the Thirteenth endorsed candidates in primary elections. It had an endorsement procedure that on the face of it was a model of fairness. The executive board appointed a committee to interview candidates who requested endorsement. After completing the interviews the committee made a recommendation to the executive board. At this point the executive board could request more information. Once it had received answers to all its questions, it presented the recommendations of the interviewing committee to the elected precinct delegates, with or without a recommendation of its own. The membership then decided which candidates would receive the endorsement of the district. Normally, the recommendation of the interviewing committee was supported by the executive board and approved by the membership. This was especially true when one of the candidates was an incumbent. In 1968, however, an incumbent failed to receive the endorsement. The reason was his race.

In 1964, Tom White was elected to the state house of representatives from a Detroit district that included Wayne State University and a large black minority, a sizable portion of which lived in the Jeffries housing project. Two year later, White faced a black opponent in the primary. Aided by the district endorsement, and by the fact that his opponent was involved in a barroom shooting just before the primary election, White was reelected. By that time the district was at least half black, and it was expected that the percentage of blacks would continute to increase. Moreover, the war on poverty, an effort White fully supported, had made the people who lived in the projects more politically astute; the projects were quickly becoming an organized political force. As the 1968 election approached, it was certain that the district had a black majority, and that White would face a black opponent in the Democratic primary.

At first it appeared that White would manage to get the district endorsement once again. His voting record in the state legislature contained nothing to which black voters could object. He had done as much as anyone else to establish a state housing authority, and residents of the Jeffries project would benefit from that more than most. After the interviewing committee had met with both White and his black opponent, Nellis Saunders, its recommendation was to endorse White. The executive board brought the recommendation before the membership; but the membership, which, reflecting the racial composition of the entire congressional district, had a higher black percentage than White's district, refused to follow. It endorsed Saunders, and Saunders won the election. She did not, however, have the help of the UAW. White was an incumbent who had a decent record as a legislator, and the UAW saw no reason to withhold its endorsement on the basis of race. The Thirteenth District, on the other hand, saw no reason not to insist on having a black represent a district that contained a majority of black voters. White voters were not needed.

What had happened in the Thirteenth District was a small indication of what was taking place in Detroit altogether. It had been advantageous for black leaders in the UAW to support Jerome Cavanagh in 1961 when the city's black population was not quite 30 percent. By 1969, when blacks were already close to a majority in the city, support for a white candidate, no matter how liberal, would not do a black any good at all. The UAW, with its interest in holding blacks and whites together in a working coalition, faced a dilemma. If it decided to support a black mayoral candidate, the community might be split on racial lines, and victory might well go to a white candidate who owed his election to antiblack sentiment. On the other hand, if it failed to support a black candidate the union itself might be split on racial lines, and in at least some circles its dedication to racial equality would be drawn into serious question. That in turn would make it even more difficult for black Democratic leaders in Michigan to continue to refuse to leave the Democratic party for independent, and sometimes separatist black political movements. That the UAW would have to make a choice became evident the day Richard Austin became the first black candidate for mayor of Detroit.

When Austin announced his candidacy on June 4, 1969, Jerome Cavanagh was still mayor and had not made any announcement about his intentions. There were some who believed that Cavanagh needed a few more years in city hall to recover from the political setback he sustained when he failed to win the Democratic nomination for the U.S. Senate in 1966. Others believed that Cavanagh would not run for reelection, and would instead devote all his time and energy to a gubernatorial campaign for 1970. Perhaps because his congressional candidacy had suffered greatly from its late beginnings, Austin did not wait to see what Cavanagh would do. He could not afford to wait; it had already been decided that a black would be in the race. In March, fifty-five blacks had gathered at the home of Congressman John Conyers and decided to run a black against Cavanagh. Austin, however, was not the candidate they had in mind. The general preference seemed to be William Patrick, Jr., a member of the Common Council. Others were mentioned, but Austin was not high on the list of possibilities. Among the more militant black leaders, Austin, who held the position of Wayne County Auditor, was considered too conservative. Another and perhaps more important cause for displeasure with Austin was his attempt to obtain the newly created First District congressional seat in 1964. "Many people say," reported the *Detroit Free Press,* "Conyers has yet to forget that close call."[3]

Austin seemed to face very difficult obstacles, and the absence of support from Conyers was not the most formidable among them. Charles Diggs, Jr., the other black congressman, was also disposed to see William Patrick as the best possible black mayoral candidate. Even worse for Austin's prospects was the decision of Horace Sheffield, who had been perhaps his strongest ally in the 1964 congressional campaign, to give his own support, and that of the TULC as well, to Cavanagh. In the same month Conyers was trying to forge an alliance of the black leadership as the basis for a black candidacy, Sheffield put his political influence on the line and made certain that Cavanagh obtained "an early endorsement from TULC."[4] On the day Austin announced, the only thing that seemed clear was that there was going to be at least one black candidate in the race and that that candidate did not have the support of the most powerful members of the city's black leadership. But Austin did have something that was of immense importance, the announcement itself.

The black population of Detroit, as near as anyone could know before the next census appeared, was slightly less than half the total population; as a percentage of the voting-age population it was thought to be somewhat lower. Although a general election in which one candidate was black could be expected to produce a high turnout among black voters, the primary, out of which the top two candidates would be selected for the runoff, would probably receive less attention. What the turnout would actually be was any-one's guess, but a fact that could not be ignored was the decline in the black vote in Detroit between the 1964 and 1968 presidential elections; it had fallen an incredible 35 percent. The entry of a second black into the contest might very well split a black vote that could be considerably less than the percentage of blacks in the total population. Austin was the first black candidate. A second faced the prospect not only of failing to survive the primary because of a split in the black vote, but of being blamed for the inability of *any* black candidate to survive it. There were no takers. Austin was the first and only black candidate for mayor. What that was worth against Jerry Cavanagh was far from certain.

Cavanagh had the promised support of Horace Sheffield and the TULC. There were also indications that the UAW was leaning in the direction of the incumbent mayor. But three weeks after Austin became a candidate, Cavanagh announced that he would not seek reelection to a third term. After Cavanagh, the most powerful white candidate appeared to be Ed Carey, president of the Common Council. A UAW organizer, Carey had served several terms in the state legislature before running for the council. However, he suffered a heart attack and had to stay out of the race. Mary Beck, a member of the Common Council and a "persistent critic of Mayor Cavanagh," announced her candidacy, which she assured the voters would be devoted to the issue of "law and order."[5] Mary Beck, however, was not the candidate most likely to be the strongest opponent for Richard Austin. The most powerful white candidate from the moment he announced was a Polish Catholic and the Wayne County Sheriff, Roman Gribbs.

Not since 1949, when Albert Cobo defeated George Edwards, had there been a mayoral election in Detroit without the presence of an incumbent seeking reelection. The record of the Cavanagh administration would not be nearly as important a campaign issue as it would have been had the mayor been a candidate. The broad directions of city policy would still be discussed, but specific measures adopted by the administration would be immune from attack because none of the candidates was in any sense responsible for them. Without a record to attack, candidates would necessarily have to address themselves to the large and rather general issue of what they would like the city to concentrate its energies and resources on in the future. Without a record to focus on, not only would campaign issues tend to be general and even vague, but the issue of race would almost certainly become the dominant question in the election. It clearly was the central and most anguishing issue for the UAW.

Before Cavanagh removed himself from the campaign, the UAW had been leaning in his direction, but even then it was reported that the union was "disturbed at the idea of opposing a black."[6] With Cavanagh's withdrawal, it was still not certain that the UAW would endorse Austin. The *Detroit Free Press* ventured the prediction that the UAW "may now endorse Austin or perhaps remain neutral."[7] There were some union leaders who believed neutrality the better part of valor. Austin stood a decent chance of losing, and the UAW was not eager to find itself once again in opposition to the candidate who became mayor. There was an even more persuasive argument for neutrality. If the contest became one based largely on race, the union might be able to prevent or at least mitigate division within the community, to say nothing of racial discord within the union, by pressuring all the candidates to suppress the racial issue as much as possible. On the other hand, neutrality had its disadvantages. It was difficult enough to argue for an endorsement of Jerome Cavanagh, a liberal incumbent with considerable black support, against the challenge of a black opponent. To withhold the endorsement after Cavanagh's withdrawal, in favor of a policy of neutrality, might easily be interpreted as reflecting a hidden bias on the part of the UAW itself. More than a few members of Detroit's black community would have been willing or even eager to make precisely this interpretation, and to do it with as much publicity as possible.

There was another reason not to opt for neutrality. Four UAW regions drew at least part of their membership from the city. Only one of the four had a black regional director, but in each of the others the percentage of blacks among the membership was increasing. Already eleven local union presidents were black, and it was only a matter of time, according to one observer, before most Detroit plants would have black majorities.[8] Because each of the four regional directors had constituencies in which blacks were a majority or a growing minority, none of them could afford not to support Austin. Failing to back him might seriously jeopardize a director's ability to retain his position, and that was something too valuable to risk.

Pressure that might have been irresistible to the regional directors in the

Detroit area had no direct impact on the highest leadership of the UAW. The union's membership numbered 1.7 million; of these, a quarter of a million were black—a substantial minority, but still a minority. Nevertheless, it was something like the same calculation that had such force with the four regional directors that led the UAW to decide against neutrality and in favor of Austin. When the UAW executive board met to take up the question of endorsement in the Detroit mayoral election, Walter Reuther presided. He asked each member of the executive board to state his preference and the reasons for it. Some, like Austin's boyhood friend Emil Mazey, were passionate in their recommendation that the UAW endorse; others argued for neutrality; a few suggested an endorsement of Gribbs. After everyone had spoken, Reuther did not bother to either summarize the opinions presented or take a vote. Instead, the president of one of the most democratic unions in America simply announced that since a majority of the UAW members who both worked and lived in Detroit were black the UAW would endorse Austin. He asked if anyone had anything to say. The question was greeted with complete silence and Reuther left the room. Richard Austin had just become the endorsed candidate of the United Automobile Workers of America.[9]

Two weeks before the primary election the candidates seemed devoted to the proposition that the least offensive campaign would be the most successful one. Each was trying to attract as many voters as possible while alienating as few as necessary. The campaign was, in the words of one of the city's two major newspapers, "deliberately dull."[10] For Austin it seemed a most intelligent strategy. One UAW official explained: "He's running a campaign designed not to disturb anything. He wants to campaign quietly, then get his black vote out and steal a victory."[11] The UAW, however, seemed to have decided on another strategy. As many as seventeen headquarters were to be established by the UAW throughout the city. These would be the centers of activity for the union's campaign for Austin and other endorsed candidates. It was going to be a citywide campaign, not an effort aimed only where it would do the greatest amount of good with the least harm. Austin's name was to be carried not into black areas alone, but into white areas as well, "despite fears that as many whites might be aroused to vote against him as for him. 'We can't agree to a strategy where we campaign among only a segment of our membership or the community' the UAW official says."[12] Injecting Austin's name into predominantly white areas did not seem entirely consistent with an attempt to conduct a quiet campaign that relied heavily, if not exclusively, on the mobilization of the black vote. In fact, the inconsistency was more apparent than real. Austin might survive the primary with the black vote alone, but in the general election against only a single opponent that would not be sufficient. A campaign to attract white voters could not begin too early. Moreover, the expressed fear that carrying Austin's name into white precincts would antagonize one voter for every one it attracted was scarcely anything to fear at all. On the contrary, it was something much to be hoped for: if half of the white vote, or anything close to it, were cast for Austin, the election would be a runaway for the black candidate.

Both Austin and Gribbs were Democrats, although the latter's credentials were subject to question. Because both were members of the same party, and because the city had given 70 percent of its vote in 1968 to Hubert Humphrey, it has been said that "party politics were not really involved."[13] It is true that the election itself was nonpartisan, but the Democratic party was much involved in the campaign, and that involvement was itself eminently political. Each of the four congressional districts that were either entirely or largely within the city's boundaries had Democratic committees that took an active part in the campaign. Two of them, the First and the Thirteenth, were completely within the city and had large black majorities. Both of them endorsed Austin with no discernible opposition. The other two districts, the Fourteenth and the Seventeenth, were largely but not entirely within the city limits. Both possessed populations that were overwhelmingly white and both were represented in congress by liberal Democrats. But the extent of liberal sentiment among the constituencies differed considerably.

The Seventeenth District was unique in several respects. It was the only district in the state represented in the congress by a woman, Martha Griffiths; it was the only district in Wayne County where, since the beginning of the liberal-labor coalition, there had never been a chairman who was associated directly or indirectly with the labor movement; and of all the districts in the county, it was the one where white liberals exercised continuing influence within the party organization. Throughout the long tenure of chairman Al Meyer, party affairs were conducted strictly in accordance with the principle that members of the district organization, no matter what institution or association they might be connected with, represented only themselves.[14] Under Meyer's aegis no separate labor caucus—in fact, no caucus of any sort—was permitted to exist. All this ended in 1964 when reapportionment placed Meyer outside the boundaries of the Seventeenth District. With his removal, a major source of support for a party organization made up of interested individuals, rather than individual interests, disappeared. In the following four years organized factions began to develop. Organized labor, which for the most part had agreed with Meyer's conception of party organization, failed adequately to combat the emergence of organized interests. In part this failure was caused by the diminished activity of the UAW's district coordinator who was nearing retirement and no longer had any great incentive to oppose the drift of things.

When a new coordinator was appointed in 1968, he found the district divided among five factions. Grouped under the district chairman, William Gladstone, were "the Al Meyer type independents," who were in what might be called the liberal mainstream of the Democratic party. Opposite them in political outlook was a group calling itself the Democratic Forum. This was the repository of the "old line Democrats" for whom the economic policy of FDR was decidedly more attractive than the civil rights platform and programs of the party under Kennedy and Johnson. A third group was identified by its allegiance to Mayor Cavanagh. Led by Jack Casey, one of the mayor's assistants, the "Cavanagh group" was composed of the predominantly "Irish City Hall bunch." Their primary interest was to increase the mayor's influence in the party structure. They attempted without success to replace Gladstone with one of their own as chairman in 1966. Labor was the fourth faction, and the Concerned Democrats the fifth.[15]

The Concerned Democrats had come into being almost inadvertently. In 1966, labor had run 65 candidates for precinct delegates in the district and elected 60 of them. This meant that labor had elected delegates from one-fifth of the district's 299 precincts. At the same time, 30 or 35 delegates were elected who found themselves to the left of the Gladstone group. They proceeded to form a separate faction, and called it the "liberal conference." In the spring of 1968 the members of the new caucus, now called the Concerned Democrats, began a concerted effort to capture control of the district. No fewer than 170 candidates were recruited to file for precinct delegate. Labor, in an attempt to prevent the takeover, ran 120 delegate candidates. Labor elected 58.3 percent of its candidates while the Concerned Democrats elected 64.7 percent of theirs. This rather small differential provided the Concerned Democrats, who had run 50 more candidates, with 110 delegates to labor's 70. The Concerned Democrats were now the single most powerful group in the Seventeenth District.[16]

Though they were short of a majority, it seemed likely that the Concerned Democrats would obtain a sufficient number of the votes scattered among the district's other three factions to replace Gladstone with a chairman of their own selection. Likelihood, however, was not certainty. Two of the three factions were obviously unsympathetic. The few votes controlled by the Democratic Forum were not about to be cast to elect a chairman further to the left than the one they already had. Gladstone's group, by definition, was committed to him. Only the Cavanagh group, which controlled about 15 percent of the elected delegates, remained a possible source of the needed number of votes. The Cavanagh group was willing and an agreement was reached. As the year ended the Concerned Democrats looked forward to the January district meeting with absolute confidence. They had formed a coalition and that coalition possessed more than enough strength to defeat Bill Gladstone.

When the Seventeenth District Democratic organization convened for the purpose of electing party officers, 227 delegates were in attendance. They voted 114 to 113 to reelect Bill Gladstone. The securely tied alliance between the Concerned Democrats and the Cavanagh group had come apart. Instead of voting for Jim Jackson, candidate of the Concerned Democrats, the Cavanagh faction went with Gladstone, almost to a man. There had been no falling out between any of the members of the Cavanagh and Concerned Democrats factions; there had not even been any maneuvering within the district. The decisive step had been taken at another level altogether. It was the result, as one of those involved put it, of "an approach made at higher than precinct level."[17] What had occurred was the employment of pressure and persuasion directly on the mayor's office by organized labor. It is not known what form that pressure and persuasion took, but Cavanagh's people in the district were instructed to switch their support to Gladstone. Cavanagh was mayor, and if he did not seek reelection in 1969 it was almost certain he would seek statewide office in 1970 or soon after; he had little interest in antagonizing labor over a district chairmanship. Labor, with both a citywide and a statewide political apparatus, was able to circumscribe and curtail the power of a group that had no effective organizational base beyond the district itself.

With a majority coalition labor could have systematically excluded the Concerned Democrats from any participation on the district executive board. There was little doubt that had the Concerned Democrats won they would have removed most if not all of those who had previously occupied positions of authority within the district organization. There could not have been any legitimate complaint if labor had proceeded to do to them what they had been more than willing to do to labor. But instead of driving the Concerned Democrats out, labor did everything short of giving them majority power to keep them in. It agreed to a system of proportional representation under which the executive board would be apportioned in strict relation to the delegate strength of each faction. Far from being excluded, the Concerned Democrats found themselves in control of 49 percent of the seats on the executive board. From a policy of prohibiting the formal recognition of groups, a policy initiated and jealously protected by Al Meyer, the Seventeenth District had now effected the institutionalization of factionalism.[18]

Labor had gone to some lengths to prevent the Concerned Democrats from seizing control of the Seventeenth District. It had exercised influence on city hall to secure enough allies to form a majority coalition. It had succeeded, but the margin might have been greater and the work less troublesome had it simply run more candidates. If labor had elected a majority of precinct delegates on its own, there would have been no need to negotiate with the mayor's office or to enter into a coalition with any other group. To have done this, however, would have violated the main intention labor had in the district. It was largely through the efforts of the UAW that factions had been given formal recognition in the district in the first place. It had done that in order to identify clearly the contending power blocs, so that negotiation would become the accepted method of resolving disputes between them. It was only through accommodation of what were sometimes divergent interests that, in the union's judgment, a stronger, more effective political organization could be built in the Seventeenth District. One UAW operative claimed that "in the Seventeenth we have never shot for a labor majority. What we have wanted, and we have usually been able to get it, is a strong minority."[19] With a majority labor could have its own way, but, it was feared, it would have its own way only with labor. Participation of those not associated with the labor movement would dwindle and perhaps even disappear. A strong minority would prevent things from getting completely out of hand while allowing and, because labor never took party offices in anything like the proportion to which its delegate strength entitled them, encouraging the active participation of others.

By entering into a coalition, or more precisely by preventing the Concerned Democrats from making an alliance with the Cavanagh group, labor had protected its own position in the district organization. By agreeing to proportional representation, it deprived the Concerned Democrats of any justification for refusing to continue as active members of the Democratic party. And the Concerned Democrats did not desert the party. Though their numbers diminished as the passions of 1968 began to subside, they were still able to continue as one of the two largest factions in the district. This had the effect of making the district stronger than it would have been otherwise. The Seventeenth District would have echoed the UAW's endorsement of Richard Austin if the union had simply driven the Concerned Democrats out and taken over. But because that did not happen, and because the Concerned Democrats were at least as eager to endorse Austin as the UAW was, the district endorsement was something more than a formal ratification of a labor decision. The endorsement now carried with it more resources and more manpower, and perhaps most importantly, it was a symbol of a broader range of community support. To the people in the district who were not political activists but for whom the endorsement of a political party was influential, the inclusion of the Concerned Democrats—not because they were the Concerned Democrats, but because they were not members of organized labor—gave the endorsement more credence than it would have had otherwise. At the very least, it deprived those opposed to Austin's candidacy from using the endorsement to claim that labor intended to take over the city of Detroit, an accusation that could still have a pronounced effect on a considerable segment of the citizenry.

Austin had been able to obtain the endorsement of the Democratic organizations of three congressional districts without any real difficulty. The First and the Thirteenth, both predominantly black, had given their backing to the city's first black mayoral candidate. The Seventeenth district, with the UAW and the ultraliberal Concerned Democrats in agreement, had gone for Austin. Taking the three districts together, blacks, the UAW, and liberals of the "new politics" persuasion were the major political components. In the Fourteenth Congressional District, the fourth of the four districts that were entirely or largely within the city boundaries, there were few blacks and even fewer adherents of the "new politics." There were instead large numbers of Irish Catholics and one of the largest Polish populations in any congressional district in the country.

In 1961, in what was then the First Congressional District, Congressman Thaddeus Machrowicz died. The district chairman, Lucien Nedzi, entered the special election called to fill the vacancy. He faced formidable opposition. T. John Lesinski had decided that the life of a congressman was preferable to that of the state's lieutenant governor. Nedzi contributed his own life savings of 6,000 dollars and waged a vigorous door-to-door campaign, but it was generally expected that the lieutenant governor, who by virtue of his office was much better known than any of the other candidates, had a very great advantage. Lesinski's apparent advantage, however, proved to be a real disadvantage. To many of the district's Polish constituents the issue was simple. One Polish voter expressed what seems to have been the prevailing sentiment when he informed one of Nedzi's workers: "There is no good reason to vote for Lesinski. He is the lieutenant governor. If I vote for Nedzi, he goes to Washington and we have a Polish congressman and a Polish lieutenant governor. Why should I vote for one when I can have two?"[20] In addition to this eminently sound ethnic logic, Nedzi had another pronounced advantage. At the time the district was 60 percent white and 40 percent black. With the help of John Luster, a black UAW political activist who was very influential among the black working class, Nedzi ran ahead of Lesinski in the black community. The black vote, and the desire of Polish voters to have both a congressman and the lieutenant governor, gave Nedzi a seat in Congress.

In the 1961 special election the Teamsters backed Lesinski and the Wayne County AFL-CIO adopted a formal position of neutrality. By enabling John Luster and other black unionists to work for the candidate of their choice, neutrality had been more of a benefit to Nedzi than to Lesinski. Something very similar happened in 1964 when the same reapportionment that gave Detroit two black congressional districts provided Nedzi with a district that was 90 percent white and included another incumbent congressman, Harold M. Ryan. In the primary election in the new Fourteenth District, the UAW refrained from endorsing either of the two incumbents. Nevertheless, the union leadership was decidedly in favor of Nedzi. The UAW coordinator in the district was then Ted Pankowski, and as a member of the district committee put it, "You could tell by his name who he was for." Pankowski, one of the union's most able political operatives, was a great asset. According to Paul Donahue, who became Nedzi's district representative, "Pankowski had such great personal relationships built up in the district that he used to be able to get people to march for civil rights who really didn't believe in civil rights at all."[21] Perhaps even more important than Pankowski's assistance, however, was the support of Emil Mazey.

Mazey's support was derived, at least in part, from a division within the district between labor and liberals on the one hand, and predominantly Irish Catholics on the other, a split which in turn had its origins within the labor movement itself. In the early days of the UAW the battles within the union were generally perceived to be between the communist and the Reuther factions. There was a third force, however—the Catholic trade unionists.[22] In the eyes of the church, communism and socialism (and in its judgment Reuther was certainly a believer in one or the other) were equal doctrines of sin. In Detroit, Cardinal Mooney attempted to develop a body of Catholic workers who would put the labor movement on the proper course. Church funds, for example, were used to underwrite the costs of training sessions in parliamentary procedure for Catholic workers. The Catholic group never came close to presenting a serious threat within the union, but the struggle between Catholics and the UAW leadership carried over into the internal affairs of the Democratic party. This was nowhere more evident than in the Fourteenth District.

The Catholic opposition to Nedzi faced serious difficulties. A majority of the district's precinct delegates were controlled by the UAW and its allies. In addition to the precinct delegates, the liberal-labor caucus, as it was called, had all the party offices. Liberals held them, and the UAW, in the person of Emil Mazey, "called the shots." Catholic difficulties were compounded by the political leanings of the candidate they supported. Harold Ryan's vote against the 1964 Civil Rights Act, along with his publicly expressed opposition to the American Civil Liberties Union, intensified Mazey's determination to remove him from Congress. In addition to everything else, Ryan was seen by the UAW leadership as an "anti-semite who saw everyone in Solidarity House as Jewish or atheistic Communists." This point of view had not been such a great political liability when his district had been completely white and mainly conservative, but it now brought down on Ryan's head everything the UAW leadership could unload. Finally, the Catholic opposition to Nedzi and the union leadership could not carry with it all Catholics. Irish Catholics might go along with Ryan, but Polish Catholics were not about to forsake one of their own. Nedzi won going away.

Two years later, Nedzi had the formal endorsement of the UAW. He also had Harold Ryan as an opponent in the primary. Ryan waged a bitter campaign comprised almost exclusively of charges that Nedzi was the tool of the UAW and of Emil Mazey in particular. The accusations did no discernible damage. Nedzi defeated Ryan by over 10,000 votes, 29,197 to 18,886.[23] By 1968, neither Ryan nor any other Democrat thought it prudent to run against the incumbent congressman. Nedzi's ability to secure reelection was accompanied by a continuation of UAW influence in the district. Throughout the sixties the liberal-labor caucus controlled 70 percent of the elected precinct delegates. Of these approximately two-thirds were labor and one-third liberal. Irish Catholics continued to oppose labor in the belief that the union was altogether too far to the left, but labor's hold on the district was unshaken and seemingly unshakable. Even the election of Jerry Dessert, one of Mayor Cavanagh's lieutenants, to the district chairmanship in 1967 appeared to be only a brief exception to the general rule. In the Fourteenth District, the UAW's endorsement of a candidate seemed a certain precursor of what the Democratic party would do.

In the early summer of 1969 Jerry Dessert, an Irish Catholic, resigned the district chairmanship to work in the mayoral campaign of Roman Gribbs, a Polish Catholic. Unlike the congressional campaigns between Nedzi and Ryan, the mayoral contest between Gribbs and Austin furnished no basis for a split among Catholics. Catholics were for Gribbs; the union was for Austin. Dessert's successor in the chairmanship, Helen Irving, was a UAW employee, but a majority on the executive board supported the Wayne County sheriff. With the executive board for Gribbs and the UAW for Austin, the key to the district endorsement was the meeting of the district membership. Both sides set out to pack it with their followers.

When the meeting opened at the Detroit Street Railways (DSR) Hall, Helen Irving was in the chair but the presence of Jerry Dessert was felt. Under Cavanagh the former district chairman had been secretary to the city fire board. As the meeting got underway in the relatively cramped quarters of the DSR Hall, two fire marshals arrived. They announced that the hall was too crowded and in the interests of safety would have to be cleared. One of Austin's supporters, John Kanachuk, suspecting that the two were not really fire marshals, asked to see their credentials. This request, reasonable in itself, was refused. When it was refused, the police were called. The police arrived and the self-proclaimed fire marshals fled. They did not go far. Police pursuit ended in a nearby alley where, according to the police—who some believed were very much in favor of Gribbs—the proper identification was shown. The hall was cleared, and because no meeting was held no endorsement was made.

The Fourteenth was the only district in which Gribbs even came close to getting the party endorsement, and it was the only one that failed to endorse Austin. It was a failure that had significance far beyond whatever importance the district endorsement might have had by itself. Even though Austin might very well have received the district endorsement had not considerable chicanery been employed, support for Gribbs among a majority of the membership of the district executive board demonstrated that the Catholic voters, whether because Gribbs was Catholic or because he was white, were not about to follow the lead of the UAW or anybody else and give Richard Austin their support. Once the primary vote had been cast it seemed reasonably clear that it was not Gribbs's religion that was the major motivation for the support he received. Austin finished first in the balloting with 37.7 percent of the vote. Gribbs finished second, with 32.9 percent, and thus won a place in the general election. Mary Beck, who like Gribbs was Polish, came in third, with 21 percent of the ballots cast. This was disturbing. Austin had finished on top, but 54 percent of the vote had been cast for two white Polish candidates, one of whom had pounded away on law and order, while the other, because he was the county sheriff, scarcely needed to emphasize that issue. Moreover, Austin had been able to attract only 7.6 percent of the vote in predominantly white areas.[24] In predominantly black areas his vote was "nearly unanimous."[25] In the only city in the country that had two black congressmen, that had the highest incidence of union membership, and that had given Hubert Humphrey and the rest of the Democratic slate 70 percent of its vote in 1968, blacks, the Democratic party, and the UAW were almost unanimous in their support for Richard Austin. White voters seemed almost as united in their opposition.

Two years before Austin set out to become the first black mayor of Detroit, Carl Stokes had become the first black mayor of Cleveland. In 1967, Stokes had won the Democratic primary against a white opponent in the face of a white majority, because 73.4 percent of the registered black voters turned out while only 58.4 percent of the white voters bothered to go to the polls. Even this differential would not have been sufficient by itself to overcome the three-to-two white majority. Stokes was able to win only because he received 15.4 percent of the white vote.[26] If Stokes had needed white votes to be elected, Austin was going to need them at least as much and perhaps more. Indeed, "Austin's campaign supporters realized that to win Mr. Austin had to mop up the bulk of the black vote plus capture between 20 and 22 percent of the white vote."[27]

The need to obtain a fifth of the white votes while at the same time doing everything possible to bring out the greatest possible number of black voters required the most delicate maneuvering. Austin would attract black voters to the polls to the extent that his black candidacy was emphasized; he would attract white voters to the extent that it was not. Shortly after the primary both Austin and Gribbs "promised to keep racism out of the campaign and direct their appeals to all of Detroit, black and white. . . ."[28] This was the first of many statements made during the campaign by both Austin and Gribbs that had the effect of keeping the question of race at the forefront by declaring it irrelevant.

On election day it appeared that the Austin strategy was going to work. Gribbs, with all his talk about law and order, had gotten the endorsement of the *Detroit News,* but Austin had been endorsed by the *Detroit Free Press.* Gribbs had the support of the Building Trades Council, but Austin had the backing of the UAW. Walter Reuther had written a letter urging the election of Austin to over 100,000 union members living in the city. Sixty prominent liberals, including former governor G. Mennen Williams, had run a full-page ad entitled "Can you vote for a Black Mayor?" that gave every reason not only why you could but why you should. The turnout that day was unusually high for a city election; in many districts over 70 percent of the registered voters cast their ballots.[29] In black precincts Austin received 94 percent of the vote; in white and mixed precincts he obtained 21 percent. The percentage indicated an Austin victory but the numbers did not. By a margin of 7,000 votes out of slightly more than half a million cast, 257,312 to 250,020, Roman Gribbs defeated Richard Austin. The eventual and inevitable election of a black mayor had been postponed.

There would never be absolute certainty about the cause of Austin's defeat. It was clearly important that "turnout rose substantially in Slavic areas for the runoff, and Gribbs won five out of six votes cast there."[30] It may also have been the case that, as a member of the Fourteenth District Democratic committee believed, "Austin simply did not spend enough time campaigning in white areas out here on the east side." In the judgment of many of the most experienced observers, however, the most important thing of all was something no strategy could affect. It rained. Worse yet, it rained in the late afternoon. This "sharply reduced voter turnout in most downtown Negro districts."[31]

Notes

1. *Detroit News,* May 24, 1967.
2. *Detroit News,* May 19, 1967.
3. *Detroit Free Press,* May 6, 1969.
4. B. J. Widick, *Detroit: City of Race and Class Violence* (Chicago: Quadrangle Books, 1972), p. 206.
5. *Detroit News,* April 18, 1969.
6. Ibid.

7. *Detroit Free Press,* June 25, 1969.

8. Widick, *Detroit,* p. 222.

9. In the internal workings of the union, Walter Reuther did not always give complete license to the workings of democratic procedure. Perhaps the most interesting example is supplied by the fortunes of Paul Schrade, who was for some years director of the UAW's western region. Schrade was defeated in his bid for election to another term in 1970. At least one regional director thought this the height of incompetence. "Anyone who becomes a regional director and can't hang on to it is an idiot," he declared. "A regional director who has any sense at all won't let any challenge get off the ground. You appoint to staff positions people who will work for you. They know their careers depend on you and they spend as much time as necessary to make certain that no one gets into position to take you on." Schrade paid too little attention to union affairs and too much to other things. Reuther, however, had not been unwilling to involve himself in the election of regional directors; while he lived he made certain that Schrade was reelected. After Reuther's death, Leonard Woodcock took over, and the new president refused to intervene on Schrade's behalf. Woodcock simply felt that if you could not get elected on your own, you should not be elected. Schrade, it has been suggested, "got all caught up in the Kennedy thing. His mistake was that he did not understand that the Kennedys were not interested in Paul Schrade, they were interested in a regional director. While Schrade was spending all his time working for them he got out of touch with his own region and some other guys got together and beat him. Now I hear that Schrade has asked the Kennedys to get him some kind of job and they won't." (Quoted from interview with George Merelli, July 11, 1973.)

10. *Detroit Free Press,* August 15, 1969.

11. Ibid.

12. Ibid.

13. Widick, *Detroit,* p. 207.

14. Meyer was fanatical in his devotion to the principle that party affairs were to be conducted on the basis of individual participation. This meant that no one was to have any influence beyond his own vote and his individual power to persuade. All were to be equal. The chairman never departed from that principle in practice, and that had at least one unfortunate result. After her first election to Congress, Martha Griffiths apparently did not think it necessary to go through the formality of requesting the district endorsement when she sought reelection. Meyer, however, saw no reason to permit anyone to avoid established procedures because of their position. The district did not endorse Griffiths, a fact that had almost no effect on the outcome of the election, but relations between the member of Congress and her own district committee never fully recovered.

15. Michael Kirwin, interview with author, October 16, 1971.

16. Ibid.; Philip Gorak, interview with author, October 21, 1971.

17. Michael Kirwin, interview with author, October 16, 1971.

18. Within only two years proportional representation had reached the extremity of mathematic precision and perhaps also the height of political impracticality. Labor, with 42 percent of the precinct delegates elected in the 1970 primary, was entitled to 37.8 seats on the 90-member executive board. Reality was accommodated by per-

mitting 38 seats to be filled. These 38, however, could among them cast exactly 37.8 votes.

19. Michael Kirwin, interview with author, October 16, 1971.

20. Paul Donahue, interview with author, April 14, 1973.

21. Ibid.

22. The Catholic influence in American trade unionism goes back at least to the early AFL, where there is some evidence that Catholics were instrumental in preventing a takeover by the socialist faction. See Marc Karson, *American Labor Unions and Politics, 1900–1918* (Carbondale: Southern Illinois University Press, 1958) (especially chapter 9, "The Roman Catholic Church and American Labor Unions"). See also James Weinstein, *The Decline of Socialism in America, 1912–1925* (New York: Vintage Books, 1969).

23. State of Michigan, *Official Canvass of Votes 1966,* p. 13.

24. *Lansing State Journal,* September 11, 1969.

25. Mark R. Levy and Michael S. Kramer, *The Ethnic Factor: How America's Minorities Decide Elections* (New York: Simon and Schuster, 1972), p. 149.

26. Jeffrey K. Hadden, Louis H. Masotti, and Victor Thiessen, "The Making of Negro Mayors in 1967," *Trans-action,* January/February, 1968, pp. 21–30.

27. *Christian Science Monitor,* November 6, 1969.

28. *Lansing State Journal,* September 11, 1969.

29. Widick, *Detroit,* p. 207.

30. Levy and Kramer, *The Ethnic Factor,* p. 149.

31. *Christian Science Monitor,* November 6, 1969.

CHAPTER 8
White Suburbs:
The Politics of Reaction

The 1969 mayoral election in Detroit was decided on the basis of race. The election demonstrated that where the candidates were not perceived to differ on issues that had a direct economic impact on the electorate, the division between black and white was still too great to be bridged by the old coalition of liberals, blacks, and labor. Since its formation in 1948, the coalition had been held together by a common desire to bring about some redistribution of wealth. So long as the objectives had been clearly economic, members of the white working class were an indispensable and reliable component of the coalition, no matter what their feelings might be on the question of race relations. But when, as in 1969, the issue was seen as one of race alone, no allegiance, whether to the Democratic party or to the union, was strong enough to overcome racial antipathy. Still, it could be argued that this analysis is too severe. The mayoral election was not a partisan contest, and both candidates considered themselves Democrats; party allegiance therefore was not really an issue. It was hoped that in contests for Congress and the state legislature—contests that were partisan and necessarily involved basic economic issues—the old coalition would continue as it had before. This hope was short lived. Within a year a new issue had arisen that would prove more divisive and durable for the coalition than a single contest between a black and a white candidate for the same office. The issue would divide not only Detroit but all of Wayne County. Nor would it stop there; the entire state would be affected by it. Though at bottom an issue of race, it caused as much division among whites as between the races. Communities that had no black candidates for elective office, and in some cases no black voters among the electorate, would be as divided by it as any biracial town or village. One of the ugliest issues in recent American political history, it was symbolized by one of the most innocent objects in American life, the school bus. Setting party against party, race against race, neighbor against neighbor, busing would arouse the citizenry in ways the best-intentioned public servants feared

and every public official understood. Busing left no room for even the semblance of compromise; in the Detroit suburbs in Wayne, Macomb, and Oakland counties especially, no compromise seemed possible.

In the western end of Wayne County more than 96 percent of the population was white and the two congressional districts, the Fifteenth and the
Sixteenth were heavily Democratic. In 1968 Congressman William Ford had
been reelected by a margin of two-and-one-half-to-one from the Fifteenth; in
the Sixteenth, John Dingell had been reelected by a margin of almost three-
to-one. While the ultraliberal New Democratic Coalition (NDC) was causing
serious difficulties in other areas of the state, its influence in western Wayne
County was almost insignificant. In the Sixteenth District, for example, the
NDC was never able to obtain more than thirteen of the ninety seats on the
Democratic committee executive board.[1] The two congressional districts together included nearly three dozen communities, almost every one of which
was a working-class suburb. With the exception of Ecorse in the Sixteenth
and Inkster in the Fifteenth the communities' populations were almost uniformly white. After most of the state legislators from the two districts voted
against open housing legislation in 1968, the UAW withheld its endorsement
in the next election, but the voters, in almost every case, reelected them by
margins as large as or larger than before.

When the busing controversy began, there was little doubt what position
the overwhelming majority of the citizenry would adopt. Both Dingell and
Ford quickly made public statements condemning busing as a means of
achieving racial integration. The chairman of the Fifteenth District Democratic committee, John Canfield, estimated that if it were possible to recall
a U.S. Senator, Philip Hart, who followed his conscience instead of his
constituency on the issue, would have been recalled in that district by a
margin of at least nine-to-one.[2] In Taylor, 4,000 turned out in October, 1971,
for an open-air rally sponsored by an organization calling itself Citizens
Against Busing. At one meeting in Dearborn Heights, 460 turned out; at
another, 728 showed up. Canfield suggested the significance of these numbers
when he said, "You can't get that many to show up for nothin' in Dearborn
Heights."[3] Feeling was so intense that even opposition to busing was not
enough to turn away criticism. In 1972, Ford, for the first time since he was
elected to Congress in 1964, found himself with serious primary opposition.
He was somehow to be held responsible for the fact that the issue had ever
come up.

In the Fifteenth and Sixteenth Districts both Dingell and Ford received
the endorsement of the UAW and used it as an important part of their successful reelection campaigns. In the Fourteenth District, however, where Lucien Nedzi was seeking reelection to his sixth full term in the Congress, it
was decided that the UAW endorsement would lose more blue-collar votes

than it would gain. Unlike the Fifteenth and Sixteenth Districts, the Fourteenth, as we have seen, had had most of its constituency in Detroit. Most of what was not in Detroit was in Hamtramck. In 1972, however, the Fourteenth District was not what it had been two years earlier. Under the congressional reapportionment plan adopted by the state legislature, Nedzi's district had apparently been strengthened by the inclusion of the most heavily Polish segment of Macomb County. When the plan was drawn no one anticipated the almost savage reaction of white blue-collar workers to the busing controversy. Nowhere was this reaction more pronounced than in Macomb County where, in a referendum, busing to achieve racial balance was rejected by a margin of fourteen-to-one.[4] Nedzi, a strong advocate of civil rights, was not blind to the political implications of the busing issue. He quickly and publicly expressed opposition to it, and, together with several other Democratic congressmen from the Detroit area, including Dingell and Ford, introduced legislation designed to foreclose the possibility. In the minds of many white voters, however, no opposition to busing, no matter how vehement, was sufficient to efface the fact that Nedzi was a liberal Democrat, and liberal Democrats were the ones who had decided the federal government should compel white children to attend black schools.

Many white blue-collar workers had come to see in the Democratic party the political vehicle for preferential treatment for blacks; many had also come to see the leadership of the UAW in the same light. This attitude was not simply derived from the union's traditional support for civil rights; it was, rather, a product of what white workers were beginning to witness in the internal affairs of the union. Sixty-five percent of the UAW membership in Detroit was black. At the same time, the top leadership of the union was predominantly white, not only within Solidarity House, but in the regional offices as well. With the exception of Marcellius Ivory, the only black director, the regional directors attempted to retain their hold on office by propitiating possible black challengers. In the eyes of many white workers, as a Nedzi assistant explained, the white leadership "has gone overboard trying to go with the blacks." This perception had led to the assumption that, "if you have the UAW endorsement you are pro-black."[5]

The UAW was not slow to recognize that Nedzi had become politically vulnerable and that his prospects would only be diminished by flourishing the banner of a UAW endorsement. As a matter of course, it did endorse him, but that became one of the best-kept secrets of the 1972 campaign. Although it was made almost covertly in order to prevent an unnecessary loss of votes, the endorsement brought Nedzi his greatest single source of the sinews of any political campaign, money and manpower. For the primary election, the UAW provided Nedzi with $4,000 in direct financial assistance, 200,000 copies of a "kicker" card (with the candidate's name and office printed on it), and poll watchers, at a cost of $25 a day, to cover ninety polling places on election day. In addition, six UAW members were taken from the plants to help the union's effort in the district, and two UAW retirees were assigned to the campaign.

The CAP campaign in the district was carried on in accordance with the silent endorsement strategy. Nedzi's name was not even listed on the "UAW CAP Voter's Guide" card handed out in the district. Instead, the UAW at first passed out cards that stated simply "Re-elect Congressman Lucien N. Nedzi." The UAW was not mentioned on the card; the sponsoring organization listed was the "Fourteenth District Official Democratic Organization." Nedzi himself had the CAP organization replace this with another card that had as its lead line "Congressman Nedzi is Trusted." Three endorsements were then listed, from the non-partisan Civic Searchlight, the *Detroit News,* and the *Detroit Free Press.* The UAW's endorsement was discreetly omitted. Below the endorsements, enclosed in a box and in bold letters, were the words "No Busing." At the very bottom of the card was the name of the sponsoring group, "Citizens for Nedzi Committee." Not only the mention of the UAW but allusion to the Democratic party had come to be considered politically dangerous. If these precautions seemed excessive, the result made them appear reasonable. The incumbent congressman, who had not even had a primary opponent in the previous two elections, managed to survive the 1972 primary election by less than two percentage points.[6]

The Fourteenth District had undergone a significant alteration since Lucien Nedzi was first elected to Congress; the black population had decreased from nearly 40 to less than 10 percent. In order to create two black congressional districts, boundaries had been redrawn in 1964 in such a way that over 90 percent of Detroit's black population was included within the First and the Thirteenth districts. In the Fourteenth District, blacks, who had been a substantial minority, disappeared as a group with significant political power. The creation of a second black congressional seat destroyed black influence in the Fourteenth, and cleared the way for political appeal on racial grounds. Instead of a situation in which the presence of both blacks and whites in substantial numbers made moderation possible and perhaps even necessary for political success, the congressional constituencies came to be made up overwhelmingly of one race or the other.

In Detroit and (although to a lesser degree) in Wayne County as a whole, the division of political power on the basis of race was a decision consciously arrived at. In the suburbs of Macomb County no decision was made by anyone about anything; Macomb County simply happened. In 1950 the population of Macomb County was 184,961. Warren, with 727 residents, was little more than a village. But several forces were at work that would combine to bring about an almost phenomenal population increase. First was the expansion of the state highway system. During the Williams administration highway construction had been given a high priority and federal money was supplied in lavish amounts. By 1960 Michigan had one of the nation's best highway systems. This developing transportation system had the effect of extending the area within which automobile production could be carried on. Transportation made this possible, but another consideration seemed to require it. Most of the automobile plants in the Detroit area were the original facilities that had been created when the industry first entered the era of mass production. Many of these were in a state of disrepair and could not, without exorbitant expense, be converted to the largely automated plants that were being developed in other industries and in the auto industry itself in other countries. The cost of converting existing facilities and of acquiring land within the city for expansion provided a powerful incentive for the automobile companies to look to outlying areas where transportation was good, land cheap, and the tax rate low. Macomb County, which at its closest point was less than ten miles from the heart of Detroit, offered everything. The highways, the suburban housing development, and the automobile itself made it possible for the auto companies to locate industrial plants and let labor follow the job, instead of building industrial facilities where labor was available. In 1955, three old factories in Detroit were phased out and two of the replacements were opened in Utica and Warren, then two of the smaller towns in Macomb County.

Between 1950 and 1960, more than half a million people left Detroit and moved to the suburbs; a substantial number found their way to Macomb County. In the course of that single decade, the county population went from 184,000 to 405,000, an increase of 125 percent. Warren, which had been populated by 727 residents in 1950, grew to nearly 100,000 men, women, and children as "new Chrysler, Ford, General Motors and feeder plants were built there."[7] The increasing population, combined with the fact that much of the increase was due to the heavy influx of automobile workers from Detroit, carried unmistakable political implications. By the middle fifties "everyone knew it was only a matter of time before we would be able to elect a Democratic congressman."[8]

As part of a multicounty congressional district, Macomb County had been represented in Congress by a Republican for so long that Blackstone's phrase "the memory of man runneth not to the contrary" seemed to describe the fortunes of the Republican and the failures of the Democratic party. The first sign that Republican control might be weakening occurred in 1954 when the incumbent congressman, Jesse P. Wolcott, defeated the Democratic challenger Ira McCoy, "an old war horse who had run against Wolcott for years,"[9] by the comparatively small margin of 8,000 votes.[10] When Wolcott announced he would not be a candidate in 1956, McCoy's prospects brightened, but only temporarily. Once again a Republican, Robert J. McIntosh, was sent to Congress. After more defeats than he cared to remember, McCoy decided enough was enough; he would not be a candidate for Congress in 1958. Had McCoy not decided to stand aside, he would probably have found himself in a contested primary. A growing number of politicans had come to the conclusion that the district had changed sufficiently to make it possible for a new Democratic candidate to be elected. However, there was nothing even close to unanimity about who that candidate might be.

The logical choice for the Democratic nomination appeared to be State Senator George Steeh. After one term in the house, Steeh had won election to the senate, where he represented all of Macomb County. Steeh's ambitions were not exhausted by service in the state legislature. When he announced that he was likely to become a candidate for Congress, however, his Lansing roommate, State Representative John Bowman, was upset. Bowman, one of the two members of the house from Macomb County, argued that when both of them were serving together in the house, and the senate seat had become available, he had stepped aside for Steeh; it was time for Steeh to repay the favor. Whether from a feeling of obligation or fear of a contested primary, Steeh did what Bowman asked. Bowman, who was a good campaigner, proceeded to line up considerable support among active Democrats. Then Bowman had another conversation with his roommate. Bert Wagner, the Macomb County clerk, had predicted that between eighty and ninety thousand votes would be cast in the county in the 1958 elections. Bowman asked Steeh whether he thought this would be enough to offset the vote in the rest of the district. Steeh expressed the opinion that a Democrat could win only if one hundred thousand votes were cast in Macomb. At this point Bowman had a sudden change of heart. He now suggested that Steeh run for Congress, and he would run for Steeh's seat in the state senate. Steeh declined. Bowman could not get an opening into the state senate, but he could keep a safe seat in the state house, and more than anything else he did not want to find himself out of office. The candidacy of John Bowman for the U.S. Congress came to an end, at least for that year.[11]

When Bowman withdrew he asked those who supported him to endorse Joe Mihelich, a young lawyer from East Detroit. Mihelich got the endorsement of the UAW and the assistance of Howard Knute, president of the Macomb County AFL-CIO; he also obtained the support of the elected Democratic county officials. From the union halls to the courthouse Mihelich was being called the next member of Congress from Macomb County. His major opponent in the Democratic primary was also a young attorney. Unlike Mihelich, however, James O'Hara had no political connections and no real acquaintance with the leadership of organized labor. In fact, O'Hara had lived in the district for two years without knowing it until he was approached by a small group of party activists who wanted to know if he had any interest in running for Congress. Among the members of that group, and in many respects the leader of it, was John Bruff, who like O'Hara had been in the district for only two years, but knew it. Bruff also knew something else: the name O'Hara was a very great political advantage. A year earlier, a Republican candidate for the state supreme court, D. Michael O'Hara, had run exceptionally well. Mihelich, who had run once for a minor office and lost, was not well known in the district. With an opponent whose name was not widely recognized, and in a district where many of the voters had only recently arrived, some believed that O'Hara might be able to win just because he was named O'Hara.[12]

O'Hara ran and lost to Mihelich in the Democratic primary by twenty votes. But the election result was disputed and a recount demanded. The recount lasted for a full month. It began with the precincts adjacent to Eight Mile Road, the boundary of Detroit, and went all the way to Huron County in the Thumb. (The Lower Peninsula of Michigan is shaped somewhat like a right hand held palm up.) Every day, as the lead went back and forth between them, O'Hara and Mihelich were interviewed on the radio. That publicized the Democratic primary recount, and more importantly, made the names of both candidates better known to the electorate that would vote in the general election. When it was all over, James G. O'Hara, by the really impressive margin of exactly five votes, 11,097 to 11,092, had won the Democratic nomination for Congress.[13]

After the primary, labor, which had done everything it could for Mihelich, proceeded to do everything it could for O'Hara. The UAW sent in Russ Leach to assist the O'Hara campaign full-time. Mildred Jeffries, also of the UAW, was largely responsible for bringing in Hubert Humphrey to campaign for O'Hara. Almost everything on registration and the get-out-the-vote drive was done by labor. Its contributions in money and manpower were, in the assessment of O'Hara's campaign manager, John Bruff, "tremendous." More than anything else, and perhaps more than everything else combined, organized labor was responsible for sending Jim O'Hara to Congress in 1958.[14]

Labor had quickly and easily forgotten the defeat it had sustained in the Democratic primary and had concentrated its energies on electing a Democratic congressman. Electing O'Hara, however, was not the same thing as entering into a perpetual political alliance with him. An early indication that the district was not going to become automatically responsive to the wishes of its new congressman occurred shortly after the election, when the new county Democratic committee was selected. In 1958, the members of the county committee were appointed by a committee made up of the elected Democratic county officials and the Democratic state legislators. This group of eight decided not to appoint O'Hara's campaign manager, John Bruff, to the new county committee. Labor did not attempt to intervene, and did nothing to object. The only group among elected Democratic officials or the labor movement that showed any sign of irritation was the Building Trades Union, which had endorsed O'Hara in the primary.

Although O'Hara and Bruff were not on the best of terms with the Democratic county organization, and were unable to obtain much support from the labor leadership on matters pertaining to the internal politics of the Democratic party, no real opposition emerged to challenge O'Hara in the 1960 primary election. Nor was there any substantial threat in 1962. O'Hara was reelected by increasing margins, while control of the county committee remained in the hands of those who were, if not open enemies, scarcely friends. In 1964 O'Hara decided that it was time for a change, and set about to organize a takeover of the Macomb County Democratic party.

O'Hara's decision to try to take over the county organization was based on two considerations. First, by 1964 the population of Macomb County had grown to 411,000. Through reapportionment the congressional district had become almost coincident with the county boundaries; only four precincts from Detroit were included from outside. This alone would have made the county political situation a matter of immediate and important interest to the congressman; the intrusion of John Bowman into congressional politics added a sense of urgency. Bowman was now in the state senate from a district that encompassed more than half the county, and he had managed to acquire a reputation that extended far beyond the confines of his own district. In 1962 there had been serious discussion at the state level about whether Detroit's taxing power should be permitted to reach the increasing number of people who worked in Detroit but lived in the suburbs. Bowman, who cared little for Detroit but a great deal for his own career, introduced a measure to prohibit this form of taxation. What quickly became known as the Bowman Bill passed the legislature but was vetoed by Governor Swainson. In the judgment of many political observers, that cost Swainson his chance for reelection, but introducing the measure made John Bowman the darling of the suburbs. Although some local politicians believed he could defeat O'Hara, Bowman, whose senate seat was up in 1964, decided, as he had decided in 1958, that the guarantee of a place in the state legislature was more attractive than the doubtful prospects of a run at higher office. O'Hara was not challenged in the Democratic primary, but the fact that a challenge had been contemplated was a warning for the future that had to be heeded without delay.

The second consideration in O'Hara's decision to try to control the county organization was simply that for the first time it was possible to do so. In 1958, as noted earlier, the county committee was appointed by the elected

Democratic county officials and state legislators. This system had continued until 1964, when by an act of the legislature the elected precinct delegates were authorized to select half the members of the county committee. With passage of the law, O'Hara and his allies set out to acquire as many precinct delegates as they could. The crucial question was what organized labor would do. Although the UAW had gone with Joe Mihelich in the 1958 primary, O'Hara had received the union endorsement in every succeeding election. As a member of the House Education and Labor Committee, O'Hara had established himself as one of the most knowledgeable and effective proponents of labor legislation. Labor could scarcely oppose O'Hara in a contest for control of the county organization on the basis of any disagreement over public policy. It was not public policy, however, but personal power that was at issue.

George Merelli, the UAW regional director with responsibility for Macomb County, was not enthusiastic about what O'Hara proposed to do. Several days before the county convention was scheduled to meet, Merelli met with the county officials and the O'Hara forces. He let it be known that he was not about to participate in any takeover of the county organization.[15] Neither did he offer to use his good offices to bring about some compromise arrangement that would protect the interests of the congressman while at the same time retaining representation for the political allies of the county officials and the state legislators. The meeting settled nothing. It served instead to put all parties on notice that the county convention would be an all-out battle in which everything would go to the victor.

It was clear that Merelli was not going to support O'Hara, but it was not immediately clear what that would mean in terms of those precinct delegates who were members of the UAW. The regional director was opposing the O'Hara forces, but Solidarity House was not. Indeed, Ed Purdy, director of the UAW citizenship department, was supporting O'Hara, as were Russ Leach and most of the other political operatives who worked out of the international headquarters.[16] The question was whether the regional director or the international could deliver more. The question did not wait long for an answer.

When the county convention convened, more than two hundred precinct delegates were assembled. The first order of business, and the question that would decide everything, was the election of a convention chairman. John Bruff was the O'Hara candidate. He was opposed by Joe Snyder, who had the support of George Merelli. The precinct delegates were almost evenly split, with Bruff having a slight edge of one or two. The elected officials were not so evenly divided. Of the twelve officials present and voting, ten went for Snyder and only two for Bruff. Snyder's election signaled the beginning of a process in which O'Hara's supporters were systematically eliminated from any participation on the county committee. Merelli had done his work well. Years later John Bruff recalled:

> That night we learned the power of a regional director. Merelli had done his work well. Merelli really put on the screws. Once he decided not to go along with O'Hara he pulled out all the stops. Some of the UAW activists had worked for O'Hara in campaigns. Merelli simply threatened them with loss of their jobs if they didn't oppose us in the convention. He showed us that all the support from Solidarity wasn't worth a damn thing if the regional director was against you.[17]

Merelli's opposition did not go so far as to support a challenge to O'Hara's congressional seat. But if Merelli did not actively oppose O'Hara in congressional campaigns, neither did he provide much direct assistance. Labor continued to supply a preponderance of the money and manpower that went into the general Democratic campaign every two years, but the regional director consistently provided more assistance for state legislative campaigns than for O'Hara's congressional campaigns. Thus, for example, the UAW regional office was somehow never able to release a staff member to work on the congressional race. Whether this lack of support was because Merelli had never gotten over O'Hara's primary victory in 1958, or because he saw in the congressman's attempt to gain control of the county organization in 1964 a direct attack on his own political influence, relations between the two never really improved.

The UAW's failure to participate fully in O'Hara's congressional campaign was accompanied by a continuation of the enforced nonparticipation of O'Hara's supporters on the county committee. Leon Garwood, who had been elected county chairman in 1964, was reelected in 1966. O'Hara and Bruff did not even try to oppose him. In 1968, however, the situation changed. O'Hara was one of Hubert Humphrey's earliest supporters in the 1968 presidential race, and John Bruff became the director of the Humphrey campaign in Michigan. Bruff's involvement in the Humphrey campaign substantially altered the attitude of the Democratic county officials. They might have their differences with O'Hara and Bruff over questions of political power in the county, but to them the adherents of Eugene McCarthy in 1968 were practically the embodiment of the Red Menace. Anyone who ran Humphrey's campaign was a regular. Bruff's newly acquired popularity opened up the county committee to the friends and allies of Jim O'Hara. For the first time since he went to Congress, O'Hara found that his supporters were not completely shut out of the county organization.

When Leon Garwood announced that he would not run for a third term as chairman, the question of Garwood's successor was a matter of direct interest to O'Hara. Reapportionment was coming up in 1970 and John Bowman was once again expressing an interest in becoming a congressman. The next county chairman would be able to exercise some influence on the way in which the new reapportionment plan would be drawn. If the position were to be occupied by an ally of Bowman, O'Hara might find himself with a district that could be won only by a Republican, while Bowman resided in another district occupied by most of O'Hara's former Democratic constituents. Bowman, however, had not thought so far ahead. Indeed, no one made much of an effort to line up support in the county committee, and no one seemed to have given any thought to the possibility that O'Hara's best friend might even be a candidate. To the surprise of just about everyone, John Bruff was nominated for the chairmanship, and against almost nominal opposition was elected the new chairman of the Macomb County Democratic party.

The first term of Bruff's tenure as chairman of the Macomb County Democratic party produced increased success at the polls and a broader participation within the party. Following the 1970 general election, the chairman reported that in Macomb County the Democratic party had achieved results "that in many respects surpassed the 1964 Johnson landslide." Every incumbent Democrat had been reelected, and every one of the twenty-one members on the county board of commissioners was now a Democrat. Five Republican supervisors in townships in the northern portion of the county had been defeated; only two townships in the county had Republican supervisors. The entire Democratic statewide ticket had carried the county. Bruff concluded that "sound candidates, legitimate issues, and hard work from the grass roots of the party produced the best Democratic victory this county has seen in its history."[18]

Immediately after the 1970 general election the party structure was broadened considerably. Delegates to the county convention met to select half the membership of the executive committee. Twenty-six county officials, five state representatives, two state senators, and one nominee for state representative made up the nonelected half of the executive committee. The thirty-four places the precinct delegates were to fill by election were not contested separately. A carefully selected slate of candidates had been chosen by the county chairman and recommended to the convention. This slate, which, according to Bruff, had been drawn up "with the sole purpose of giving equitable balance to all areas of the county," was approved in its entirety. The executive committee was clearly much more representative of the party's rank and file than it had been in the days when the county officials and state legislators formed half of it themselves and named the other half. But the executive committee was broadened still more, and Bruff's influence extended further yet, by the adoption of "an ex-officio committee of nearly 100 members which is to 'participate in all executive committee meetings . . . with full voice only.' "[19]

Macomb County Democrats now had an executive committee that was "one of the first to increase its membership beyond what is required by law." By including "seventy-eight rank and file Democrats as ex-officio members," the county chairman expected an increase in participation and a more accurate reflection of "the thinking of the community." "A political party," according to Bruff, "must be responsive to the majority. Sixty people cannot express the needs of the Macomb County population of over 600,000. Our new, broader base will improve our communications."[20] Improved communication with the growing population of Macomb, however, was scarcely relevant to the two major problems Bruff and James O'Hara were to face in 1972. It was not a failure of communication but an irreconcilable conflict of political and personal interests that separated the incumbent congressman from his potential opponents on the question of proper congressional apportionment. Nor could any system of communication between the Democratic party and the overwhelming white population of the county ignore or prevent the explosive and politically destructive reaction to court ordered busing to achieve racial integration.

Under a provision of the state constitution, the state legislature reapportions the state's congressional districts after each decennial census by means of a bill passed by both the house and senate and signed by the governor.[21] By the beginning of 1972 Democratic legislators had a reapportionment plan, approved by the state Democratic party, that would bring the party's statewide voting strength and the number of Democratic congressional districts into closer correspondence. Republicans, on the other hand, had a plan of their own that would preserve so far as possible the twelve-to-seven advantage they enjoyed in the congressional delegation. Each party wanted an apportionment scheme that produced the greatest possible number of congressmen of its political persuasion; each party argued that its plan was the only one that met the test of fairness and disinterest; each party argued that the other was pursuing only its own narrow partisan advantage. Few believed anything that was said by either side. Several members of the legislature cared little for what their party wanted and even less for what the public had a right to expect. State Senator John Bowman did not even bother to mask his ambitions with verbal generalities. Bowman's duty was, according to Bowman, "to defend the Constitution of the United States, uphold the Constitution of the State of Michigan and to do everything I could to get a seat in Congress."[22] He very nearly succeeded.

Neither party alone could get its own apportionment plan through the state senate. Because the thirty-eight members of the senate were divided evenly between the parties, each party needed to keep all of its own votes and attract the support of at least one defector from the opposition. Bowman was more than willing to defect, if the price was right. The Republicans knew his price and were willing to pay it, especially since it cost them nothing. He was permitted

> to amend the Republican plan with a proposal which redraws the Twelfth District, now represented by Democratic Congressman James G. O'Hara, of Utica. Bowman's amendment puts O'Hara in the Fourteenth District and pits him against Congressman Lucien Nedzi, of Detroit.

Bowman had removed O'Hara and given himself a district in which he could "run without having to face an incumbent."[23]

Bowman's dream of an uncontested seat in Congress was shattered in less than a day. O'Hara quickly announced that "I don't feel obligated to run for re-election from where my home is now. I could easily move and challenge Bowman in his brand new district."[24] Still, Bowman did not relent. With the assistance of two Democratic state representatives from Macomb County, both of whom were far closer to Bowman than O'Hara, the Republican plan was passed in the House by a vote of 57 to 48.[25] The house version, however, was not identical to that passed in the senate. Before both houses could agree on a bill, the matter was removed from their hands on Friday, May 12, by the intervention of federal district court judge, Damon Keith.

For nearly nine months the state legislature had considered the question of congressional apportionment. The senate and the house had passed two different bills, and agreement between the two houses had never been reached. Only thirty-eight days were left before the filing deadline for congressional candidates when Judge Keith ordered adoption of a redistricting plan. "The plan adopted by Judge Keith, most clearly met the equal population or one person one vote requirement of the Constitution. This plan did not originate with Judge Keith but with the Michigan Democratic Party."[26] Judge Keith's order seemed to end one dispute only to give rise to another. Under the apportionment plan, not only was John Bowman left with Jim O'Hara as an obstacle to his congressional ambitions, but Macomb County was divided among three different congressional districts. Some presumed to find in this division both a punishment for the attitude taken by the residents of the county toward busing and, as if by coincidence, a means for continuing the political attacks on Bruff and O'Hara. State Representative Thomas Guastello found Judge Keith's order an irresistible invitation to announce the existence of a black conspiracy against the white citizens of Macomb County. Arguing in a *Macomb Daily* interview that the county had been "deliberately short-changed" because of its refusal to tolerate interdistrict busing, Guastello claimed Keith's action was "a deliberate move on the part of the black caucus in the Democratic Party to deny Macomb County its proper representation in Congress." This denial took the form of dividing the county among three districts although its population was sufficient "to warrant two seats in Congress."[27] According to Guastello,

> the black caucus said openly to us in the legislature that they were not going to vote for any plan that gave Macomb County another congressman. They were concerned about the county's strong stand against busing, the HUD issue and the fact that John Bowman of Roseville might be a serious contender for Congress in one of the districts.[28]

Guastello's version was extraordinary. Nowhere did he mention that the plan by which Macomb County was divided among three congressional districts was the very scheme devised by the state Democratic party. Nor did he even bother to indicate that the plan that would have given John Bowman his much-coveted congressional seat was the scheme devised by the Republican party that had been supported by only eight Democrats in the house. Moreover, far from being a sinister revenge on the part of the black caucus, the tripartite division of the county had been supported by a majority of the county's own legislative delegation.

An accurate description of what had transpired was not Guastello's purpose. By suggesting that the reapportionment plan was the product of a conspiracy of black legislators, all of whom were from Detroit, Guastello put himself on the side of all those who opposed busing and any other form of compulsory desegregation. He also attempted to place the incumbent congressman firmly on the other side. "It is pathetic," Guastello charged, "that John Bruff and Jim O'Hara exhibited not one ounce of leadership in this redistricting situation except to save their own jobs." Not content with accusing Bruff with an indifference that by implication worked to the advantage of the black caucus, Guastello added what he may have hoped more than expected, that O'Hara might not be able to survive in his redrawn district. "I think we may end up with no congressman. I see O'Hara's district as a swing district. It's no longer a Democratic stronghold."[29] The article in which Guastello unleashed his attack on Bruff and O'Hara contained a brief rejoinder from State Representative Warren Goemaere. With the blunt directness that characterized almost every public declaration he made, Goemaere cut right through to the basic issue: "The party leadership would have been able to decide this but Bowman went over to the Republicans to work out a deal for himself."[30] Bowman, on the other hand, was quoted as saying simply, "It has to be a political disadvantage to Macomb in that we will be so fragmented that we will lose our effectiveness as a strong political force."[31]

Neither Bruff nor O'Hara had been contacted by either the *Macomb*

Daily or Representative Guastello before the latter's allegations were published. Two days later Bruff responded. In a letter to the editor, he took Guastello and his allegations apart piece by piece. Guastello's charge that Judge Keith's action was related to the desires of the black caucus was "a discredit to him as a lawyer and a member of the Michigan Bar Association." The accusation that Bruff and O'Hara had failed to provide leadership was absurd on the face of it. Neither of them were "members of the Michigan Legislature while Guastello is a member of the House who voted on redistricting bills." No doubt was permitted as to precisely what kind of bills Guastello had energetically, if ineffectively, supported.

> In fact, Rep. Guastello . . . supported the ambitions of Senator John Bowman to go to Congress by voting for a House passed bill which attached the western half of Macomb County to a portion of St. Clair County and Wayne County. This bill would have placed Congressman Lucien Nedzi and Jim O'Hara in the western district. Coincidentally, it left the other district with no incumbent congressman for Senator Bowman's candidacy.[32]

If Guastello could refer to the imagined dominance of the black caucus in the plan actually adopted, Bruff, with far more accuracy, could recite the record of the strange alliance his adversary had entered into. "Representative Guastello joined with 51 Republicans and 7 Democrats to pass this bill which would have endangered Congressman Jim O'Hara's seat in Congress."[33]

Guastello might complain that Macomb County had been politically fragmented, and John Bowman's ambitions thwarted, through the machinations of a black caucus intent on the eventual integration of the county through the despised medium of forced busing. Bruff might argue that Bowman and Guastello had ignored the legitimate ties of party affiliation to further the political career of the senator by threatening with extinction the political life of the incumbent congressman. Judged on the merits of their arguments, Bruff was clearly the victor. He gave an entirely factual account in reply to a thoroughly fabricated allegation. Judged on the political consequences of their presentations, the issue was far less certain. Bowman and Guastello had done everything necessary to declare open political warfare on Bruff and O'Hara. Bowman had lost on the crucial question of reapportionment, but the charge that the new apportionment was the result of a court order by a black judge acting in concert with the black caucus did nothing to lessen the determination of the white population of Macomb County to oppose busing by any means available. Local officials were quick to voice their suspicion, whether they believed it or not, that the apportionment plan was, as Guastello said, connected with the county's antibusing sentiment. Eleven days after Guastello's initial charge, the city council of Warren, the largest community in the county and the center of the most outspoken opposition to busing, declared its intention to fight the redistricting plan. "Councilman Montgomery echoed State Representative Thomas Guastello's sentiments, saying the new boundaries may have resulted from Warren's and Macomb County's strong vocal stand against forced busing across school district lines."[34] As if to demonstrate an infinite ability to detect a conspiracy to promote busing, the *Macomb Daily* added as factual background that the "busing concept was proposed by Philip Roth, also a Federal district judge and Judge Keith's colleague."[35] Black robes and black skins had entered into a conspiracy of color.

The division of Macomb County among three congressional districts was not the result of a conscious attempt to diminish its political influence; it was simply the consequence of the fact that by 1970 the county population had become almost two-thirds of a million. Numbers alone, however, did not account for the savage reaction of county residents to the notion of interdistrict busing; nor did it account for the apparent willingness with which they came to believe that almost any political event might be a vehicle by which busing would be forced upon them. Not the increase of population, but the kinds of people who made up that increase, determined what came to be the central fact of Macomb County politics in 1972.

In 1970 blacks made up 11 percent of Michigan's population and 44 percent of Detroit's population, but there were only 7,572 blacks among the 626,938 residents of Macomb County.[36] Concentrated on the east side of Mt. Clemens, one of the oldest communities in the county, and in Clinton Township, north of 14 Mile Road, blacks had little political influence, and even less contact, with the almost completely white suburbs in the southern part of Macomb. If the county population came close to being uniformly white, there was within the white population considerable diversity. It is almost astonishing that nearly 37 percent of the county population were either first- or second-generation Americans. The three major nationalities among them were German, Italian, and Polish. Larger than any of those three groups, however, was the number of whites who had emigrated from the southern states. Of even greater importance than where they came from was where they settled. It was almost impossible to find a concentration of German-Americans, but Poles, Italians, and southern whites tended to live in close proximity to members of their own groups. Italians were found in greatest numbers in East Detroit, and both southern whites and Poles were concentrated in Warren.[37]

East Detroit and Warren were both close to the city limits of Detroit. Many of those who lived in those communities had crossed Eight Mile Road, the boundary between Detroit and Macomb County, as if they were refugees. For many of them the move to the suburbs was more than a change of address;

it was an escape. "People in Macomb left Detroit because they thought it was a bad situation. They don't want to be bothered with problems. They want to be left alone north of Eight Mile."[38] All the city problems, crime, and conflict were behind them, and, they thought, would stay behind them so long as Eight Mile Road remained an invisible but impenetrable barrier. The busing of school children back and forth across Eight Mile would mean that Detroit had somehow managed to follow and bring them back.

Congressman O'Hara was one of the first to understand the political implications of the busing controversy. Elected to his seventh term in 1970, O'Hara had become one of the most knowledgeable and able members of the Congress. Throughout the sixties, his record on civil rights was as good as any and better than most. While Philip Hart was the floor manager of the 1965 Voting Rights Act in the senate, O'Hara played a major part in its passage through the house. O'Hara's liberal credentials were impeccable; he had helped organize the Democratic Study Group in the house and had served as its chairman. He had given his vote and his effort to every major piece of civil rights and welfare legislation initiated during the Kennedy and Johnson administrations; some, like the Manpower Training Act, he had authored himself. Busing, however, was another matter. It might make good sense to judges with life tenure, and it might become a principled position for liberals who held no office, but for a congressman facing an election in 1972 in an almost entirely white suburban district, supporting it was equivalent to defeat.[39] Nor was busing itself such a clear matter that conscience could dictate only one course of action.

Those who had strongly supported civil rights legislation in the previous two decades had been mainly concerned with preventing overt acts of discrimination. Segregation, whether in public schools, public accommodations, or public transportation, was a clear abuse that had to be ended, and perhaps could only be ended by federal action. The most flagrant discrimination, because tolerated and even encouraged by the public authorities, occurred in the South. It is only a seeming paradox that because discrimination was so blatant in the South it was more easily remedied there than it would be in the northern states in the seventies. Segregation in southern schools had been rigorous and complete: whites went to all-white schools, blacks went to all-black schools. But because segregation was enforced not only by law but, more powerfully, by custom and habit, the social separation of the races did not keep blacks and whites from living in close physical proximity. As a result, the 1954 Supreme Court decision in *Brown v. Board of Education,* by striking down the doctrine of separate but equal, meant that the neighborhood school would become an integrated school. In many southern communities the busing of school children, which had been used to perpetuate school segregation, came to an end. Outside the South the situation was almost reversed. Black citizens were not prohibited by law from public facilities or public schools; they were, however, often prevented by social, and sometimes physical, pressure from entering white communities as residents. But the greatest constraint on black citizens was economics. Blacks came from the South to the industrial cities of the North to look for employment. They remained in the cities while their white neighbors, unable to prevent the intrusion, left in growing numbers. The white exodus to the suburbs often carried with it a substantial portion of the tax base from which city services and public education were funded. De jure segregation was not permitted by law; de facto segregation seemed impossible to prevent.

As a remedy, busing seemed of questionable utility. That schools should be integrated was taken as a premise that was never really examined. If the racial composition of a school was not to reflect the racial balance of the neighborhood it served, it was not clear what it should reflect. If district lines had been drawn in an effort to separate black from white, and some clearly had, what racial balance should obtain in a properly drawn district? But busing was not a fit subject for detached inquiry; it contained more emotion than Macomb County public officials had seen in their lifetime. It was an issue, according to one union official, that "got people involved in politics who never had been, people who perhaps had never even bothered to vote before. It was the worst issue I've ever encountered."[40]

O'Hara had two choices. He could suggest, as Philip Hart did, that busing was a remedy that could not be denied the courts. That would cause him to be replaced in the Congress by someone who would be against busing and also against most of the economic programs that O'Hara believed held out the greatest promise of eventually eliminating most of the differences and much of the antagonism between the races. His other choice was to oppose busing and avert defeat. O'Hara chose the second alternative, and was still almost defeated. He was quick to give public expression to his opposition to busing, but his opposition was not immediately as vehement as his constituents demanded. When the Congress was considering a proposed constitutional amendment prohibiting busing, O'Hara, under pressure, announced he would vote for it if it came to the floor. When it was discovered that he had not signed the discharge petition to bring it out of committee, three hundred enraged citizens assembled before his district office demanding he do so. He followed their advice.

Through this whole ordeal O'Hara was getting little real assistance from the UAW. On the busing issue itself, the union had adopted the position that it was a matter for the courts to decide, and had then suggested that attention should be directed to what was really the major problem, quality education. This might have been a moderating influence had the UAW in Macomb County accompanied it with a serious political effort. George Merelli, the

UAW regional director, was not inclined to get involved. Although no group was more vociferous in its attacks on busing than those who supported George Wallace within the county, the UAW did not even attempt to prevent them from taking over the county Democratic convention in the summer of 1972. Seventy-eight delegates from labor did not bother to attend and, as a result, a remarkable alliance of Wallace supporters and "kids for McGovern" temporarily took over the county party and used it as a platform for extreme statements on both sides of nearly every issue, but with busing the most prominent. The UAW was completely excluded; no representative of the labor movement from Macomb County was sent to Miami as a delegate to the Democratic national convention.[41]

Without any serious effort by labor to direct the attention of his constituents, or even its own members among them, to other issues; and without a presidential candidate acceptable to even a substantial minority among those who would decide his political fate, Jim O'Hara was on his own. Two years earlier he had seemed one of the most secure Democrats in the Congress; his Republican opponent had received only 22 percent of the vote. Had his district not been altered by reapportionment, had he continued to represent most of Macomb County, O'Hara would surely have been defeated in the electoral upheaval that associated busing with the Democratic party and failed to distinguish between those Democrats who opposed and those who supported it. As it was, O'Hara won his eighth term, but he won it with only 50.8 percent of the vote.[42]

With a large and growing population comprised to a great extent of union members, Macomb County had throughout the sixties seemed a safe source of increasing Democratic majorities. Fastened together by a common attachment to the economic programs of the Democratic party, a coalition of blue-collar workers, blacks, and liberals was expected to grow in strength and power. When busing disrupted and threatened to destroy this alliance, many among the leadership of the state Democratic party believed that it was a temporary difficulty that could be solved by greater emphasis on common economic problems. The New Deal coalition, however, had come up against not so much a problem as a condition. That social issues such as busing or abortion could arise in the first place was more a consequence than a cause of the growing disagreements among the major elements of the Democratic party. Blue-collar workers were no longer struggling for job security and enough money to keep themselves and their families from starvation; they were now a well-established part of the American middle class. Blacks were no longer a group which required white assistance, much less white leadership, to receive even the most basic rights of citizenship. They were now asserting their rights on their own, and were actively pursuing positions of political leadership. Liberals seemed to have lost a following and a cause.

Vietnam was something to oppose but within America there seemed to be no overriding objective, shared by a large segment of society, to which they might devote their talents and considerable energies. Macomb County, with its white blue-collar suburbs, had adopted a politics of reaction to black Detroit. Oakland County, with some of the nation's most affluent suburbs, seemed, as will be seen, to have adopted a politics no less discouraging for the continued maintenance of the liberal-labor coalition.

Notes

1. Clarence Contratta, interview with author, November 6, 1971.
2. John Canfield, interview with author, October 21, 1971.
3. Ibid.
4. Theodore H. White, *The Making of the President 1972* (New York: Atheneum, 1973), p. 161.
5. Paul Donahue, interview with author, April 14, 1973.
6. Ibid.
7. White, *Making of the President 1972*, p. 141.
8. John Bruff, interview with author, June 6, 1973.
9. George Steeh, interview with author, June 20, 1973.
10. State of Michigan, *Official Canvass of Votes 1954*, p. 51.
11. George Steeh, interview with author, June 20, 1973.
12. John Bruff, interview with author, June 6, 1973.
13. State of Michigan, *Official Canvass of Votes 1958*, p. 10.
14. John Bruff, interview with author, June 6, 1973.
15. George Merelli, interview with author, July 11, 1973.
16. Russ Leach, interview with author, December 15, 1971.
17. John Bruff, interview with author, June 6, 1973.
18. John Bruff, memo to Macomb County Democratic precinct delegates, December, 1970.
19. *Macomb Daily,* November 13, 1970.
20. John Bruff, press release, March 11, 1971.
21. Constitution of the State of Michigan, Article 4, Section 22, requires that "all legislation shall be by bill. . . ."
22. *Detroit News,* March 1, 1972.
23. Ibid.
24. *Community News,* March 8, 1972.
25. *Macomb Daily,* May 4, 1972.
26. John Bruff, letter to the *Macomb Daily,* May 15, 1972.
27. *Macomb Daily,* May 13, 1972.
28. Ibid.
29. Ibid.
30. Ibid.
31. Ibid.
32. John Bruff, letter to the *Macomb Daily,* May 15, 1972.

33. Ibid.

34. *Macomb Daily,* May 24, 1972.

35. Ibid.

36. U.S. Census, 1970. Cited in Michigan Democratic Party, "Macomb County Elections" (internal document, May 4, 1974).

37. Michigan Democratic Party, "Macomb County Elections."

38. Daniel Newman, interview with author, July 6, 1973.

39. Ten years earlier, when President Kennedy was considering whether to issue the executive order prohibiting racial discrimination in federally assisted housing before or after the 1962 congressional elections it was not Jim O'Hara but Martha Griffiths who urged that it be done only after the election. The liberal Democrat wrote White House congressional liaison chief Lawrence O'Brien, that "she knew of no Democratic congressman from suburbia who believed that he was in danger of losing colored votes; but he does feel such an order could cost white votes." Carl M. Brauer, *John F. Kennedy and the Second Reconstruction* (New York: Columbia University Press, 1977), pp. 206–7. Kennedy delayed the order and, unlike O'Hara in 1972, Griffiths in 1962 was able to enjoy the luxury of supporting equal opportunity without the danger of losing votes through its practical application.

40. Daniel Newman, interview with author, July 6, 1973.

41. Ibid.

42. In 1972, the percentage of Democratic straight-ticket voters declined all over Michigan. Fully half of the twenty-four Detroit suburban communities where the decline was 25 percent or more were in Macomb County. This included every one of the communities south of Fourteen Mile Road and Sterling Heights as well. As many as 35,000 voters who had cast straight Democratic ballots in the county in 1968 cast straight Republican ballots in 1972. From 66 percent of the straight ticket vote in 1968, the Democratic share decreased to 47 percent in 1972. In the part of Macomb County that remained within O'Hara's district the basic Democratic strength dwindled to less than 44 percent. Only by attracting the votes of ticket splitters was O'Hara able to win. The ticket splitters he managed to get were not to be found in the communities in the southern half of Macomb County. Only in communities further removed from Detroit and with a longer established population did he run substantially ahead of the party vote. The election may very well have been won in Roseville and St. Clair Shores, where O'Hara received 61 percent and 53 percent respectively, a result which exceeded the party vote by 6 percent in the first and 9 percent in the second locality (Michigan Democratic Party, "Macomb County Elections.").

CHAPTER 9

Oakland County:
The New Politics and the Old

In the 1948 election, in which the liberal-labor coalition elected a governor and began refashioning the Michigan Democratic party, two residents of Oakland County who in their own ways would eventually make significant political contributions played parts that scarcely foreshadowed their later activity. On the day of the primary election one of them spent the day in his Detroit office practicing law. Few if any of those who knew him then could have anticipated the chain of events that would one day make him the most respected member of the U.S. Senate. Philip A. Hart had not taken part in the organizing activity that was about to culminate in the nomination of G. Mennen Williams as the Democratic candidate for governor. He had not even taken part in the organization of his own precinct in Birmingham. In fact, no one had. Late in the morning of primary election day he received a phone call from a local Democratic party worker who explained to him that no one had bothered to file for precinct delegate and inquired whether he would allow his name to be used as a write-in candidate. The future senator had no objection. He called his wife, and after first asking her to ignore the apparent irrationality of the request, asked that she call all their Democratic friends in the precinct, if indeed they had any in that heavily Republican area, and ask them to write his name in for the high office of precinct delegate. Late that evening Hart received another phone call. It was the same Democratic activist who had called him earlier in the day. With some laughter in her voice she reported that G. Mennen Williams had been given eleven votes by the precinct's voters. Hart, as a write-in candidate, had received twenty-seven.[1] From such improbable beginnings sprang the impressive political career of Philip A. Hart.

Late on the day of the general election in November, it was raining heavily in Madison Heights. Few communities in Oakland County were further removed from the charm and affluence of Birmingham than this suburban town filled with its white blue-collar inhabitants. An obvious mark of the discrepancy between the two was the relative absence of paved roads in Madison Heights. With the dirt roads made almost impassable by the heavy downpour, John Dewan's wife suggested that perhaps they ought to give up trying to get to the polls and turn around and drive home. Dewan, however, was adamant. Though he had not yet become politically active in the UAW, he was a union member, and the prediction that morning in the *Detroit Free Press* that Thomas Dewey was certain to be elected had only intensified his determination to cast his ballot for Harry Truman. Telling his wife that "we're going to vote no matter what," Dewan got to the polls and cast a straight Democratic ballot.[2]

With remarkable speed, Hart left Oakland County politics for larger pursuits, first with the federal government, then with the Williams administration, and then, finally, in the senate of the United States. Dewan never left the union and hardly ever left Oakland County. Dewan's vote in the 1948 election was motivated more by the fact that he was a Democrat than by his membership in the union. Within two years, however, he had developed a serious interest in the union and in the union's involvement in politics. Two events transformed him from a union member to a union activist. In 1950 he went to a meeting at the Dodge Main local and for the first time heard Walter Reuther speak. Reuther's appeal for greater participation in the affairs of the union on the ground that only a strong union could preserve jobs and improve conditions made a powerful impression. Dewan had recently begun a family and the prospect of unemployment had become a far more serious matter to contemplate. "After I had a family I became concerned with security. When the guy came down the line laying off it would scare the hell out of you. The young guys who were married were very concerned."[3]

When John Dewan became an active union member through the persuasive power of Walter Reuther and the force of his own personal circumstances, Oakland County was a predominantly Republican area. What there was of a Democratic party was concentrated in Pontiac, and what there was of a Democratic party in Pontiac was under the control of Willis Brewer. Nothing was done without Brewer's approval and no one ran for office without his endorsement. Brewer's lieutenant, Carlos Richardson, was chairman of the county Democratic party, and Brewer's friend, Art Law, became mayor of Pontiac. Labor's influence in politics can be gauged by the fact that Law, who was president of Local 596, depended on Brewer and not on the union for the advancement of his political career. Still, the labor movement in Oakland County was almost synonymous with labor in Pontiac. In the mid-1950s the Pontiac CIO council was the Oakland County CIO council.[4]

The Pontiac CIO council was run by Fred Haggard, whom a growing number came to believe was not "doing the job politically." William Mc-Cardy, the UAW regional director, was not so much unskilled at politics as indifferent to it. Far from attempting to build the union's influence within the Democratic party in order eventually to refashion the party on a more liberal pattern, McCardy was quite content to go along with the drift of events. The status quo, whatever it might be, was the appropriate standard to observe. But while power seemed concentrated in Pontiac, and labor and the Democratic party appeared content with the existing distribution of political power, forces were at work that within a few years would radically transform party politics in Oakland County.[5]

Pontiac was an established community in which people lived and worked. Nearly thirty miles northwest of Detroit, the city had an independent existence. Any population increase it might experience would be the result of expanding employment opportunities in the city or its immediate environs. The significant population increases in Oakland County, however, were not to take place in Pontiac. Instead, by the mid-1950s an immense increase began in the southern half of the county. After 1950, as we have seen, the Detroit population began a decline that has not yet come to an end. At the same time that Macomb County was becoming a series of suburban communities for the blue-collar employees of the automobile companies, southern Oakland County began to receive a large increase in white-collar employees. The Fishers, the Briggses, the Fords, and most of the other founding families of the auto industry might retain their baronial estates in Grosse Pointe, but the new managerial class preferred the more spacious suburbs of Birmingham and Bloomfield Hills, where new money was more important than old family. What the upper middle class did by choice, the middle-level managers did for convenience. As the older plants in Detroit became outmoded, newer, more automated facilities were situated not only in Macomb County but in southern Oakland County as well. Both white- and blue-collar employees swarmed into suburban developments that had been built, it often seemed, overnight.

As the center of population moved from the northern to the southern half of the county, a shift in political power was perhaps inevitable. The size of the new population, however, was less important for the future political development of the Oakland County Democratic party than the kind of people included in it. They were, on the whole, wealthier, better educated, and, at least among those who were Democrats, more liberal than their northern neighbors. It was one thing to have an increased number of liberals in the county; it was quite another to assemble them as a political force capable of exerting influence within the established party organization. Even as an organized force they were doubtful candidates to challenge the old guard's control of the party. Not only did they need to be organized, they needed an ally.

If the liberals were to have any chance of gaining control or even significant influence in the Oakland County Democratic party, they needed the support and the active assistance of labor. This was scarcely a novel situation; what was true in the county had been true on the state level a decade earlier. But perhaps the situation was not entirely similar. Those who had helped build the liberal-labor alliance that had elected Williams governor and eliminated opposition within the state party apparatus were now coming to be viewed, in their turn, as impediments to progress. Indeed, the leader of the old guard in Oakland County, Willis Brewer, had been one of Williams's earliest followers. Labor, having altered the composition of the state party, had no apparent incentive to join a struggle against those who had been needed allies in the past. The union leadership in the county was established, believed itself effective, and saw nothing to gain by attaching itself to a new group of liberals whose wealth was suspect and whose politics were unclear.

The same growth that brought a large influx of middle-class liberals also brought a new group of union leaders into the county. With every new automobile plant constructed in Oakland County, a new union local was created. One of the presidents was Sam Fishman of Ford Local 36 in Wixom, which, though new, was already one of the largest in UAW Region 1-B. Fishman was soon deeply involved with labor's political arm in the county, the Oakland County CAP, and deeply disappointed. Far from attempting to move the Democratic party in a more liberal direction, the labor leadership, especially the regional director, seemed more than willing to follow whatever lead Willis Brewer cared to give. Millie Burns, secretary of Local 36, put Fishman in touch with Harriett Phillips, who was the moving force among those liberals who wanted to replace the old guard in the leadership of the county party. Phillips and Fishman agreed on the desirability of an alliance between labor and the liberals. The key question, and the major obstacle, was the attitude of the labor leadership.[6]

Though both Phillips and Fishman were persuasive advocates, persuasion alone would never have changed the attitudes of those who had authority in the union's regional office. That could come about only if a new regional director came to power. The prospects of that did not seem good; regional directors, like incumbent state legislators, were almost never denied reelection. But just as shifts in population were coming to be seen as the proper occasion for reapportioning state legislative districts, the great increase of automobile plants and auto workers in Oakland County led to the redrawing of the UAW's regional districts. The old Region 1-B was eliminated and a new district created that included virtually all of Oakland County, including Pontiac. The new region got a new regional director. McCardy, with his close connections with Willis Brewer and the party's old guard, was replaced by Ken Morris, who was already convinced of the desirability of an alliance between labor and the new liberals.

In the 1950s, liberal Democrats were held together by a belief that the nature of politics must change from the pursuit of self-interest to a commitment to the public welfare. Only then could politics provide a means for eliminating the complacency permeating the government and for solving the great social problems that seemed, to those Democrats, to have been deliberately hidden from view. In their view this required above all else the participation of well-educated and well-meaning men and women. Adlai Stevenson had convinced them that politics could not be ignored and could only be improved by their full participation. Stevenson had also demonstrated that a liberal of intelligence and cultivation could become the nominee of his party. Though twice nominated, the eloquent governor of Illinois had been twice defeated for the presidency. If the future prospects of liberalism within the Democratic party were not to be diminished by Stevenson's failures, and if liberal Democrats were ever to have the opportunity to capture not only the leadership of the party but the governance of the country, liberal Democrats had to both exercise influence within the party and strengthen the party's position with the electorate.

None of this could be accomplished without a liberal organization. Although a seemingly endless number of organizations already relied on liberals for membership, to say nothing of financial support, the organization of the Democratic party did not include any place likely to attract those people, and liberals were decidedly among them, who were more interested in the discussion of public policy than in the mechanics of party functions. Even for those who did not find the details of party organization the ultimate in tedium and inconsequence, the number of positions available was limited. Except for the few dozen places on a county central committee, whose members might occasionally deliberate a proposed resolution on some matter of public moment, the only position available was that of precinct delegate. But while several hundred delegate positions might be available in a county as large as Oakland, the delegates really did little but attend two county conventions during their two-year terms. If liberal Democrats were to become heavily involved in the party, and if the party was going to be influenced by liberals, another form of organization would have to be devised.

A political party, as defined by Edmund Burke, is an assemblage of men devoted to a common principle.[7] The internal organization of political parties in the United States has been characterized by the principle of self-interest; patronage in one form or another has often been its lifeblood. Among those liberal Democrats who entertain the hope, if not always the expectation, of one day obtaining public office, self-interest may still be said to be a moving force. But in the lives of the great majority of liberal Democrats who neither seek elective office themselves nor have any need or desire for employment by a public official, patronage is irrelevant and wholly ineffective as a spur to political activity. White-collar liberals had no interest in patronage.

Liberals were, however, interested in public policy—and, perhaps even more, in the discussion of it. Clearly the only organizational form that would entice liberals to enter was one designed specifically to encourage not only the discussion of political issues but the belief that discussion could lead, directly or indirectly, to some actual influence on what elected officials did. One of the first attempts to harness the energies of liberal Democrats took place in California. There, a notoriously weak party organization and the almost complete lack of patronage of any sort made the creation of a structure that would attract people to politics imperative, if not inevitable. In the early 1950s Alan Cranston, who would later become a U.S. Senator, and State Senator George Miller, Jr., the northern California Democratic chairman, established the California Democratic Council. The CDC was organized through Democratic clubs scattered around the state. These clubs were established to promote discussion of political issues and were kept going by the social ties that gradually developed in them.[8] In Michigan, as we have seen, the founders of the liberal-labor coalition established Democratic clubs as an alternative structure to the formal party apparatus. Once the coalition had captured the party organization, however, most of the clubs dissolved of their own accord. Those in Oakland County were among the exceptions. As the number of college-educated liberal Democrats increased and were dispersed over larger portions of the county, the Democratic clubs gradually grew in number and in membership.[9]

In the gubernatorial primary of 1960, the liberals, organized in Democratic clubs throughout the county, were overwhelmingly in favor of the candidacy of John Swainson; James Hare was supported only by what had become the old guard. Those who had been part of the liberal-labor coalition in 1948 and had acquired and exercised political power within the county during the long tenure of G. Mennen Williams, now found themselves faced with another coalition of liberals and labor. The difference between the two groups seemed to have little if anything to do with substantive questions of public policy. The differences, in the judgment of one of the most energetic of the new liberals, were "less ideological than style."[10] It is not immediately obvious what a difference in style really meant. It appears to have signified nothing more or less than the difference between an older and more established group that held power and a newer younger group that was ambitious to get it.

Just as the 1948 primary victory of G. Mennen Williams had marked the beginning of a campaign to take control of the state party, so Swainson's victory in the 1960 primary was part of the effort to capture the county party. Having carried Oakland County for Swainson, the liberal-labor coalition turned its attention to carrying the county for themselves. It had already prepared to do so. At the same time that the Swainson campaign for the Democratic gubernatorial nomination was being waged in the county—and indeed as a part of that undertaking—liberals recruited candidates to run for precinct delegate positions. Labor leaders who supported Swainson were not slow to follow. Harold Julian, then codirector of the UAW's Chrysler Department, Clayton Johnson from the union's social security department, and Howard Arnold, vice-president of Local 653 in Pontiac, were among the main labor leaders encouraging their friends and followers to elect Swainson and become precinct delegates.[11] Perhaps more ominous for the future political prospects of the established party leadership was the encouragement given by the UAW regional director, Ken Morris.[12]

After the general election had been held and Swainson elected governor, the Oakland County Democratic party met in convention to elect the county committee that would lead and control the party for the next two years. There were a great many new faces at the convention, and all of them were intent on removing Carlos Richardson from the chairmanship and as many of his followers as possible from the committee. The faces may have been new, but the methods employed were not. With neither reluctance nor remorse, the liberals and their union allies beat and very nearly banished what for a dozen years had been the ruling power and force in Democratic politics in Oakland County. Richardson was replaced as chairman by a Southfield attorney, Jim Grim, and a new generation of liberals had predominant power within the county organization. What they would do with it remained to be seen.

After only a year, the newly elected county chairman decided that party politics brought more trouble and consumed far more time than he had anticipated. Though he was already halfway through his two-year term, Grim resigned. The recently victorious coalition of liberals and labor had now to win another victory. The old guard had been defeated, but it had not disappeared; half of the county committee was then composed of those who had been nominated for public office, and more than half of these were still loyal to Carlos Richardson. If the new coalition was to retain control of the county organization, it had to retain the allegiance of each of the members of the county committee it had elected and all the party nominees it had supported. This required that the coalition put forward a candidate for chairman that all of them would accept.

One evening in the late 1950s, John Dewan attended the monthly meeting of the Berkley Democratic Club. As the meeting wore on he noticed that at almost every opportunity the same person rose to speak. Finally Dewan asked someone "who the little guy was who was talking all the time." Sander Levin was "up and down the whole meeting."[13] By his interest and his persistence

Levin soon established first a reputation and then a predominance within the club. Finally, with the considerable assistance of Harold Julian, Levin was elected the club's chairman. When Grim resigned, Levin was more than willing to become a candidate for county chairman. At this stage in his political career he had few enemies, if any, and more importantly, maintained good relations with all of the major factions within the county party. Liberals saw him as one of their own, while labor, in the person of Harold Julian, treated him almost as a protégé. Moreover, unlike some liberals, Levin appeared more interested in broadening the base of the party than in advancing the cause of liberal principles to the exclusion of political success.

With labor and the liberals united on a single candidate for chairman, the party's old guard had no chance to win and knew it. Levin was elected chairman without opposition and began to build the county party into a powerful political organization. One of the first steps Levin took in this direction was to build the county's annual Phil Hart Dinner into a larger and more lucrative event. With the added revenue generated by this and other enterprises, Levin was able to become the first county chairman to have a paid staff year-round. The new chairman also attempted to bring back into the party the old guard that had been defeated and embittered. With remarkable insight into the willingness with which many will forgive a reduction of actual power if given the appearance of prestige, Levin began referring to Willis Brewer as "Mr. Oakland County Democrat" whenever the former power of the Oakland County party was present at a public event. The tactic proved irresistible. If Brewer and his followers did not do much to contribute to the fortunes of the county party, neither did they any longer present an opposition to be dealt with.[14] With this accomplished, Levin was now able to turn his undivided attention to the problem of strengthening the party in the electorate.

One of the keys to attracting people to a political party is the quality of the candidates that party puts forward. A county organization can influence the selection of the top of the ticket only in an indirect fashion, but can have a direct and a very significant influence on the choice of local and countywide candidates. In Oakland County in the early 1960s, as in numerous other counties in the state, many areas were heavily Republican and contests for many local offices failed to attract any Democratic candidates at all. Levin spent much of his time as chairman encouraging Democrats to become candidates for local and county offices, convincing them that even where it was impossible for a Democrat to win it was important to have a Democrat run.

Any candidate will attract at least a few voters among his own circle of relatives and acquaintances who would not otherwise bother to go to the polls. Each additional candidate also means an additional campaign, which adds additional campaign volunteers. If the number of campaigns in the county increases, the overall county effort increases, and that effect does not end with the election. Those who are attracted to politics by involvement in a particular campaign can become the primary source of party activists in the future. Under Levin's leadership, Oakland County adopted the strategy of building the county organization on the foundation supplied by the organizations each candidate brought into being for his own purposes.[15]

Elected to a full two-year term following the 1962 election, Levin began to look forward to the 1964 campaign less with an eye toward furthering the growth of the county organization than with an ambition to run for public office. Legislative reapportionment had created a senatorial district in the county that a Democrat might and very probably could win. With labor's endorsement, Levin won the primary and easily defeated his Republican opponent in the general election. Levin was now a state senator and the chairmanship of the Oakland County party passed, with the approval of labor, into the hands of another liberal, George Googasian.

While Levin had dissipated the hostility of the old guard by calculated deference to Willis Brewer, Googasian, as Art Law's son-in-law, had the actual support of at least some of them. It was not the old guard but the new liberals that presented the most serious problem during his tenure as county chairman. In 1968, as Googasian neared the end of his second term, the coalition of liberals and labor almost dissolved into warring factions over the presidential candidacy of Eugene McCarthy. The three factions into which the county party was divided, labor, the liberals, and the old guard (or, as they had now become known, the populists), each had approximately one third of the elected precinct delegates. Though evenly divided countywide, each faction drew a large portion of its strength from particular areas in the county. Labor's influence at the precinct level was largely related, if not entirely restricted, to where its members lived; the southeastern quadrant of the county, along with the city of Pontiac, furnished the great majority of its delegates. Populist support, on the other hand, came mainly from the rural areas, and these were found almost entirely in the Nineteenth Congressional District, which encompassed the western and northern sections of the county. Liberals were located in both the Eighteenth and Nineteenth districts. It was in the Eighteenth, where almost none of the populist faction resided, that the battle lines between liberals and labor were most clearly drawn.

McCarthy's adherents in the Eighteenth District did extremely well in the August election of precinct delegates. Nowhere did they do better than in those precincts that were heavily Republican. There, a concerted effort was often enough to win a majority of the relatively few Democratic voters. Perhaps the best example of this tactic, and easily the most embarrassing to labor, occurred in the home precinct of the UAW regional director, Ken Morris. Morris was the incumbent precinct delegate, but a McCarthy supporter defeated him by four votes. The loss (in an 85 percent Republican precinct) was even more painful because it resulted from a write-in campaign. And Morris's defeat was not unique; it happened all over the district. Labor's precinct delegate strength seemed shattered. But no matter how many precinct delegates the McCarthy cadre was able to elect, the delegates elected two years earlier were the ones who would meet in district conventions to select delegates to the Democratic national convention. The district was entitled to a total of four national convention delegates and all four, Fay Weiss, Gene Kuthy, Ken Morris, and Allen Zemmol, had been picked by labor.[16]

The delegates elected by the McCarthy forces could not participate in the process by which the Democratic presidential nominee was selected; after the general election, however, they became a very formidable body within the Eighteenth District organization and within the county party as a whole. Almost immediately after their official terms of office began in January, the district met in convention to select a new set of officers. The McCarthy delegates nominated Jean Leopold as their choice for district chairman. Labor countered with Allen Zemmol. On all the other offices labor and the liberals compromised; with the exception of the chairmanship, both sides had agreed to a single slate of candidates. On the chairmanship there was to be no compromise. The highest office in the district organization was to be decided between the two nominees by a vote of the contesting factions. Labor would have preferred a compromise, less because it was interested in party unity than because it was clear to both groups that the liberals had the votes to win. Both sides, however, had miscalculated. By the narrowest margin ever recorded in a contest for the district chairmanship, labor's candidate, Allen Zemmol, was elected.[17]

Having narrowly averted defeat in the Eighteenth District, labor faced another battle for control of the Oakland County organization. Once again the two sides appeared to have almost identical strength. The chairmanship was not an object of contention, for the McCarthy forces chose not to oppose George Googasian for a third term. Googasian, who had gone to the national convention as a delegate from the Nineteenth District, had voted for George McGovern, an action that mollified the liberals without antagonizing labor. But the chairmanship was the only office that was not contested. No compromise had been entered into and no common slate had been agreed to. Each side ran a full complement of candidates. When the executive committee met to elect party officers, the slate of candidates supported by labor was elected by three votes.[18] Labor had preserved its influence in both the district and the county party organizations, but only by the smallest of margins. What labor's victory would mean for the Democratic party in Oakland County was a question still to be decided. The question would hinge largely on whether labor used its strength to diminish liberal influence or to conciliate the defeated and encourage their continued participation.

No one had any desire to relive 1968. One of the most able political activists in the county put it simply: "Everyone was strung out in 1968."[19] Many of those who had been intense partisans of Eugene McCarthy were new to party politics, and some of them withdrew from any active part in politics after the election. Others remained active and decided that only by working within the existing party organization could they have any real influence in the selection of candidates or on the policy of the Democratic party. Labor, while in favor of including as many of its former adversaries as possible in the party, was at the same time determined that an infusion of new liberals would not result in a diminution of its own influence. Participation was one thing; power was something else.

In the past, labor's strength within the party had depended on its ability to elect precinct delegates. That ability, in turn, depended on nothing so much as its success in persuading its own members to fill vacant delegate spots. In Oakland County, it had not been uncommon to have half the 400 precincts without an elected delegate.[20] After the 1968 election of precinct delegates, in which many positions were contested and many contested positions won by liberals, labor decided it had to make a concerted effort to run as many candidates as possible. In 1970, labor did all it could to elect precinct delegates whose loyalty or at least sympathy was with the union. Although only 233 of the 400 precincts had candidates for delegate, labor elected enough to preserve its power and perhaps even to extend its influence. Labor's drive to elect precinct delegates was based on its desire to protect its position. That was quite compatible with a willingness, and even an eagerness, to see the county and district organizations perform their functions in a spirit of compromise. As one of the union's political operatives put it: "We were determined to get along with anyone and to do almost anything to prevent a repetition of the 1968 battle."[21] For the most part, compromise and conciliation succeeded in moderating the tensions between the major factions. Only once did the spirit of cooperation seem imperiled.

In 1970 the Eighteenth Congressional District was scarcely a Democratic stronghold. In fact, even by the wildest stretch of the imagination it was not a district in which a Democrat had any real chance of winning: so long as the district lines remained unchanged, nothing short of an act of God was likely to unseat the Republican incumbent. But if God moves in mysterious ways, the ambitions of candidates for public office are often even more difficult to understand. Perhaps on the theory that the advocacy of principle is eminently superior to the acquisition of office—a theory some see as the best preparation for defeat—two of Eugene McCarthy's most devoted followers decided to become candidates for Congress. So long as Annetta Miller and James Elsman were campaigning only against each other in order to win the opportunity of losing the general election, no one was greatly disturbed.

Liberals might line up behind one or the other of the candidates, but labor was quite content to remain a neutral observer of what was a strictly liberal affair. Labor, it was publicly announced, would be more than glad to give its support to whichever candidate became the party nominee against the Republican incumbent, Congressman William S. Broomfield. Unity seemed assured.

For more than twenty years those who sought office as Democratic candidates had been compelled to take notice of the very formidable figure of Gus Scholle. As president of the Michigan AFL-CIO, Scholle had been the recognized political spokesman for almost all of organized labor in the state; only the Teamsters consistently refused to follow his lead. Scholle decided which candidates received assistance from labor, and if they received assistance he decided how much they should get and what form it should take. No one was more powerful within the liberal labor alliance, and no one was more conscious of that power than Scholle himself. By 1970, however, all of that was already a rapidly fading memory. With the withdrawal of the UAW from the AFL-CIO, Scholle was in charge of an organization that had only a small fraction of the money and manpower he had once directed. From the single most powerful man in the Democratic party and one of the most influential men in the state, he had been reduced almost overnight to a figure of at best secondary importance. Overshadowed by the immense strength of the UAW, Scholle seemed condemned to a political life of increasing obscurity. There was little if anything he could do to redress the balance between the AFL-CIO and the UAW in Michigan, but there was a way to at least recapture some of the publicity and notoriety that had been his for more than two decades, if only for a short time. Rather than go through another campaign in which he was unable to direct events, he did what no one expected. Gus Scholle became a candidate for Congress in the Eighteenth Congressional District.

The last hurrah of Gus Scholle was not greeted by liberals with even the slightest touch of nostalgic sympathy. Those who had been among his earliest opponents responded to the candidacy of one of Lyndon Johnson's last adherents with intense and even livid dissatisfaction. The carefully created mood of concession and cooperation within the Eighteenth District and the county organization threatened to explode. Still, Scholle had entered the race very late, and both his liberal rivals had already put together working campaigns. Scholle's solitary prospect for victory in the primary seemed dependent on the presence of two candidates who might divide the liberal constituency and permit him to win with less than a majority of the vote. There was, of course, an easy and an obvious way to preclude this possibility; one of the liberal candidates would have to withdraw. But both Miller and Elsman believed that the proper subject of politics was principle, and both refused to believe that principle could be as well served by the other. Neither could be enticed to withdraw. When the final vote was counted, Elsman received 9,355 votes, Miller 10,900, and Scholle 12,566. With little more than 38 percent of the vote cast, Gus Scholle became the Democratic nominee for Congress.[22]

If the liberal candidates prided themselves on their fidelity to principle, Scholle was faithful to the tenets of practical politics. Liberal hostility to Scholle was caused less by his leadership of the AFL-CIO than by his continued support of American involvement in Vietnam. Faced with the choice of continued opposition within his own party or consistency in his Vietnam position, Scholle abruptly changed course; one of the last of the hawks was metamorphosed into the latest of the doves. What the Democratic nominee did out of political expediency, liberals viewed with some satisfaction as the vindication of political principle. The restoration of party unity was not left to the uncertain force of an agreement on principle, however. With a shrewd suspicion that at least some liberals could not distinguish between the acceptance of their principles and the advancement of their own ambitions, Oakland County Democrats went into the August state convention and obtained a nomination to the state board of education for Annetta Miller. She was now convinced that the Democratic party stood for something after all.

The general election went as might have been expected. Scholle was defeated in the Eighteenth Congressional District contest, 113,309 to 62,081, a margin that had become typical in that decidedly Republican district.[23] The county's other congressional district, the Nineteenth, returned the incumbent Republican, Jack McDonald, for yet another two-year term by the smaller but still substantial margin of 28,588, 91,763 to 63,175.[24] Both Democratic defeats were expected, and no one except perhaps the candidates themselves felt any particular anguish over the results. In fact, on the whole, county Democrats took considerable satisfaction in the election outcome. For the first time the county board of commissioners had a Democratic majority; with sixteen of the twenty-seven positions, the Oakland County Democratic party had control of county government.[25] Moreover, Oakland Democrats had waged the most active county campaign in the state on behalf of U.S. Senator Philip Hart. The young man in charge of the county's Hart campaign was about to emerge as a power in party politics.

Morley Winograd's effective leadership of the Hart campaign led the county chairman, George Googasian, to begin to think seriously about his own successor. Googasian was not interested in a fourth term as chairman. He had not really been interested in a third term, but labor had persuaded him that his retirement following the divisive 1968 campaign would only cause further difficulties between the factions. The possibility of a factional fight over the chairmanship remained a concern, so Googasian indicated that he would retire only if Winograd's candidacy was supported by all the major groups within the party. Having run the Hart campaign, Winograd was on good terms with party liberals. The major question was what labor would do.

Winograd was not the only one interested in becoming the next chairman of what was the most powerful county organization in Michigan. After several terms as chairman of the Eighteenth Congressional District Committee, Allen Zemmol was eager to acquire broader responsibilities and increased power. The choice was clearly going to be between Winograd and Zemmol and, just as clearly, the choice was going to be dictated by labor. Labor wanted Googasian to run again, but Googasian was emphatic in his reluctance to continue and assured the UAW that Winograd could both handle the job and work well with the union. John Dewan, the UAW's Oakland County coordinator, had observed Winograd during the campaign and had reached the same conclusion. Telling a disappointed, and somewhat astonished, Allen Zemmol, "We're going to go with young blood," labor chose Winograd, and the election of the next county chairman was decided even before the new county executive committee had been elected.[26]

Winograd inherited a county organization that was in many ways almost unique. Oakland County was the only county in the state beside Wayne that had more than one complete congressional district within it. And in Wayne County the congressional district organizations were autonomous; the county committee had no functions to perform and no power to perform them if it had. The two congressional districts in Oakland County, the Eighteenth and the Nineteenth, each had official committees, but neither alone nor in combination could they rival the authority of the county organization. The basis for that authority rested on the year-round activity made possible by the existence of a full-time staff. In turn, the staff and all their efforts toward expanding the influence of the county organization depended on a constant supply of money. The wealthiest county in the state was the home of many of the state's wealthiest Democrats. In 1971, when few if any of the state's county organizations could even afford to have a regular headquarters, the Oakland County Democratic party was working with a $40,000 annual budget. Three quarters of this amount was raised by the county party and one fourth came from labor.

Winograd took over a well-established organization, but the main business of that organization was no longer self-evident. It had been almost an article of faith that the major function of the county party was to identify Democrats and make certain they were registered to vote. Ever since Sander Levin's tenure as chairman, the county party had developed and maintained one of the most elaborate and effective voter identification programs anywhere. But almost from the beginning of the program a new phenomenon was noticed. Each year fewer people were willing to identify themselves as either Democrats or Republicans. Moreover, it was progressively less certain that there was any necessary correlation between the party chosen by those who were willing to do so and the party or the candidate they voted for in an election.

Both the 1968 and the 1970 elections demonstrated that exclusive reliance on straight-party voters was a sure guarantee of defeat. From 1960 to 1968 Democratic percentages increased in nearly every community in Oakland County.[27] Beginning in 1968, however, a new tendency became apparent. Some "types of communities show increases for one party and other types of communities show increases for the other."[28] The vote cast for the state board of education candidate made it clear that many who were counted as Democrats were not supporting all Democratic candidates. Among southern whites living in the county the percentage of falloff in the Democratic vote was remarkable. In three sample precincts, each of which was mainly southern white, the vote for Hubert Humphrey was far behind the base Democratic vote. In the Forty-second Precinct of Pontiac, Humphrey's vote was 24 percent less, in the Fifth Precinct of Hazel Park, 14 percent less, and in the Fourth Precinct of Madison Heights, 17 percent less. The 1970 election proved that southern whites were not the only group whose votes were not being cast for every Democrat on the ticket. The Eighth Precinct of Madison Heights, which was both blue-collar and Catholic, cast 18 percent less of its vote for the Democratic gubernatorial candidate than for the Democratic candidate for the board of education. The Fourth Precinct in Berkley, upper-middle-class Catholic, cast 10 percent less. The Third Precinct in Farmington, upper-class Catholic, cast 16 percent less.[29]

For a county that had a 48 percent share of the base party vote in 1968, the defection of large numbers of southern white and Catholic voters, all of whom identified themselves as Democrats and voted Democratic for candidates at the bottom of the ballot, required a reevaluation of traditional methods. Not the professed Democratic voter but the independent voter, no matter how he identified himself, had to become the target of party efforts. In 1971, at the August meeting of the county committee, a decisive break was made with past policy. The whole notion of a voter identification program was dismissed as "not a profitable use of time."[30] A new policy was adopted that on the surface seemed to have little if anything to do with the problem presented by the great and growing number of independent voters. The Oakland County Democratic party "became the first organization in the state to recommend endorsement of local candidates in the party primary."[31] Every Democratic club in the county was now empowered to endorse candidates for local office and supply them with financial backing. The county organization, in turn, was authorized to endorse and provide financial assistance to primary candidates for county office.

The decision to endorse primary candidates was not only related to the problem of independent voters, but was adopted as a strategy for attracting independents to the party. In the belief that independent voters were attracted more to a candidate than to a party, the county chairman concluded that independent voters who supported a candidate endorsed by the party could more easily be induced to support other Democratic candidates.[32] By endorsing those candidates with an appeal beyond the party faithful, the party would at least have a chance at reaching out to those who had no real allegiance to either party. Moreover, giving local Democratic clubs the power of endorsement in local elections would provide additional incentives to political activity. Labor was in full agreement with Winograd's new strategy. John Dewan had been saying for years that the central problem of political organization was the absence of patronage. A substitute was perhaps to be found in the provision of political power to Democrats whose only position was membership in a Democratic club in a small Oakland County township, and giving such organizations the power to endorse local candidates seemed a step in that direction. Within eighteen months, however, Morley Winograd would no longer be much concerned with attracting new participants to the Democratic clubs of Oakland County. The problem presented by the political defection of white and Catholic voters in the Detroit suburbs, however, continued to intrigue and to bedevil him as he began, in February, 1973, his first term as chairman of the Michigan Democratic party.

Notes

1. This account was given by Senator Hart at a luncheon meeting of the women's caucus of the Michigan Democratic party at the Democratic state convention held in Detroit in February, 1975. It was also given by the Senator at other places and times while the author had the great good fortune to serve as his special assistant.

2. John Dewan, interview with author, October 14, 1971.

3. Ibid.

4. Sander Levin, interview with author, May 5, 1971; Harold Julian, interview with author, February 23, 1973.

5. Sam Fishman, interview with author, June 6, 1973; Harold Julian, interview with author, February 23, 1973.

6. Sam Fishman, interview with author, June 6, 1973.

7. According to Burke, "Party is a body of men united for promoting by their joint endeavors the national interest upon some particular principle in which they are all agreed." Edmund Burke, *Works*, Vol. 1, 1865 ed. (Boston: Little, Brown and Co.), p. 530. For an account of Burke's understanding of the relation between political parties and free institutions see Harvey Mansfield, Jr., *Statemanship and Party Government* (Chicago: University of Chicago Press, 1965).

8. See James Q. Wilson, *The Amateur Democrat: Club Politics in Three Cities*

(Chicago: University of Chicago Press, 1962). The importance of social ties for the maintenance of liberal Democratic clubs was emphasized in comments made by California State Senator George Miller, Jr., to the Danville Democratic Club, Danville, California, in September, 1964.

9. Sander Levin, interview with author, May 5, 1971; Morley Winograd, interview with author, August 31, 1971.

10. Sander Levin, interview with author, May 5, 1971.

11. Harold Julian, interview with author, February 23, 1973.

12. Sam Fishman, interview with author, June 6, 1973.

13. John Dewan, interview with author, October 14, 1971.

14. Sander Levin, interview with author, May 5, 1971.

15. Ibid.; Morley Winograd, interview with author, August 31, 1971.

16. Morley Winograd, interview with author, August 31, 1971.

17. Ibid.

18. Ibid.; John Dewan, interview with author, October 14, 1971.

19. Morley Winograd, interview with author, August 31, 1971.

20. Every county in Michigan except three apportioned delegates according to the number of party voters within a precinct. In Wayne, Oakland, and Kent counties the apportionment was one delegate for each precinct no matter how many Democratic or Republican voters had cast ballots within it.

21. John Dewan, interview with author, October 14, 1971.

22. State of Michigan, *Official Canvass of Votes 1970,* p. 10.

23. Ibid., p. 69.

24. Ibid.

25. In 1968 a bare majority of the commissioners were nominally Democrats. Two of these, however, voted with the Republicans, and actual control passed out of Democratic hands.

26. John Dewan, interview with author, October 14, 1971; Morley Winograd, interview with author, August 31, 1971.

27. Michigan Democratic Party, "Voting Trends in Oakland County, 1969–72: A Brief Summary" (internal document, 1973).

28. Ibid.

29. Ibid.

30. *Pontiac Press,* August 11, 1971.

31. *Royal Oak Daily Tribune,* August 11, 1971.

32. Ibid.

PART 4

The Liberal Failure and the Labor Challenge

CHAPTER 10

The Threat to the Center

For twenty years, from the beginning of the liberal-labor alliance in 1948 until the general election of 1968, the UAW and the AFL-CIO had acted together within the Michigan Democratic party. Their growing divergence of opinion on matters of public policy, best exemplified in the field of taxation, had remained for the most part an internal dispute. Even when Walter Reuther led the UAW out of the AFL-CIO in the early part of 1968, the establishment of a separate UAW political organization did not carry with it an opposition of purpose. During the 1968 campaign, the UAW and the AFL-CIO were in complete accord and fully cooperated with each other to elect Democratic candidates to the state legislature and to Congress. In the presidential campaign the two labor organizations formed the major component of the coalition that gave Michigan's electoral vote to Hubert Humphrey. If the UAW's withdrawal from the AFL-CIO had not been made public no one who observed the 1968 campaign would have guessed that the two were no longer part of the same organization. Within a few months of the election, however, the two unions found themselves in public opposition over the selection of the next chairman of the state Democratic party. For the first time in the history of the liberal-labor alliance, labor did not speak with a single voice.

It will be recalled that after Zolton Ferency was driven out of the chairmanship in 1967 the party officers appointed state senator Sander Levin acting chairman. Levin wanted very much to be governor, and the chairmanship provided the best means for him to broaden his contacts within the party and extend his influence beyond the confines of his own legislative district. To remain chairman for more than the unexpired portion of Ferency's two-year term would add nothing to his prospects, and might become an actual hindrance to his ambitions. The next regularly elected chairman would serve a two-year term during which the next gubernatorial election would take place. Levin had taken the party through one election; he wanted to lead the ticket in the next. To combine the chairmanship with a gubernatorial candidacy might have been possible, but the example of Zolton Ferency, who had done it in 1966, did little to encourage emulation. Whatever advantages the chairmanship might have provided in the way of political organization could still be his so long as his successor had an interest in seeing Sander Levin governor of Michigan.

When Levin accepted the temporary position as state chairman he did so with the understanding that because of his legislative duties he would not be expected to devote all his time and energy to party affairs. To handle the day-to-day duties of the office, Levin was permitted to appoint a deputy chairman. He knew who he wanted. James McNeely had been his deputy when he chaired the Oakland County Democratic party, and Levin gave him the same function at the state level. As deputy chairman, McNeely had been in the best possible position to acquire the experience and the support necessary to become a formidable candidate for the elected chairmanship, and he was clearly Levin's choice for the office. With his friend and former assistant occupying the leading position in the state party, Levin's gubernatorial candidacy could at the very least look forward to benign neutrality from the party leadership during a contested Democratic primary. All of this made sense. It only remained to get McNeely elected.

The year 1968 had been one of the most politically divisive any Democrat or for that matter any citizen could remember. The physical violence at the Chicago convention seemed only to bear witness to the sudden inability of the party to engage in the time-honored processes of compromise and conciliation. Nowhere was the party more divided and hostility more open than in Michigan. Humphrey and McCarthy supporters held each other in contempt, and each proclaimed its intention to bring about the political destruction of the other. The only way anyone could keep open a line of communication to both camps was by refusing to become the ally of either. As acting chairman of the state party, Levin had been able to do this in 1968 by withholding his vote as a delegate to the national convention from both Humphrey and McCarthy. Without announcing his intention beforehand—not even to Walter Reuther, who spent an hour with him arguing the wisdom of a vote for Humphrey—Levin cast his ballot for George McGovern. Because McGovern was then perceived as an amiable senator from South Dakota without a prospect in the world of securing the Democratic nomination for the presidency, Levin's vote made neither of the two major camps happy— but far more important for the future, neither was greatly offended.[1]

Levin had managed to walk a political tightrope during the 1968 campaign by acting impartially and professing as his overriding ambition the unification of the party. The AFL-CIO, which had been intensely partisan on behalf of Hubert Humphrey, and the NDC, which had been at least as zealous in its support of Eugene McCarthy, both agreed on the need to restore unity. There was never any clear agreement, however, determining under whose direction unity would be imposed. Once the November election had become

a bitter chapter in party history, the AFL-CIO and the New Democratic Coalition each decided that the chairmanship of the state party ought to be
occupied by someone who instead of remaining neutral would serve as a
spokesman for its own point of view. By the end of the year both had found
candidates. The NDC put forward the candidacy of one of its founders, Otto
Feinstein, and the AFL-CIO agreed to support the deputy secretary of state,
William Hettiger.

Once the third candidate, McNeely, decided to seek the chairmanship
he immediately began to seek the UAW's support. In his judgment it was
only a matter of time before the UAW would decide to throw its considerable
weight behind him; there simply was no other candidate it could support.
Hettiger and Feinstein both suffered from being too closely aligned with
factions that despised each other; victory for either would guarantee the continuation of political division. That was only the beginning, and indeed only
the surface, of an analysis that the UAW would be compelled to make. The
union had only recently become independent because in Walter Reuther's
opinion the AFL-CIO was no longer as progressive as it had once been.
Hettiger's candidacy seemed to confirm Reuther's appraisal; the AFL-CIO's
candidate had a great deal of practical political experience and no discernible
political principles. If he was altogether too pragmatic, Feinstein was just the
opposite. Perfectly expressive of the organization he represented, Feinstein
had little in the way of experience and seemed convinced that politics could
only be elevated by an unyielding commitment to principle. The injury this
attitude would inflict on the prospects of building a coalition formidable
enough to win elections was only compounded by the fact that many of the
principles Feinstein and the NDC proclaimed were not shared by the UAW.
Feinstein had too many principles and Hettiger not nearly enough—and neither of them owed their first allegiance to the UAW. With twice as many
members in Michigan as the AFL-CIO and the NDC combined, the UAW
was not likely to be content with anything less than the undivided loyalty of
the next state Democratic chairman.

McNeely was taking no chances. In each of the six Michigan UAW
regions he entered into regular communication with the most influential local
union officials. He gave particular attention to the western part of the state,
where Democrats had frequently felt left out of party affairs and where the
Democratic vote had begun to show signs of a major increase. Union officials
in the area had been among the most vocal Democrats to point this out and
complain of the relative absence of concern and attention by the state party.
McNeely spent six weeks traveling through the state talking not only to UAW
officials but to party leaders at all levels. He publicly announced his candidacy
at press conferences held on the same day in Detroit, Lansing, and Grand
Rapids. In Grand Rapids one of that city's leading Democratic attorneys asked

McNeely why he was announcing then; for the attorney it made no sense to even launch a candidacy before the UAW made an official endorsement.[2] McNeely, however, did not have long to wait. Two weeks later the union endorsed him and for the first time in the twenty-year history of the liberal-labor coalition, the UAW and the AFL-CIO went into a Democratic state convention prepared to do battle over the chairmanship of the Michigan Democratic party.

When the convention opened in Detroit on the morning of the second Saturday in February, it was already clear that McNeely could count on the largest single block of votes among the assembled delegates. Of the 2,500 delegates, at least 650 were either members of the UAW, or close and reliable friends of the union. McNeely needed an additional 600 to obtain the majority required for election. His campaign had spent several hours in a suite at the Cadillac Hotel on the previous evening examining the strengths and weaknesses of each of the candidates. Based on the best information available, it was believed that McNeely would fall approximately 175 votes short of a simple majority on the first ballot. On a second ballot, however, McNeely's vote would almost certainly increase; he had already obtained a number of second ballot commitments from delegates pledged on the first ballot to one of the other candidates.

It was almost impossible to believe that McNeely could lose. Any defection from the other candidates would almost certainly go to him. No one supporting Hettiger and the AFL-CIO was likely to go with the NDC, and it was if anything even more unlikely that the liberal wing would pass over McNeely in favor of Hettiger. Moreover, the NDC was no longer a solid block. The relatively late entry of a fourth candidate, Bernard Klein, comptroller of Detroit and the candidate of Mayor Cavanagh, had siphoned off some of the strength previously enjoyed by Otto Feinstein. In addition to causing some defections from the ranks of liberals from the university communities of Ann Arbor, East Lansing, and Kalamazoo, Klein's candidacy challenged Feinstein for support among black delegates from the First and Thirteenth Congressional Districts. In the First District in particular this seemed, at least before the convention actually got under way, to be of great importance.

John Conyers, the congressman from the First District, could be counted on to oppose McNeely simply because McNeely was supported by the UAW. He had not yet overcome the hostility toward the union evidenced in his first campaign for Congress. Unlike most Democratic congressmen, Conyers took an active part in the district organization and had considerable influence within it, but no one could be quite certain how far that influence extended. When Conyers decided to support Feinstein, McNeely believed that at best the UAW might be able to deliver half of the district delegation, and that most of the other half would belong to Feinstein. The few votes that were left would be scattered between Hettiger, who would have the backing of a handful of appointees of the secretary of state, and Klein, who would pick up what little support Mayor Cavanagh might have in the district.

After each of the four candidates had been placed in nomination, the convention began balloting. At the end of the first ballot McNeely had failed to accumulate a majority, but was only 119 votes short instead of the anticipated 175. That he had come closer than predicted was largely because the UAW delivered not 50 but 80 percent of the vote in the First District. Before the first ballot had ended, McNeely was approached by Walter Elliott, an assistant to the secretary of state and one of Hettiger's floor leaders. Elliott told McNeely that it was clear no one was going to win on the first ballot and proposed a meeting behind the podium with Jim Hare, the secretary of state, Gus Scholle of the AFL-CIO, and Bill Hettiger. Elliott vaguely suggested that the purpose of the meeting would be to work something out. McNeely knew he had enough second ballot commitments to win, but he knew also that if he refused to meet with the AFL-CIO and its candidate before the second ballot began he would antagonize people he would have to work with as chairman. On the other hand, he was completely convinced that the real purpose of the proposed meeting was "to permit the AFL-CIO to extract its pound of flesh in exchange for second ballot support."[3] McNeely wanted to avoid, if at all possible, being held hostage by Scholle, Hare, and Hettiger. There was an alternative.

After the Eighth and the Eleventh Districts had cast their votes on the first ballot, McNeely approached each delegation and told them that if those who had voted against him changed their votes at the end of the roll call their district could take credit for the election of the next chairman; on the second ballot every district would change over and there would be no credit to claim. This appeal to self-interest succeeded in the Eleventh. The district chairman, Tom Baldini, got the delegation to change its vote to a unanimous declaration for McNeely. Once this happened almost every other district fell into place. Gus Scholle, who could recognize a political fact as well as anyone, turned the Fifteenth and Sixteenth Districts around for McNeely. And while he claimed the credit for this, he knew that the Eleventh had gone first and he also knew that McNeely knew it. All that was left to the three other candidates was the chance to address the convention and move that the election of Jim McNeely be made unanimous. Otto Feinstein, on behalf of himself and, it is to be presumed, the NDC, told the assembled delegates that he looked forward to working with the next chairman in a unified Democratic party. Not everyone believed him.

On the surface, the party appeared to have achieved a greater measure of harmony than might have been expected during the turbulent months of the 1968 presidential campaign. Both the left and the right wings had been denied control of the state organization and deprived of the power to exalt themselves at the expense of their opposite numbers. The middle or moderate section of the party, supported mainly by the UAW and sharing the union's belief that only a party that could at least be tolerated by both its left and right wings could possibly obtain majority approval in the electorate, had elected the new chairman. Nor was there any immediate danger that either wing would bolt the party. The right, which was scarcely reactionary or even conservative, had been inspired mainly by the desire of the AFL-CIO to continue as the predominant labor power in the party after it lost the UAW. Leaders of the AFL-CIO might continue to blame the NDC for causing Hubert Humphrey the problems that elected Richard Nixon, but the Democratic party they had helped to build was still their political home. The left (the NDC) however, had not been involved in the early battles to create the liberal-labor coalition, and had no very great attachment to it. Party allegiance was for them largely contingent on how well the party served as a vehicle for the reform of American politics. They had failed to capture the chairmanship of the party; it remained to be seen whether they might still influence the direction the party would take.

Those who believed that the reform of American politics depended on the reform of the Democratic party—and few adherents of the new politics doubted that dependency—had been provided with evidence that this might be a real possibility a month before McNeely's election when the acting chairman, Sander Levin, announced the formation of a commission to study political reform. The Democratic Party Commission on Political Reform was headed by Dr. William Haber of the University of Michigan. Its fifty-four members represented what was then viewed as a comprehensive cross-section of the party. The party leadership, the UAW, and the AFL-CIO, as well as blacks and Latinos, were all represented; Otto Feinstein was a member; Levin, who was about to end his period of service as acting chairman, appointed himself associate chairman. That only four of the fifty-four members were women was a fact no one then perceived as either out of the ordinary or as the potential source of any serious objection.

The establishment of a commission on political reform, especially one that included in its membership the major forces within the Democratic party, seemed to suggest agreement with the NDC that there was a need for reform. Everyone might agree that reform was needed, but it was not nearly as certain that there was any common understanding of what those reforms should be. There was not even a clear statement about what was actually to be reformed. Levin, who appointed the commission's members, and Haber, who agreed to chair it, seemed to have somewhat different opinions on what the commission was about. In announcing the formation of the commission, Levin stated, "The role of this commission will be to scrutinize every aspect of the political process to determine what changes need to be made to guarantee every citizen the chance to participate fully and fairly in the political system."[4] While Levin seemed to hold out the promise that the commission would discover ways and means of ensuring every citizen a direct part in politics, Haber appeared concerned with having the commission investigate methods by which to ensure that citizens were represented in the system: "Both parties have a vital stake in a political process in which the people know they are being fully and fairly represented."[5] The difference between Levin and Haber was nothing more nor less than the difference between reforms to bring about *direct* participation and reforms to produce *fair* representation.

The difference pointed to a basic dilemma: Should a political party be the organized expression of the opinion of those who directly participate in it, or should a party somehow organize itself to represent the opinion of those who, for whatever reason, do not directly participate? The answer to this question would have enormous consequences. To adopt the second alternative and attempt to make a party the representative of those who did not directly participate raised the obvious questions of who was to be represented, and by whom. To increase their appeal to the electorate, parties have traditionally adopted public positions that were not always identical with the opinions of the active party membership. But the normal and ordinary methods of compromise and conciliation were not at issue. Instead, the question that came to dominate discussion was whether, in addition to a fair opportunity for individuals to run for party office at every level, some groups should be guaranteed representation regardless of the outcome of those elections. But before this question could be addressed, or for that matter even clearly formulated, the state Democratic party, at the insistence of its liberal wing and with the support if not the enthusiastic approval of the UAW, supplied at least the beginnings of an answer.

When the party met in convention at the end of August in 1970, there were two agendas, one written and the other too well known to require formal acknowledgement. The written agenda outlined the order and procedure for the selection of the party's nominees for lieutenant governor, secretary of state, attorney general, two supreme court justices, two members of the state board of education, and two members of each of the governing boards of the state's three largest universities. There were also provisions for the adoption of resolutions expressing the position of the Democratic party on a variety of public issues. The unwritten agenda, which served as the constant backdrop for the written one, contained the double imperatives of electoral politics: the election of the Democratic candidate for governor and the reelection of Senator Philip A. Hart. This agenda had as its most important priority the retention of the support of the party's liberal wing. Ever since the debacle of 1968, the party leadership constantly had in mind the need to do whatever was necessary to avoid a repetition of the division that had preceded and presaged defeat. No one had expended more energy or contrived more carefully to avoid a rupture with the liberal wing than Sander Levin. He had steered a middle course between the Humphrey and McCarthy campaigns at the national convention and had established a commission to investigate and remedy the abuses liberals had complained about. Now, as the winner of the Democratic gubernatorial primary earlier in the month, he was especially reluctant to do anything that might antagonize the left.

Levin's interest in conciliating the left was more than a simple continuation of the policy he had followed as acting chairman. He was now the Democratic nominee for governor, but he had gotten that nomination only by defeating Zolton Ferency, one of the most articulate and outspoken advocates of the new politics. His victory, moreover, had been achieved with the active assistance of organized labor. Faced with the possibility of a second Ferency candidacy, the UAW had taken the unusual step of making a formal endorsement in the primary. In the 1960 primary contest between Hare and Swainson, labor had taken no official position and much of the secondary leadership had proceeded to give assistance to Swainson. In the two succeeding elections no serious primary contest had developed and no decision by labor was required. Fearful that without its intervention Ferency might once again become the Democratic nominee, and convinced that a Ferency candidacy would end as it had in 1966 with a Republican victory of major proportions, the UAW endorsed Levin in the primary and helped to deprive Ferency of a second chance.[6]

Levin wanted no trouble with the liberals, and for their part the liberals really wanted no trouble with Levin. He had, they believed, dealt with them fairly as chairman and he was, if not their first choice, at least an acceptable candidate for governor. From their own point of view the liberals only wanted the adoption of several resolutions that were nothing more than what reasonable and decent people of principle could all agree on. First, the war in Vietnam was clearly immoral if not actually criminal, and therefore a refusal to take part in it was commendable if not heroic. This issue seemed to matter a great deal to the NDC and not very much to many others. In the absence of any powerful arguments to the contrary, the Michigan Democratic party called the draft "destructive of individual freedoms," and adopted a resolution that concluded:

> Whereas the Democratic Party of Michigan has taken a strong stand acknowledging our distress with the current warfare in Indochina; and, Whereas, there are U.S. citizens now in prison, under indictment or without the country who

also have expressed distress with our policy in Indochina; Be it Resolved that the Democratic Party of Michigan supports a general amnesty for all opponents of said warfare.[7]

Having proclaimed that "the very essense of selective service is involuntary servitude" and therefore, presumably, in violation of the Thirteenth Amendment, the convention finished with amnesty and moved on to abortion. Under the temporary tutelage of its liberal wing, the party asserted the existence of an inalienable right in addition to those detailed in the Declaration of Independence. The convention concluded that beside life, liberty, and the pursuit of happiness, "it is an inherent natural right of a woman to control her own procreativity." It was then only axiomatic that a woman could curtail that procreativity. From this premise it seemed simply logical to conclude that abortion could not be prohibited. The convention put the Democratic party on record against existing state abortion laws and in favor of "legislation which permits any woman to obtain an abortion in a hospital accredited by the State of Michigan on the recommendation of a physician licensed by this State."[8] At the time there were some who thought that the amnesty resolution might not be attractive to those voters, especially white blue-collar workers, who believed that the failure to punish draft resisters was to implicitly approve the refusal to bear arms in defense of the country. There was also some doubt that a resolution calling for the legalization of abortion would contribute much to the continuation of Catholic attachment to the Democratic party and its candidates. At the time, however, the immediate potential source of opposition was the liberal wing, and the immediate method of gaining support was to let their resolutions pass.

On the surface, neither amnesty nor abortion seemed to have anything to do with the question of political and party reform. In fact, however, both resolutions were closely related to it. The resolution on abortion was only a part, if an important part, of a broad program put forward to diminish so far as practicable the differences between male and female members of American society. Eight separate resolutions were incorporated into a women's rights platform.[9] Seven of the eight points were directed toward eliminating various forms of discrimination that could be remedied by state or federal legislation. The remaining demand dealt with a matter that was entirely within the authority of the Democratic party, the representation of women within the party itself. Nothing less than absolute parity between the sexes was called for. Half the members of the county and district executive boards were to be women, and in addition the state delegation to the national Democratic convention in 1972 was to be made up of equal numbers of men and women. Moreover, every committee at state conventions would be composed of one male and one female from each of the state's nineteen congressional districts. The demand for numerical equality at what was in effect every level of party organization was not based simply on the numerical division within the general population. That statistic could as easily have supported the claim that there was no real danger of women being systematically excluded from participation in party affairs. With half the population, women faced no apparent obstacle to providing at least half the precinct delegates and, therewith, at least half of those delegated to represent the lower levels at the higher levels of the party organization. Thus something beside numbers had to be invoked as the rationale for a demand that a series of elections within the party be required to produce equality between the sexes.

Abortion had been advanced as a right that had been denied. It was an inherent right and could not have been voluntarily surrendered; if not voluntarily given up it must have been wrongfully taken away. It was not difficult to conclude through this reasoning that women had been subjected to some kind of oppression, and that conclusion was precisely the premise of the women's rights platform. The opening clauses read:

> Whereas we recognize that women have traditionally been placed by society in roles which denied them full realization of their potential; and Whereas today's events and circumstances have created a more significant awareness of the role that women must play in social and political action. . . .[10]

Women were oppressed and were only beginning to realize just how oppressed they really were. Precluded from realizing their full potential because of the place to which society had traditionally assigned them, women could not secure their rightful position and power within the Democratic party if they were only provided equality of opportunity. If that were sufficient, their numbers within the various bodies in the Democratic party would already be in the same (roughly equal) proportion that they were within the population. The absence of equal representation, in other words, was proof positive that the oppression of women could be ended only by requiring equality of result.

It was exceedingly difficult, and as it turned out, impossible, for the Democratic party to resist this claim for equality. For years the Michigan party, in compliance with the rules of the national party, had elected a national committeeman and a national committeewoman. The extension of this division to every level of party organization did not seem in any sense a radical departure from any reasonable principle. No one seemed to notice that at one blow the Democratic party had adopted the principle that representation should correspond not to the proportions of membership in the party, but to the proportions found in the electorate. Moreover, it had accepted the principle that the outcome of elections to party office must comply with a preordained result. Nor did anyone inquire what might be the potential consequence of an arrangement that established, at least in this one instance, a quota system in the Democratic party. Having accepted the claim that women were entitled to power within the party in strict proportion to their numbers in the population, how could the claim of any other group for equal treatment be resisted, especially if the claim was accompanied by the allegation of oppression and oppression was proven by the absence of that representation now demanded?

This was not merely a question for idle speculation. The state convention also adopted a series of resolutions designed to remedy past injustices to another group. Though the precise category was nowhere defined within them, the "youth resolutions" claimed that youth, like women, had been deprived of its rightful place in society: "Whereas youth has not been given equal or even partial representation in the process of making decisions affecting their lives" the Democratic party went on record in favor of proposals that would guarantee that representation. Interestingly enough, however, there was no proposal to guarantee participation in party affairs in proportion to their numbers in the population; there was instead a tepid suggestion that "it is a policy of the Democratic Party of Michigan that students and young people must be welcomed into all activities of the American political system." Presumably this included the activities of the Michigan Democratic party. However, not party but public office was to be subject to the requirement that the outcome of elections comply with a specified result. Under provisions of the resolution adopted, the Michigan Democratic party was to

> demand immediate action on a number of . . . bills and resolutions including the following two: Election of a student at a state institution of higher learning to the State Board of Education, and election of a student member to the governing boards of state operated institutions of higher learning.[11]

With the youth resolutions and the women's rights platform, the Democratic party established the basis upon which any group could lay claim to representation both within the party and within the government. If the latter was impossible to satisfy, it could easily be translated to a demand for proportional representation on the slate of candidates selected by the party in convention every two years. Still, these were problems which, if they ever developed, would only occur in the distant future—that is to say, after the 1970 election. And in that election the resolutions on abortion and amnesty were far more significant.

With considerable assistance from the UAW, Sander Levin had won the nomination for governor and had managed to preserve peace in the Democratic party. In light of the events of 1968 this seemed to be a noteworthy achievement. A divided party had been the constant nightmare of every major political figure who had its well-being at heart. By supporting the resolutions of the liberal wing, Levin and the union had done what was apparently required to prevent substantial defections by the left. Unlike the presidential campaign of Hubert Humphrey, the gubernatorial campaign of Sander Levin was going to begin with the support of both labor and the liberals. Levin had every reason to be pleased with the outcome of the convention, and every right to look forward to a general election in which opposition would come from the Republican and not the Democratic party.

One of the lessons of 1968 was that the Democratic party could not win a national election if it was deeply divided. It was not the only lesson, however, and the UAW had drawn several others. In an internal document analyzing the 1968 election, it made two major points. The first was that there now existed "a great big new political constituency out there waiting for political parties to understand, to organize, and to weave into the organizational fabric." This group, "the affluent middle class constituency" which had responded to the appeals of McCarthy, Kennedy, and Rockefeller, would constitute 35 percent of the electorate by 1972. Their concerns were with "environmental issues and the whole 'quality of life' syndrome which loom big in Kennedy and Rockefeller tactics. They were virtually missing from Humphrey's and Nixon's appeal to voters."[12] To the extent that this group was represented within the party by those liberals who had supported McCarthy or Kennedy in 1968, Levin and the UAW had done everything possible to give them the feeling of full participation within the party organization.

The other major lesson drawn from 1968 seemed to look in an entirely different direction, one that was perhaps not completely compatible with the policy of retaining the allegiance of the new affluent liberal: "The real key to success in future political contests is to bridge the gap between the old hardrock Democratic core of blue collar, urban voters and the white collar suburban voters." The white-collar suburbanites mentioned here are not to be confused with the affluent liberals mentioned earlier. These suburban voters, and the blue-collar urban voters, "can be both suckered into voting for a Wallace as 1968 shows." Indeed, it was likely that the cause of this phenomenon would continue and intensify: "There is bound to be more alienation and disgruntlement with the existing political system among some blue collar types who cozied up to Wallace and then eased off in the final stages of the campaign."[13]

A number of lessons resulted from 1968, but there did not appear to be any serious attempt to decide what conclusion should be drawn from them. The nomination of Hubert Humphrey was unacceptable to the left, but it was also not agreeable to those on the right who believed in George Wallace. The agreement between left and right on the deficiencies of Humphrey might be explained by a few ingenious intellectuals as reflective of a common feeling of alienation from the American political system, but the plain fact was that in 1968 the left thought Humphrey too much of a hawk on Vietnam and the right thought him not nearly hawkish enough. And that was only the beginning of the differences between them. The left thought it only proper to interrupt Humphrey's speeches with demonstrations against the war; the right loved it when Wallace suggested he would never stop his speech, or his automobile, for a demonstrator. Within the party, however, the right was not an organized force. There simply were no spokesmen for those Democrats who had supported or came close to supporting George Wallace. The right had a constituency of an undertermined size and no spokesman in the Democratic party; the left had spokesmen in every corner and in every caucus. Sander Levin had managed to convince Democratic liberals to remain in the party; after the August convention he faced the more formidable difficulty of retaining the electoral support of Democratic conservatives.

By adopting the resolutions for amnesty and abortion, the Democratic state convention provided the opposition with two potentially powerful weapons. A fair number of Republican candidates running for the state legislature in conservative districts were quick to label their Democratic opponents members of a party that was willing to turn its back on the sacrifice of life made by patriotic servicemen. Governor William Milliken, the Republican incumbent, did not join in the attack; he had no need to call attention to the Democratic position so long as others were so eager to do it for him. Milliken claimed to be a moderate, and knew full well that in a contest with a moderate Democrat that claim would not cost him conservative support. The abortion issue was a more difficult matter. It did not follow normal or traditional divisions between liberals and conservatives—it seemed mainly to divide Catholics from Protestants and Jews. Moreover, it was not an issue that could in any real sense be compromised. You were for the legalization of abortion or you were not. The question was nothing more nor less than whether you believed that the unborn fetus was a human being and therewith endowed with a soul. The Catholic vote, traditionally Democratic, was fundamentally antiabortion, and its position was as adamant as it was clear: the fetus was a living human being and abortion was simple murder; legalization was out of the question. Whatever temptation there might have been for the governor to win favor with Catholics by adopting an antiabortion position, he managed to resist it. He did, however, select a Catholic as his running mate, and he did have ready at hand a method of attracting Catholic votes without sacrificing his own private point of view.

Abortion was an attack on the moral and theological principles of Catholics. Paying tuition for their children at parochial schools while still having to pay property taxes to support public schools was an attack on their economic well-being. It did not seem fair to the parents of children in parochial schools that they should have to pay what was in their eyes a double tax. It seemed a serious grievance given the fact that without parochial schools, the increased burden on the public schools would require a substantial increase in the public budget for education. To offset in part the cost of parochial education, the Michigan Catholic Conference had collected enough petition signatures to place on the ballot a constitutional amendment to permit some public assistance for private education. Labeled "parochiaid" by its opponents, the measure provided the means for a Republican to secure Catholic support. Adhering to the doctrine of the separation of church and state, Levin opposed the proposal, and Milliken, who thought it best to leave constitutional questions to the courts, endorsed it. Among Eastern and Southern European Catholics, a group sometimes referred to as the Slavic community, support for parochiaid brought Milliken about 42 percent of the vote. Levin had kept a majority in that group, but his 58 percent of the Slavic vote was considerably less than even Zolton Ferency had managed to collect while being beaten by George Romney three-to-two in 1966. "Had Levin run as well with Slavs as liberal Neil Staebler did in 1964 against George Romney, or Zolton Ferency did against Romney in 1966, he would have . . . won."[14] But Levin did not win. He lost to William Milliken by the narrow margin of 44,000 votes.[15]

Though perhaps decisive in the 1970 gubernatorial campaign, parochiaid could be dismissed as a political aberration that had little if anything to do with a fundamental realignment of party preferences. In the absence of a one-time issue like parochiaid, the Catholic vote could reasonably be expected to return to its traditional Democratic allegiance. Of more immediate importance for its long-term prospects, the Democratic party had entered and emerged from the 1970 campaign intact, as it had not in 1968. The nightmare of discord and division seemed to have receded into a permanent past. With the UAW using its predominant power in the party to secure continued moderation and with the liberal wing satisfied with the adoption of the reforms it had promoted, there seemed nothing to prevent a unified party effort to defeat Richard Nixon in 1972. Then it was discovered that there was no agreement at all on the precise method Michigan Democrats would use to determine who they wanted as the Democratic nominee for president of the United States.

Notes

1. For an account of Levin's ability to bridge the gap between the Humphrey and McCarthy forces before the national convention see Douglas Crase, "Michigan Democrats in Disarray," *Nation,* March 11, 1968, p. 340.

2. James McNeely, interview with author, May 14, 1973.

3. Ibid.

4. *Lansing State Journal,* January 3, 1969.

5. Ibid.

6. Levin defeated Ferency nearly two-to-one: 304,343 to 167,442. State of Michigan, *Official Canvass of Votes 1970,* p. 4.

7. "Resolution on the Draft," Michigan Democratic Party Convention, August, 1970.

8. "Resolution on Abortion," Michigan Democratic Party Convention, August, 1970.

9. "Women's Rights Platform," Michigan Democratic Party Convention, August, 1970.

10. Ibid.

11. "Youth Resolutions," Michigan Democratic Party Convention, August, 1970.

12. United Auto Workers, "What Are The Lessons of 1968?" (internal document).

13. Ibid.

14. Mark R. Levy and Michael S. Kramer, *The Ethnic Factor: How America's Minorities Decide Elections* (New York: Simon and Schuster, 1972), p. 154.

15. State of Michigan, *Official Canvass of Votes 1970,* p. 47.

CHAPTER 11
Union Domination

In 1969, Sander Levin established a reform commission as part of his continuing effort to keep the liberal wing firmly attached to the Michigan Democratic party. In that same year a national commission, the Commission on Party Structure and Delegate Selection (or the McGovern Commission), was set up. In the judgment of some observers it was designed to give liberal Democrats the decisive voice in party affairs. "From the time it was set up in early 1969 by Fred Harris . . . the McGovern Commission was an instrument of the New Politics wing of the party."[1] Most of the controversy surrounding the rules proposed by the McGovern Commission and adopted by the Democratic National Committee centered on the provisions to end discrimination within the party. Guideline A-1, entitled "Discrimination on the Basis of Race, Color, Creed, or National Origin," included a requirement that seemed by implication to call for a quota system.

> State Parties must overcome the effect of past discrimination by affirmative steps to encourage minority group participation, including representation of minority groups on the National Convention delegation in reasonable relationship to the group's presence in the population of the state.[2]

The key phrase was "reasonable relationship." If an actual quota was not required, what would be permissible within the unspecified reasonable relationship? The difficulty was scarcely solved by the apparent disclaimer that "This is not to be interpreted as a mandatory imposition of quotas."[3] That it could scarcely be interpreted any other way seemed confirmed when the commission issued an administrative memo endorsed by the national Democratic chairman Lawrence O'Brien, stating that representation of a minority group in numbers less than its proportion of the total population would constitute prima facie evidence of a violation of the guidelines.[4]

Minority groups were henceforth to be entitled to representation in the Democratic party in exact proportion to their numbers in the general population. The same treatment was to be accorded two other groups, one of which did not constitute a minority, and one of which was to be found in every minority group. Guideline A-2, entitled "Discrimination on the Basis of Age or Sex," adopted language similar to Guideline A-1, but applied it to young people and women.

> State parties must take affirmative steps to overcome the effects of past discrimination by encouraging representation on the National Convention delegation of young people (defined as people not more than 30 nor less than 18 years of age) and women in reasonable relationship to their presence in the population of the state.[5]

Despite a repetition of the disclaimer that the guideline "is not to be interpreted as a mandatory imposition of quota," once again a quota was the only possible interpretation.

The work of the McGovern Commission was made possible in the first instance by the failure of the organized Democratic party to anticipate the rising demand for participation by the liberal and affluent constituency that Eugene McCarthy and to some extent Robert Kennedy had appealed to in the 1968 presidential primaries. There was clearly a need for reform, but it was doubtful whether that reform could be carried out more competently by the theoreticians of the new politics, than by the practitioners of the old. The situation, and the consequences that followed, had more than a superficial similarity to what Tocqueville had described nearly a century and a half earlier.

> Since no free institutions and, as a result, no experienced and organized political parties existed any longer in France, and since in the absence of any political groups of this sort the guidance of public opinion came entirely into the hands of the philosophers, that is to say the intellectuals, it was only to be expected that the directives of the Revolution should take the form of abstract principles, highly generalized theories and that political realities would be largely overlooked.[6]

The adherence to abstract principle in the face of political reality was nowhere better demonstrated than in the treatment accorded minorities by the McGovern Commission rules. In the attempt to end discrimination against minorities in principle, Guideline A-1 actually diminished the potential power of minorities in the party. Under A-1, the black membership on the Michigan delegation to the national convention would be 11 percent, the percentage of blacks in the Michigan population. As even the most obtuse precinct delegate knew, however, blacks invariably gave a minimum of 90 percent of their votes to Democratic candidates. Perhaps as much as 20 percent of the Democratic vote in Michigan was black. Guideline A-1, however, was not the least bit interested in the extent to which any minority supported the party. It was easier to define a percentage of the population than to measure a percentage of the party vote or make a judgment about the importance of a particular group to the party's electoral prospects.

Guideline A-2 was if anything an even greater departure from political reality. Minorities, and perhaps especially blacks, could claim not only to have been subject to discrimination and therefore to have a common interest in the removal of obstacles to the full exercise of their rights as citizens, but to share a common set of beliefs regarding economic matters. Blacks had been attracted to and had become among the most dedicated members of the New Deal coalition precisely because they were, with few exceptions, economically disadvantaged. Women and youth, on the other hand, were present in every group and thus could have no shared opinion as such on economic issues—or, for that matter, on any substantive question of public policy. However, this was not apparent to the intellectuals of the new politics. For if, as their Michigan adherents had declared in the 1970 Democratic state convention, women and youth were both the subject of oppression, both must share an interest in the elimination of that oppression. Abstract principle demonstrated that women and youth could not possibly be advocates of the status quo—that is, they could not possibly be conservative. According to this interesting logic women and youth were necessarily liberal, and the few who did not seem to share this point of view served as further evidence of the continuation of that oppression. The false-consciousness of the oppressed would be overcome only when those who had come to understand the objective world and how to change it had greater opportunities for public expression.

Guidelines A-1 and A-2 created enormous difficulties for both the national and the state Democratic party. The greatest immediate difficulty faced by the UAW and the Michigan party, however, was caused by still other requirements of the McGovern Commission rules. One of the charges made by the new politics forces at the 1968 national convention, and one of the explanations given for their failure to defeat Hubert Humphrey, was that the selection of delegates to the convention had been made by people who had themselves been chosen long before anyone had any idea of who would be the candidates for the presidential nomination. Michigan Democrats could not deny this allegation. Members of the Michigan delegation had been selected by delegates to a state convention chosen by precinct delegates elected in the primary election of August, 1966. These precinct delegates might have had a great deal of interest in the gubernatorial election of that year, but could not possibly have argued that their selection demonstrated a clear choice for the presidential nomination of candidates who were not then running. It is doubtful that anyone elected precinct delegate in August, 1966 so much as suspected the possibility that the Democratic nominee might be anyone other than Lyndon Baines Johnson. No serious objections were made, then, when the 1968 national convention added to the call to the 1972 convention a requirement that the delegate selection process begin within the calendar year of the convention. The McGovern Commission rules were emphatic on this point. Guideline C-4 stated: "State Parties must prohibit any practices by which officials elected or appointed before the calendar year of the Convention choose nominating committees or propose or endorse a slate of delegates."[7]

The only problem with the requirement was that the state party had absolutely no legal authority to make any change in the system of Michigan elections. The only way to comply with the directive of the National Committee was to change the state law, and that required the cooperation of the governor, a Republican. From the point of view of the party leadership, including the UAW, the most desirable tactic would be to advance the date for the election of precinct delegates to the early spring of even-numbered years. That would permit the newly elected precinct delegates to meet in county and district conventions to select their representatives to a state convention that would in turn select the delegation to the national convention. The party would be able to comply with the requirement of Guideline C-4 without removing the party organization from the selection process itself. The alternative change, a direct primary, would deprive the party of any influence in the selection of the delegation to its own national convention. Voters would cast their ballots directly for a presidential candidate, and each candidate, because of Guideline B-5, which expressly excluded the unit rule, would receive a proportion of the delegation corresponding to his percentage of the total vote cast. The governor, who like every other member of his party knew Richard Nixon was going to be the Republican nominee, adopted the classic stance against politics and chose the people over the politicians. He announced that he was all in favor of letting the voters decide and for that reason would support legislation authorizing a presidential primary in Michigan. As one union official put it: "Milliken really screwed us on that one."[8]

Milliken was a Republican, but half the senate and a majority of the house were Democrats. In order to obtain the governor's consent, it might be necessary to give the citizenry a way to express its preference for a presidential candidate, but it was not clear that this had to take the form of a direct primary. The legislature could pass a bill providing for a spring election in which candidates for precinct delegate would be permitted to express a preference for a particular presidential candidate. This would satisfy the governor's insistence on direct voter participation and would also leave the party some influence over the composition of the delegation to the national convention. The UAW, at least, thought this would work and was determined to force the issue. In its judgment there was no other choice. It was violently opposed to a presidential primary because of the expense and the likely result.

Over the years, as we have seen, the UAW had built up substantial influence within the county and district organizations of the state Democratic party. With representation in virtually every county and district in the state, the union could exert influence at every level of the party and at every step of the process that began with the election of precinct delegates and culminated in the selection of the state delegation to the national convention. Groups like the New Democratic Coalition might secure significant and even majority strength in Kalamazoo County or Washtenaw County, but that strength was greatly diluted when filtered through first the district and then the state convention. Allied with the political forces of the AFL-CIO, the UAW could lead the Democratic party to select a delegation that would support almost any candidate it chose. This ability would be eliminated as a source of strength in national politics if the party organization was circumvented by a direct presidential primary. UAW influence would then depend on its ability to affect the outcome of a statewide election, and although it had the manpower and the money to do that more effectively than perhaps any other interest in Michigan politics, the price would be high. Whatever was expended on a presidential primary would reduce what was available for other campaigns. In addition, it was doubtful that the union, no matter how great its effort, could influence the electorate to anything like the same degree it could influence the party. This fear was paramount in 1972, when in the considered judgment of the UAW leadership a state Democratic primary could conceivably give George Wallace a plurality of the vote and thus the largest single bloc of Michigan delegates to the Democratic national convention.

The monthly meetings of the officers of the Michigan Democratic party normally alternated between the party headquarters in Detroit and Lansing. The problem presented by the governor's support for a presidential primary, however, could neither wait for the normal monthly meeting nor be resolved in only a single session. Three meetings were held at the Holiday Inn in Howell, midway between Lansing and Detroit, before agreement was reached on a specific proposal to recommend to the Democratic state central committee. Howell was convenient; it was also more likely to provide a cover of secrecy. The issue was too important and potentially explosive to be discussed without a guarantee of confidentality. That guarantee collapsed when an assistant to Congressman John Conyers walked into the meeting room and took a seat. The chairman, Jim McNeely, had not invited him, but he did not ask the intruder to leave. After the meeting, Conyers's assistant told *Detroit News* reporter Bob Pisor not only that the meeting had taken place but that during it Sam Fishman of the UAW had verbally attacked Sander Levin. There had been a difference of opinion between Levin and Fishman on the relative advantages of a presidential primary, but Levin had not been subject to anything that could properly be labeled an attack. The story broke, and Democrats around the state were led to believe that there was a violent disagreement among the leadership about whether to support a presidential primary. In fact, the leadership, at this its third and final meeting, had agreed to oppose a direct presidential primary and to instead recommend to the state central committee a plan for a spring election in which candidates for precinct delegate could express their presidential preference. The UAW had obtained the unanimous support of the elected party leadership for this position.

Labor was not pleased with the story that appeared in the *Detroit News,* but there was less criticism of Conyers's assistant for telling it than of Jim McNeely for permitting his presence in the first place. McNeely's credibility was about to fall much further. A few hours before the state central committee meeting was scheduled to begin, a special meeting of the resolutions committee convened. No one, including McNeely, had bothered to inform the UAW of this. Without representation from labor, the resolutions committee reported out two resolutions for the consideration of the state central committee. One embodied the plan agreed upon by the party officers in their meeting in Howell. The other called for a direct presidential primary, even though the party officers, at the insistence of the UAW, had already agreed to oppose it. Instead of acting on what the leadership had agreed to recommend, the state central committee was now asked to judge between two different proposals. What the leadership had met three times to resolve, the resolutions committee had undone. The UAW would have to begin its fight all over again.

The UAW and the NDC agreed on one thing: a direct primary would significantly decrease the influence of the organized Democratic party in the selection of a delegation to the Democratic national convention. But where labor saw a serious threat not only to its own influence over the makeup of the delegation to the national convention but to the ability of the party organization to engage in those acts of compromise and concession that would unite Democrats behind a candidate with the broadest appeal, the forces of the new politics found the promise of a more open and more responsive political system.[9] The whole problem, in the view of the new politics, was precisely in the arts of compromise that labor seemed to praise. Compromise necessarily resulted in the selection of candidates that had the broadest appeal to the established power blocs within the party, and instead of a choice between the best the parties could produce, the electorate was given a choice between the lesser of two evils.[10] The presidential campaign of 1968, which for many of the new politics adherents seemed to be the beginning and the end of American history, proved this beyond reasonable doubt. Who would argue that the choice between Humphrey and Nixon was anything other than a choice between evils?

Nor was any of this at all necessary. A party that left the selection of its nominee to the unfettered discretion of the people could count on the continued support of the people. Open up the process, permit the direct participation of the voter who was not represented by the powerful organized interests, and all the millions who had been alienated from the system would end their years of silence and take an active part in public affairs. It was hard not to detect in all this a repetition of the claim advanced by conservatives in 1964 that what the people were waiting for was a choice not an echo. But unlike the Goldwater argument of 1964 that, presented with a clear conservative choice, millions would turn out on election day who had never been inspired to vote before, the new politics argument could at least cite one substantial fact in support of the theory. In 1972 there would be millions of Americans who would vote for the first time, not because they had hitherto ignored the opportunity, but because they had never before been enfranchised. By lowering the age of eligibility from twenty-one to eighteen, the electorate had been expanded, and, in the eyes of the apostles of youth, potentially enlightened.

When the issue of a direct presdiential primary was joined at the state central committee meeting the outcome seemed certain. Those who supported the direct primary had only the votes of the liberal faction and the moral as well as the vocal support of most of those who attended but were not members of the committee. This group, composed mainly of students, was larger than normal because of the decision, made months before, to hold the meeting in the student union at Michigan State University. The opposition was led by the labor contingent and the eleven officers of the state party. Labor could expect to win, if only by a narrow margin, and at first it seemed to do precisely that. When the roll was called and the tabulation completed, the direct primary resolution failed by a single vote. At this point, troubled by the consequences of their action, two who had voted against, now asked that their votes be recorded in favor of the direct primary. One of those who switched explained his action by claiming that he had not fully understood the extent to which this question was of significance to the newly enfranchised young voters. He was cheered loudly and cursed quietly. The argument, which had been made in the debate by a student, that the action of the state central committee would determine whether youth would believe that the Democratic party was really interested in listening to the voice of the young, carried the day. The two committee members who switched were not alone in yielding to the demand that the only way to prove that one had listened to the young was to agree with what they said. Confounding those who thought there had been an agreement on the issue, seven of the eleven elected party officers voted to support the direct primary. A few of the seven later suggested they had been swayed by the public pressure generated in the course of the debate; all argued that the conclusion reached in the leadership discussions had not been binding on them.[11]

The state Democratic chairman did not desert the UAW on the presidential primary vote, but none of the officers who did suffered more for it. McNeely had permitted the situation that led to public disclosure of the private leadership meetings, had failed to notify labor of the meeting of the resolutions committee, and then, in the clearest demonstration of an inability to lead, had lost the support of seven of his own officers. The lesson seemed obvious; the party was without leadership and, as a result, had chosen a course directly opposed to what the UAW believed was in the party's best interest. This belief was communicated to the party officers almost immediately. At the next officers' meeting, Sam Fishman, representing the UAW, requested an executive session of the party leadership. Fishman and Bill Marshall of the AFL-CIO castigated the officers for failing to abide by their own agreements, claimed they had been dishonest, and stated an unwillingness to work with them in the future. Marshall blamed the chairman for failing to exercise leadership when it was necessary and when, moreover, it would not have been difficult to do so. Both the UAW and the AFL-CIO would continue to support the Democratic party, but from now on, Marshall and Fishman announced, labor would look to its own interests. Richard Austin, secretary of state, interrupted the silence that followed with a remarkable understatement. If labor felt compelled to speak that way to the Democratic party, Austin reasoned, then the Democratic party was in serious trouble.[12] Labor's attitude seemed only to be confirmed when Harold Julian, the legislative representative of the UAW, later told Bill Ryan, Democratic leader of the house, that the union did not really care what kind of presidential primary bill the legislature sent to the governor. It simply did not matter. Feelings were intense and the rupture seemed complete.[13]

One reason the UAW was so opposed to a direct primary was the belief that no one would benefit from it more than George Wallace. This was neither an irrational fear nor a reluctance to permit Democrats to choose their own presidential nominee. In the general election of 1968, Wallace had collected 10 percent of the total vote cast. This was an exceptional achievement for a third-party candidate in a presidential election. Wallace's strength, moreover, was remarkably broad; it was not at all restricted to Democrats. Several days before the 1968 election, the *Detroit News* conducted a poll and discovered that support for Wallace seemed to be almost equally divided among Democrats, Republicans, and independents. Of those who indicated they were going to vote for Wallace, 32 percent were also planning to vote for Democratic congressional candidates while 36 percent were planning to vote for Republicans. The remaining 32 percent were either undecided or were not planning to vote for any congressional candidate at all.[14] On the surface these figures seemed to suggest that the Wallace vote, precisely because 68 percent of it came from Republicans and independents, would be much less formidable in a Democratic primary. The busing controversy had no doubt greatly increased Wallace's appeal, but it could be assumed that whatever strength he had would continue to be dispersed across party lines and would not seriously affect the outcome of a Democratic party primary.

However, this analysis overlooked three important considerations. First, George Wallace was not a third-party candidate in 1972; he was running as a Democrat. Second, for all practical purposes Richard Nixon was the Republican nominee before the first primary was ever held. Pete McCloskey might believe he had a chance to do to Nixon in 1972 what McCarthy had done to Johnson in 1968, but no one else did. There would not be a contested Republican presidential primary in Michigan. Third, and perhaps most importantly, Michigan voters do not register by party. To vote in a primary election, the voter simply chooses the party ballot he desires after entering the voting booth. In short, the only presidential primary was going to be the Democratic one, and any registered voter could simply walk into the voting booth in order to participate in it. There was a very real possibility that the Democratic presidential primary would be influenced, to an extent that could only be guessed in advance of the event, by independents and members of the Republican party.

The UAW feared Wallace, but he was less worrisome to the new liberals. For them, he was simply symptomatic of the old politics and would diminish in importance as new and younger voters were attracted by an open political system. Wallace was a white blue-collar phenomenon, and that group was no longer to be the mainstay of a reformed Democratic party. This was not completely a matter of wishful thinking. At least in the category of voters who were expected to be the future salvation of the party and the country, a significant shift of attitudes had in fact taken place. Traditionally,

> the party of the left has represented the less educated against the educated, who belonged to the more "conservative" party. . . . Among the young, however, this relationship between education and party is being reversed. Based on data from the 1968 election, the Democrats are now the party choice of the educated young whites while Republicans are the party of the young, blue-collar white unionists.[15]

Moreover, if "students were included . . . the trend, if anything, would be more marked." Because voting participation increases with the level of education, this "new education mass" would have an influence on elections out of proportion to its percentage of the population. That influence would be exercised in behalf of the "progressive" side on issues such as "race, Vietnam, law and order, the ordering of national priorities." It was at least possible that the 1972 election would "involve realignments of the basic constituencies of the two major parties" as fundamental as those that had occurred in 1932.[16] The Democratic party, infused with the enlightened views of progressive youth, certainly had nothing to fear from the candidacy of George Corley Wallace in an open Democratic primary.

The white electorate might be undergoing a profound alteration of party and political allegiance, but the black voter of every age and description had no trouble deciding about George Wallace. Some black officials, however, had been having some difficulty deciding about the Democratic party. Black elected officials from all over the country had gathered in Gary, Indiana, to decide whether black interests could best be served by working in the party or outside it. A majority was ready to look toward the formation of a separate black party, but a minority, led by the Michigan contingent, refused to agree and walked out of the conference. Coleman Young, along with the other Michigan blacks in attendance, argued that only as part of the Democratic party would black Americans ever achieve equality of condition. That required some courage at the time, and any action by the state Democratic party that could be construed as even tolerating the Wallace candidacy would serve only to undermine the delegation's position in the black community. George Wallace was not a question the state party could avoid.

Since 1972 was a presidential year it seemed obvious that the Democratic candidates for the presidential nomination should be invited to speak at the annual Jefferson-Jackson Day Dinner. One month after Michigan blacks walked out of the Gary conference, the party leadership met to discuss whether all the candidates should be invited, or all of them except George Wallace. No one had any desire to have Wallace attend, and no one believed that Wallace, who was running against the Democratic party as it existed, would come if an invitation was extended. Everyone agreed, however, that if Wallace was not invited, he would come into Michigan and put on a competing event that might very well draw a larger crowd. Invite Wallace and he would not come; do not invite him, and in the judgment of the party chairman, "he will come in and nail our rear end to the wall."[17] The only rational decision was to send an invitation to Wallace immediately. Coleman Young, who was a member of the Democratic National Committee, agreed it was the only rational thing to do, but perhaps better than anyone else he understood it was also political suicide. Blacks had left the Gary conference arguing that their best prospects remained with the Democratic party. If that party now invited George Wallace to dinner, blacks would start looking for another table. Coleman Young and the rest of the party leadership agreed that George Wallace would not be invited.[18]

When 2,500 Democrats entered Cobo Hall for the Jeff-Jack Dinner, George Wallace was a few miles away at the other end of Woodward Avenue. He was not alone. Ten thousand people listened to him talk about how all those nice liberal northern Democrats would not even let him attend their dinner. When he was finished, another ten thousand who had not been able to get into the first performance took their places, and he did it again. Those who believed or pretended to believe that Wallace supporters were all fanatics and had proven their fanaticism by pouring in from all over the state to hear him bewail the bad manners of the state Democratic party underestimated his appeal. Three weeks after the dinner, Michigan voters cast their ballots in the state's first presidential primary. The worst fear of the UAW was a Wallace plurality; they had not feared enough. Wallace collected 51 percent of the votes cast and, with an absolute majority, compelled the Michigan delegation to the Democratic national convention to give him a majority of its votes. The state party that had refused to support John Kennedy's choice of Lyndon Johnson on civil rights grounds was required, twelve year later, to support the presidential candidacy of one who had made his mark in politics by uttering the cry "Segregation today, segregation tomorrow, segregation forever." It was becoming progressively more difficult to see the advantages of the new politics over the old.

George Wallace had 51 percent of the votes cast in the Democratic primary. He did not have 51 percent, or anything close to it, among the active members of the Democratic party. The leaders of the Wallace campaign were about to discover that, in this instance at least, the people giveth and the UAW taketh away. Guideline B-7 of the National Committee's new rules required that at least 75 percent of the state delegation be selected at the "congressional district or smaller unit level."[19] On June 10, when the Democratic state convention opened to conclude the process of selecting the Michigan delegation, each district had already allocated its delegates according to the vote cast within the district. This accounted for three quarters of the delegation. The remaining fourth would be chosen by the full convention, limited only by the necessity that out of the 132 votes allocated to Michigan, Wallace would have 67, McGovern 38, and Humphrey 27. As an exercise in mathematics this was a relatively easy undertaking; whether the number corresponded to a sincere commitment to a candidate was a more subjective matter.

Those who had led the Wallace campaign to a successful conclusion in the primary were themselves independent of the Democratic party and largely ignorant of its internal workings. It did not take much sophistication, however, to suspect that at least some of those chosen by the districts to participate as Wallace delegates were not fully devoted to the candidate and his cause. The state party had a committee to review and pass judgment on the credentials of delegates to the state convention, but neither this nor any other body had authority to rule on the credentials of delegates to the national convention. At a conference of the party leadership, John Bruff, chairman of the Twelfth District, suggested the formation of an ad hoc committee to deal with the problem. This suggestion was adopted and a seven-member committee hastily assembled. Three of the seven represented the presidential campaigns of Wallace, McGovern, and Humphrey. Jim McNeely, representing the state party, Harold Julian of the UAW, Paul Treska of the AFL-CIO, and a representative of the black caucus completed the membership.[20]

Every congressional district was heard from, and in all but one case the Wallace campaign received assurances that the commitment to support Wallace on the first two ballots would be honored. The Seventeenth District, however, presented a more difficult case. There, two of the Wallace delegates were well-known members of the district's Liberal Conference; one of them had even authored a series of vehemently anti-Wallace attacks in a newsletter circulated among members of the district committee. The representatives of the Seventeenth District were not prepared to make any commitments; they would go no further than to provide vague assurances that the selection process had been eminently democratic. The ad hoc committee was not impressed; it decided to recommend adoption of a resolution pledging support to a challenge to the Seventeenth District delegates at the national convention. On the surface, at least, the Wallace campaign had been treated with an even hand. With the exception of the Seventeenth, each district had promised that on the first two ballots its delegates would support the presidential candidate to whom they were pledged. The Wallace campaign did not ask, nor did anyone else inquire, what these delegates would do on any other issue that might come before the national convention. Intent on keeping what had been won at the polls, the Wallace campaign managed to overlook just about everything else. Still, even the Wallace campaign was somewhat surprised to learn that one of their delegates was Willie Felder. That Felder was the director of the UAW's political apparatus in southeastern Michigan made this unusual. That Willie Felder was black made it downright odd.

The crucial procedural question at the 1972 Democratic national convention was whether to honor the outcome of California's winner-take-all primary. McGovern had won it, and under the California law was entitled to all of the votes of the state delegation. This, however, was in apparent violation of McGovern's own rules. Guideline B-5 of the McGovern Commission rules insisted that "State parties must add to their explicit written rules provisions which forbid the use of the unit rule."[21] The California legislature, however, which was not under the jurisdiction of the Democratic National Committee, refused to change the rules of the state's presidential primary. Hubert Humphrey, who finished second to McGovern in the primary, attempted to obtain a proportional share of the delegation through the action of the national convention. McGovern, who in this instance at least preferred his victory to the vindication of his own principle, fought back. It was up to the convention to decide and, according to the calculation made by Gary Hart of the McGovern campaign, 55 of Michigan's 132 votes had to be cast in opposition to the Humphrey position if McGovern was to retain the California delegation intact.[22]

McGovern had thirty-eight votes pledged to him in the Michigan delegation; it was not immediately obvious where the other seventeen could be obtained. Humphrey had twenty-seven votes, and these presumably would take his part in the dispute. Wallace, with sixty-seven votes, shared Humphrey's interest in diminishing the strength of the frontrunner. The AFL-CIO and the UAW were divided on the issue. Bill Marshall, and the rest of the AFL-CIO for that matter, loved Humphrey and had not forgotten 1968. The UAW had not forgotten either, but drew a different lesson from it. Mc-Govern's nomination might be delayed if he lost part of the California delegation, but it could not be denied. Some UAW officials believed, though they did not discuss it publicly, that McGovern would be nominated and Nixon reelected. There was not only no point in fighting the inevitable nomination, there was a good deal to be said for cooperating now to avoid division later. The fact that the McGovernites had behaved badly after Humphrey's nomination in 1968 was no reason to follow their example in 1972. If McGovern was going to lose, no one was going to be able to blame it on the UAW. Both labor organizations pulled out all the stops. Marshall and the AFL-CIO held a majority, but the UAW got the fifty-five votes McGovern needed. Joining the thirty-eight McGovern delegates were four-and-one-half Wallace votes, and, to the great chagrin of the AFL-CIO, twelve-and-one-half of the delegates committed to Humphrey.[23] Along with Doug Fraser and Sam Fishman, Willie Felder, one of the few blacks pledged to Wallace in the convention, or in America for that matter, assisted in the effort to deny Hubert Humphrey and George Wallace the last chance to hold back the rush for McGovern.

George McGovern had captured the Democratic nomination before the national convention had even begun, but when the state Democratic party met in convention at the end of August to select nominees for the state supreme court, the state board of education, and the three university boards, the outcome was by no means predetermined. There had been no primaries or district nominating conventions in advance; the convention alone would select the nominees. The party organization, which had been reduced to an irrelevancy in the selection of a presidential candidate, retained exclusive authority to choose at least those statewide candidates. Yet there was something about the

1972 August state convention that set it apart from its predecessors. On the surface the difference was one of mood and atmosphere. Those who had been with McGovern from the beginning exhibited the enthusiasm and optimism befitting their victory. Among those who had seen presidential campaigns come and go, there was a more realistic and, surprisingly, more relaxed attitude. Nothing could be done to prevent Nixon's reelection, and the only remaining question of any interest was how bad McGovern's defeat would be. Experienced politicians believed it was going to be an unmitigated disaster. The Republican victory was going to be of such magnitude that the choice of candidates for positions that were almost always won by the nominees of the party that carried the top of the ticket was nothing to get very excited about. Labor believed the stakes were so low that at the beginning of the state convention it was not inclined to expend any real effort to secure any particular nomination. No one had a chance of winning, and there was nothing to do about it but sit back and wait for the end in order to begin again.

The air of impending defeat had never before been so prominent at a Democratic state convention, at least not since the the liberal-labor coalition had refashioned the Michigan party in 1948. But there was another and more fundamental difference between this and every preceding state convention. Labor had joined the Michigan Democratic party to construct a broad coalition capable of winning electoral majorities, an aim which most discussions of political parties, e.g., those of E. E. Schattschneider's *Party Government*,[24] and Clinton Rossiter's *Parties and Politics in America*,[25] take as a given. The new politics adherents who had begun to enter the party as an organized force in 1968 looked on this emphasis on winning with distrust if not outright disdain. For them close attention to moral principle (or what they claimed to be moral principle) rather than the prudent adjustment of conflicting interests seemed all-important. Far from being a quality unique to Michigan, it was a phenomenon noted by James Q. Wilson in his study of California politics, *The Amateur Democrat*,[26] by Frank Parkin in his investigation of the British ban the bomb movement, *Middle-Class Radicalism*,[27] and by Seymour Lipset and Earl Raab in *The Politics of Unreason: Right Wing Extremism in America*.[28] Each of these works attempted to account for the phenomenon of political absolutism in sociological terms. Broadly stated, the common conclusion was put forward by David Riesman in the following terms: "An absolute morality tends to be characteristic of people whose experience of life has not included the give and take of wide human experience and the mutual tolerance and sense for compromise that these often, but not invariably give."[29] However, this analysis failed to account for the particular point of view the new politics people adopted. If a clear conscience was the aim, abstention from politics might well be the course chosen—but the real question was: What was the basis for insisting that political practice be informed by an uncompromising moral rigor?

Whatever the psychology of those who adopted this point of view, its theoretical foundation is present in two elements of the teaching of Kant.[30] The first, the notion that the principle that guides action must be formulated without reference to particular needs, leads to the necessity never to effect a compromise, no matter how prudent, with such interests. The second, the notion expounded in *Perpetual Peace* that true political freedom will come into being through continued demonstrations of the selfish aims of governments, produces the incentive to employ unrelentingly moral principle as the ground for impugning both the policies and motives of those who pursue electoral success as their main objective. Kant, in his critique of the classical liberalism of Hobbes and Locke, was concerned to replace an arrangement in which men are permitted and even encouraged to consult their passions in determining their conduct with a condition in which men are obligated to ignore so far as possible their bodily or private needs in regulating their actions. These two strands of modern liberalism are the theoretical origin not only of the political behavior discussed above, but also of a vast quantity of the political science literature.

The running debate between the pluralists and the antipluralists paralleled, and was derived from, the central dispute of modern liberalism. The pluralist position, as stated for example in José Ortega y Gasset's *The Revolt of the Masses*,[31] William Kornhauser's *The Politics of Mass Society*,[32] David B. Truman's *The Governmental Process: Political Interests and Public Opinion*,[33] Robert A. Dahl's *Who Governs*,[34] Nelson W. Polsby's *Community Power and Political Theory*,[35] and Seymour Lipset's *Political Man*,[36] defined modern democracies as characterized by the existence of a politics of negotiation among established groups and interests. To the extent to which this signified a departure from the unfettered expression of the popular will, it was subject to attack as essentially antidemocratic. Books such as Henry S. Kariel's *The Decline of American Pluralism*,[37] Charles A. McCoy and John Playford's *Apolitical Politics*,[38] and Theodore J. Lowi's *The Politics of Disorder*[39] argued that an undemocratic status quo could be replaced only by measures that effectively brought to bear the will of the broad mass of the citizenry on public matters. Negotiation and compromise between narrow interests groups was to be replaced by a politics of direct and universal popular participation. Because it was direct it would obviate compromise; because it was universal it carried within itself the guarantee of unselfish principle.

To a remarkable degree the dispute within modern liberalism and the debate within American political science was paralleled in the internal affairs of the Michigan Democratic party. Beginning with the state convention of 1970 and culminating in the party reforms of 1972, the forces of the new politics sought to eliminate the old pluralism of the Democratic party and replace it with something that might be called the new pluralism. The new pluralism is distinguished from the old in both composition and purpose. The old pluralism was made up for the most part of self-forming groups (of which Tocqueville's description remains the best[40]) whose purpose was to secure a continued improvement of their material well-being. As none by itself constituted a majority, all were compelled to seek alliance with others, and to adjust their particular claims to comport with what was acceptable to those groups and their individual members. The desire to improve their condition thus brought about a limitation of their behavior. What had been effected in the first half of the nineteenth century in the United States through the agency of Adam Smith's well-known "invisible hand" became, with the advent of national political parties, the conscious intention of politicians.[41] Driven by the desire to win and hold office, party leaders, by compromise and concession, sought to fashion coalitions of interests sufficient to form electoral majorities.

In 1972, the new politics wing of the Democratic party opposed the idea that a combination of political interests should be the basis of a political party. Such an arrangement was in their judgment indistinguishable from an accommodation with the existing centers of power. Their attention was instead fastened upon those who lacked the power necessary to advance their claims with a reasonable prospect of success in the political marketplace. To empower the disadvantaged was their purpose, and their problem. They believed that by supporting a presidential primary they could eliminate the necessity to compromise with established interests within the party. Thus the primary was viewed by party liberals as an indispensable instrument for the expression of the popular will, while it was opposed by labor, endorsed by the state party, approved by the Democratic legislature, and, to the utter confusion of those who believed the direct voice of the people to be inherently progressive, won going away by George Wallace. Still, whatever the practical result of reform, the principle had to be asserted. Moreover, the Michigan primary could be explained away as an aberration; McGovern after all was the nominee.

In truth, though, whatever the success of the direct primary in removing obstacles to the participation of the unorganized, it did nothing to bring the powerless into positions of power within the party itself. An obvious solution would have been to follow the example set by the liberal-labor coalition a quarter of a century earlier and run candidates for precinct delegate as the first step in obtaining power within the party organization. That, however, would not only have been difficult, it would have meant accepting the legitimacy of a competitive system in which power is decisive and compromise required. The liberal-labor coalition had followed the party rules in 1948 in order to obtain political power. In turn, they used that power to make the state Democratic party the political vehicle by which to advance the principles of the New Deal in Michigan. A major principle of the New Deal, and the source of cohesion among the various groups that formed its electoral majorities, was the belief that government should enter the marketplace to remedy the condition of the economically distressed. The emphasis on working to lessen economic inequality was part of a larger and more general belief in equality itself. The political strength of the new politics faction consisted of their ability to argue that if equality was the premise, the obligation to provide equality of representation within the party was the logical consequence. And if the economic condition of a citizen was not to be left entirely to the unfettered workings of the marketplace, the political condition of a citizen should not simply be the result of open competition for power among the ambitious. Equal opportunity was as much a mask for the privileges of the powerful in the one arena as in the other.

From this proposition it was only a short step to the assertion that instead of rules providing the method of competition for place and position within the party, there should be rules prescribing the outcome of such competition. Through an apparently irrefragable logic, the new politics advocates argued that the principle of equality required that any group that did not have equality of representation within the party should be given it as a matter of right. Representation was to be in proportion to the group's presence in the general population. Any group that did not have equal representation within the party had by definition been discriminated against. What the proponents of numerical equality demanded had been granted: the Democratic state convention provided equality for women in 1970; the Democratic National Committee adopted the McGovern Commission rules and provided representation in proportion to population for youth and minorities. What had never before been prescribed was the application of the principle to the slate of candidates nominated by a party for public offices. That application, however, followed as a matter of logical necessity.

So long as it was a question of demanding proportionate representation within the Democratic party organization, there could be complete agreement among those delegates to the August state convention who believed in the principles of the new politics. They also shared the conviction that complying with the principle of political equality meant that there should be equal representation on the slate of candidates the party was about to select. However, they could not entirely agree on precisely who should be chosen to provide that representation. Mathematics could supply a formula for representation; it had nothing to say about the selection of an individual. The women's caucus could agree on the need for representation of women; likewise, the youth caucus, the black caucus, and the Latino caucus could agree that members of their groups should be selected. But *who* should be selected was a question impervious to numerical calculation. The candidates themselves made claims that far from solving the problem, merely restated it. Michael Einhauser, a student running for the nomination for Wayne State University's board of governors, distributed literature that included the statement "Support someone who knows Wayne, who will be active on the job, and who can represent those who feel they have no voice in University government." This scarcely singled Einhauser out as the automatic representative of Michigan youth.

Changing the basis of representation within the party from the open competition for power to the guaranteed possession of it not only permitted the claim that the principle should be extended to the selection of candidates; it also provided the political power through which to achieve the result desired. Women, youth, blacks, Latinos—each used the principle of equal representation to secure power within the party and then sought to use that power to obtain representation on the slate of candidates. Instead of being designed to appeal to a majority of the electorate, the ticket had now somehow to reflect the internal composition of the party. In place of the old pluralism in which a political party sought to attract a majority coalition of groups and interests by a process of compromise and conciliation, the new pluralism insisted on a strict adherence to the principle of proportional representation within the party itself. This was eminently clear when the party's traditional midnight caucus convened.

From its inception the midnight caucus was designed to resolve the differences that arose in a state convention, whether those differences had to do with issues or candidates. The party leadership, made up of the elected officers and the spokesmen of the major groups attached to the Democratic party, met together to exchange information and agree on a common position. If, for example, labor wanted one candidate to be nominated for a certain position and the black caucus wanted another, the issue would be resolved during the midnight caucus with the advice and counsel of the elected party officers. Almost invariably the principle of resolution would be the effect a particular decision was likely to have on the electorate. Membership in the midnight caucus was fairly constant. The elected party leadership, the UAW, the AFL-CIO, and the most prominent Democratic public officials were included. In 1972, however, participation was broadened to include representatives of the women's caucus, the youth caucus, the black caucus, the Latino caucus, and the NDC caucus. The problem for the midnight caucus was to construct a slate that each caucus would agree to support in place of the one it had proposed. The problem was insoluble.

Everyone who attended the midnight caucus agreed that women, youth, blacks, and Latinos should be represented on the ticket. In this the advocates of the new politics had been eminently successful. Each of these groups, however, insisted on the right to select not only their own representatives but the office to be filled by them. This led to enormous complications. The black caucus wanted Shirley Robinson to be one of the three chosen as members of the newly expanded Democratic National Committee. They also endorsed Zeline Richardson for one of the two remaining positions. The UAW, on the other hand, was upset with Richardson because as a member of the state central committee she had voted in favor of the presidential primary. The state chairman, Jim McNeely, had objections to Shirley Robinson. The Latino caucus wanted Gumecindo Salas on the state board of education, while labor wanted to move him to the Michigan State board of trustees and Zeline Richardson along with Kathy Strauss to the Wayne State board of governors. The youth caucus insisted that Mike Einhauser had to be a candidate for the Wayne State board of governors. The youth caucus, the women's caucus, and the NDC caucus all endorsed two women for the Michigan State board of trustees. Labor wanted one of the two nominations for Tom Downs. There was no agreement in the midnight caucus because none of the groups represented was the least bit willing to modify any of its demands.[42]

From the perspective of the representatives of groups based on age, sex, or race, it was impossible to compromise. Each was formed on the principle that representation was to be strictly derived from its size in the general population. Once it was accepted that representation was to be accorded on this basis, no other consideration could be permitted to enter without sacrificing the original principle. Even differences in size, as that for example between the number of women and the number of Latinos in the population, could not be allowed to interfere. Women were entitled to greater representation but they were not to be permitted to use their larger share to deprive others of their rightful, if smaller, entitlement, or to decide for others who their representatives should be or what position they should seek. The party chairman presided at the midnight caucus but was unable to persuade it to reach any agreement. Unable to keep even the party officers unified in opposition to the presidential primary, he was incapable of asserting the strength of the chairmanship to bring about, through either persuasion or coercion, the adoption of a common slate of candidates. At 3:00 A.M. the midnight caucus adjourned as divided as it had been three hours earlier.

During the midnight caucus, Doug Fraser and Sam Fishman of the UAW and Bill Marshall of the AFL-CIO had grown increasingly restive. Labor had indicated its displeasure with McNeely after the decision on the presidential primary. Its disappointment with the chairman was only intensified as the three watched demands being made without concessions being extracted. McNeely had already been told that labor would no longer work with him as before. The tactic now adopted, however, seemed less the result of design than a frustrated reaction to circumstances. The UAW informed the participants in the midnight caucus that if they could not agree labor would produce a slate of candidates and throw its support behind it on the convention floor. Though not expressed in words, it was implicitly understood that if the party leadership could not create a consensus, the UAW would assume the function of preparing the slate. Any group that disagreed could of course vote against it.

At 9:30 in the morning, the UAW caucus met and kept its promise. For the two nominations for the state supreme court, the UAW endorsed Robert Evans, a black, and Horace Gilmore. Both were unopposed for the nomination. Differences between the various caucuses arose over the nominations for the three university boards and the state board of education. The youth, women's, and NDC caucuses had all endorsed two women, Nancy Waters and Donna O'Donahue, for the Michigan State University board of trustees. The UAW endorsed O'Donahue, but replaced Waters with Tom Downs. Downs and O'Donahue won in convention. For the Wayne State board of governors, the youth caucus endorsed only one candidate, Mike Einhauser. He also had the endorsement of the NDC and the women's caucus. He was not put on the UAW slate and was not nominated by the convention. For the University of Michigan board of regents, John Reed Koza of the NDC and Marjorie Lansing had the support of the youth, women's, and NDC caucuses. The UAW, which had no graduate of the University of Michigan in its caucus, thought that Koza and the NDC lacked the intellectual ability to be put in charge of a great university. Marjorie Lansing and Thomas Roach, a graduate of the university and its law school, received the UAW's endorsement and consequently the nomination.

On the nomination of two candidates for the state board of education, the line was drawn and hostilities began with full vigor. The UAW endorsed Dr. Charles Morton, a black, and Gumecindo Salas, a Latino. Salas had been asked to run instead for the Michigan State University board of trustees. Had he agreed, the UAW would have endorsed him in place of Donna O'Donahue, and then would have endorsed a woman to run with Morton for the state board of education. Salas refused to switch and therewith removed the possibility of nominating a woman for the state board without depriving the Latinos of a place on the slate. Patricia Micklow, an intelligent and able candidate for the state board, was not impressed with such considerations. Her supporters were in fact so upset that some of them came close to physical confrontations with members of the labor caucus. In one of the closest votes of the day, Micklow finished third behind Morton and Salas.

Labor had come to the state convention privately resigned to a Republican victory in November and resolved to letting events take their course in the state convention. But events had refused to take any apparent course at all. With a party leadership perhaps unable and certainly unwilling to lead, the UAW was the only force in a position to step into the vacancy. Once it decided to fashion a slate independent of the midnight caucus, however, the UAW did not simply operate alone. Immediately after the midnight caucus ended, the leadership of the UAW, the AFL-CIO, and the black caucus agreed on a slate of candidates they would take to their respective caucuses. Moreover, the slate agreed upon accorded perfectly with the principles of the new politics. If the state supreme court nominations are disregarded on the ground that there were only two candidates, the remaining eight nominations were divided equally between men and women, and one of the eight was a black, another a Latino. However, the women's caucus and the youth caucus, or at least the members of those groups who were also part of the NDC, saw in the labor slate not a vindication of principle but the heavy hand of the old politics.

The party reforms introduced by the new politics liberals were designed to provide representation to those who on their own would not be able to acquire political power commensurate with their numbers. Underpinning every one of these reforms was the belief that open competition in the political marketplace inevitably led to the concentration of power in the hands of a few private interests that invariably used it to advance their own well-being instead of the public's. What the new politics liberal would not admit, and what labor fully understood, was that a change in the basis of representation could not replace political power with an automatic agreement on the imperatives of the public interest. A guarantee of representation was by no means identical to agreement on the purposes for which representation was to be used. Indeed, the proceedings of the midnight caucus seemed to demonstrate the exact opposite.

At its 1972 state convention, the Democratic party impaled itself on its new principle. Groups that were called into being by the principle of proportionate representation were unable to make the compromises necessary to reach common agreement without at least appearing to sacrifice that principle. A party leadership afraid to antagonize any of its constituent parts by choosing among them abdicated its responsibility to lead. Nature, it is said, abhors a vacuum, and it was perhaps inevitable that the strongest single element within the party should fill it. Starting from an often silent part in the original liberal-labor coalition, the UAW had, at least since 1968, become the major force helping to increase the strength of the Democratic party in Michigan. Now, without really wanting to, it was compelled by its own strength to assemble for the party a slate of candidates for public office. The UAW had demonstrated that it had the power to take control of the Michigan Democratic party.

Notes

1. Penn Kemble and Josh Muravchik, "The New Politics and The Democrats," *Commentary,* December, 1972, pp. 78–84.

2. Commission on Party Structure and Delegate Selection, *Mandate for Reform* (Washington, D.C.: Democratic National Committee, 1970).

3. Ibid. At a meeting of the McGovern Commission on November 18, 1969, Austin Ranney, professor of political science at the University of Wisconsin and a member of the commission, stated: "I want to suggest . . . that the commission at the very least urge . . . that there be included as members of the delegation, adequate, fair, whatever the word may be, representation of minority groups in the population." Senator McGovern responded, "I should advise you, Professor Ranney, that we discussed this matter at some length at the September meeting. The Commission, as I recall it, unanimously decided after some discussion that it was not feasible to go on record for a quota system." Ranney, however, did not give up: "I think that we would like to at least urge . . . that members of minority groups be adequately, fairly, whatever . . . represented." Senator Birch Bayh wanted to go further: "If we leave it there then I'm not sure we've moved anyplace." Bayh proposed that the commission take Ranney's "motion . . . and add two or three words to sort of give guidelines saying that to meet this requirement there should be some reasonable relationship between the representation of delegates and the representation of the minority group in the population of the state in question." The Bayh-Ranney proposal was adopted by the commission by a vote of ten to nine. Theodore H. White, *The Making of the President 1972* (New York: Atheneum, 1973), pp. 29–30.

4. Kemble and Muravchik, "New Politics and the Democrats." See also White, *Making of the President 1972,* p. 32.

5. Commission on Party Structure and Delegate Selection, *Mandate for Reform.*

6. Alexis de Tocqueville, *The Old Regime and the French Revolution* (Garden City, N.Y.: Doubleday and Co., 1955), p. 205.

7. Commission on Party Structure and Delegate Selection, *Mandate for Reform.*

8. Harold Julian, interview with author, June 14, 1972.

9. For a discussion of the effects of primary elections on state party organizations see V. O. Key, Jr., *American State Politics: An Introduction* (New York: Alfred A. Knopf, 1956), pp. 145–64.

10. Austin Ranney suggests that at least part of the explanation for the increased use of the direct primary in the United States is the "widespread belief that political parties are, at best, unavoidable evils whose propensities for divisiveness, oligarchy, and corruption must be closely watched and sternly controlled." Austin Ranney, *Curing the Mischiefs of Faction: Party Reform in America* (Berkeley: University of California Press, 1975), p. 22.

11. James McNeely, interview with author, May 14, 1973.

12. Sam Fishman, interview with author, June 6, 1973; John Bruff, interview with author, June 6, 1973; James McNeely, interview with author, May 14, 1973.

13. Harold Julian, interview with author, June 14, 1972.

14. *Detroit News,* November 3, 1968.

15. Michael Rappeport, "Party Alignment: The Biggest Shift in 40 Years," *Washington Monthly,* November, 1971, p. 21.

16. Ibid.

17. James McNeely, interview with author, May 14, 1973.

18. Ibid.

19. Commission on Party Structure and Delegate Selection, *Mandate for Reform.*

20. Harold Julian, interview with author, June 14, 1972.

21. Commission on Party Structure and Delegate Selection, *Mandate for Reform.*

22. James McNeely, interview with author, May 14, 1973.

23. *Detroit Free Press,* July 12, 1972.

24. E. E. Schattschneider, *Party Government* (New York: Holt, Rinehart and Winston, 1942).

25. Clinton Rossiter, *Parties and Politics in America* (Ithaca: Cornell University Press, 1960).

26. James Q. Wilson, *The Amateur Democrat: Club Politics in Three Cities* (Chicago: University of Chicago Press, 1962).

27. Frank Parkin, *Middle-Class Radicalism: The Social Bases of the British Campaign for Nuclear Disarmament* (New York: Praeger Publishers, 1968).

28. Seymour Martin Lipset and Earl Raab, *The Politics of Unreason: Right Wing Extremism in America* (New York: Harper and Row, 1970).

29. David Riesman, "America Moves to the Right," *New York Times Magazine,* October 27, 1968, p. 79.

30. The suggestion that the basis of moral absolutism in modern liberal politics is found in the teaching of Kant is derived from Harvey Mansfield, Jr., *The Spirit of Liberalism* (Cambridge: Harvard University Press, 1978), pp. 43–51.

31. José Ortega y Gasset, *The Revolt of the Masses* (New York: W. W. Norton and Co., 1960).

32. William Kornhauser, *The Politics of Mass Society* (Glencoe, Ill.: Free Press, 1959).

33. David B. Truman, *The Governmental Process: Political Interests and Public Opinion* (New York: Alfred A. Knopf, 1951).

34. Robert A. Dahl, *Who Governs?* (New Haven: Yale University Press, 1961).

35. Nelson W. Polsby, *Community Power and Political Theory* (New Haven: Yale University Press, 1963).

36. Seymour Martin Lipset, *Political Man: The Social Bases of Politics* (Garden City, N.Y.: Doubleday and Co., 1960).

37. Henry S. Kariel, *The Decline of American Pluralism* (Stanford: Stanford University Press, 1961).

38. Charles A. McCoy and John Playford, *Apolitical Politics: A Critique of Behavioralism* (New York: Thomas Y. Crowell, 1967).

39. Theodore J. Lowi, *The Politics of Disorder* (New York: Basic Books, 1971).

40. Alexis de Tocqueville, *Democracy in America,* ed. Phillips Bradley (New York: Vintage Books, 1945).

41. See Lloyd Ulman, *The Rise of the National Union* (Cambridge: Harvard University Press, 1966).

42. James McNeely, interview with author, May 14, 1973; Sam Fishman, interview with author, June 6, 1973.

Selected Bibliography

Adamany, David. *Campaign Finance in America*. North Scituate, Mass.: Duxbury Press, 1972.

Alinsky, Saul. *John L. Lewis: An Unauthorized Biography*. New York: Putnam and Sons, 1949.

Axelrod, Robert. "Where the Votes Come From: An Analysis of Electoral Coalitions, 1952–1968." *American Political Science Review* 66 (March, 1972): 11–20.

Banfield, Edward C. *Big City Politics*. New York: Random House, 1965.

————. *Political Influence*. New York: Free Press, 1961.

Banfield, Edward C., and Wilson, James Q. *City Politics*. Cambridge: Harvard University Press, 1963.

Barbash, Jack. *The Practice of Unionism*. New York: Harper, 1956.

Bartlett, Alton C. "How Rank and File Leaders View Union Political Action." *Labor Law Journal* 17 (August, 1966): 483–94.

Baskin, Darryl. *American Pluralist Democracy: A Critique*. New York: Van Nostrand Reinhold Co., 1971.

Beer, Samuel. *British Politics in the Collectivist Age*. New York: Alfred A. Knopf, 1966.

Bennett, Harry. *We Never Called Him Henry*. New York: Fawcett Publications, 1951.

Bernstein, Irving. "The Growth of American Unions, 1945–1960." *Labor History* 2 (Spring, 1961): 131–57.

————. *The Lean Years*. Boston: Houghton Mifflin Co., 1960.

Binkley, Wilfred E. *American Political Parties: Their Natural History*. 4th ed. New York: Alfred A. Knopf, 1962.

Blackwood, George Douglas. "The UAW of America, 1935–1951." Ph.D. diss., University of Chicago, 1951.

Bone, Hugh A. *American Politics and the Party System*. 3d ed. New York: McGraw-Hill, 1965.

————. "Political Parties and Pressure Group Politics." *The Annals of the American Academy of Political and Social Science* 319 (September, 1958): 73–83.

Brauer, Carl M. *John F. Kennedy and the Second Reconstruction*. New York: Columbia University Press, 1977.

Brazer, Harvey E. "Michigan's Fiscal Outlook." *Wayne Law Review* 11, no. 2 (Winter, 1965): 430–50.

Brophy, Jacqueline. "The Merger of the AFL and the CIO in Michigan." *Michigan History* 50 (1966): 139–57.

Bryce, James. *The American Commonwealth*. 2d ed. London: Macmillan and Co., 1891.

Bunzel, John H. *Anti-Politics in America: Reflections on the Anti-Political Temper and its Distortions of the Democratic Process*. New York: Vintage Books, 1970.

Burke, Edmund. *Works*. Vol. 1. 1865 ed. Boston: Little, Brown and Co.

Burnham, Walter Dean. *Critical Elections and the Mainspring of American Politics*. New York: W. W. Norton and Co., 1970.

Burns, James MacGregor. *The Deadlock of Democracy: Four-Party Politics in America*. Englewood Cliffs, N.J.: Prentice-Hall, 1963.

Burton, Clarence M., ed. *The City of Detroit, Michigan, 1701–1922*. Detroit: S. J. Clarke, 1922.

Calkins, Fay. *The CIO and the Democratic Party*. Chicago: University of Chicago Press, 1952.

Campbell, Angus, et al. *The American Voter*. New York: John Wiley and Sons, 1960.

Christman, Henry M., ed. *Walter P. Reuther: Selected Papers*. New York: Macmillan Co., 1961.

Cline, Denzel C., and Taylor, Milton C. *Michigan Tax Reform*. East Lansing: Michigan State University Press, 1966.

Commission on Party Structure and Delegate Selection. *Mandate for Reform*. Washington, D.C.: Democratic National Committee, 1970.

Commons, John R., et al. *History of Labour in the United States*. New York: Macmillan Co., 1936.

Cormier, Frank, and Eaton, William J. *Reuther*. Englewood Cliffs, N.J.: Prentice-Hall, 1970.

Crase, Douglas. "Michigan Democrats in Disarray." *Nation*, March 11, 1968, pp. 340–43.

Crotty, William, et al. *Political Parties and Political Behavior*. Boston: Allyn and Bacon, 1971.

Dahl, Robert A. *Who Governs?: Democracy and Power in an American City*. New Haven: Yale University Press, 1961.

Department of Research and Education, CIO. *The Truth About the CIO*. November–December, 1945.

DeVries, Walter D. "The Michigan Lobbyist: A Study in the Bases and Perceptions of Effectiveness." Ph.D. diss., Michigan State University, 1960.

Dewey, John. *The Public and Its Problems*. New York: Henry Holt and Co., 1927.

Duverger, Maurice. *Political Parties: Their Organization and Activity in the Modern State*. New York: John Wiley and Sons, 1954.

Eldersveld, Samuel J. *Political Parties: A Behavioral Analysis*. Chicago: Rand McNally and Co., 1964.

Elliott, William Yandell. *The Pragmatic Revolt in Politics: Syndicalism, Facism, and the Constitutional State*. New York: Macmillan Co., 1928.

Epstein, Leon D. *Politics in Wisconsin*. Madison: University of Wisconsin Press, 1958.

Feuer, Lewis S., ed. *Basic Writings on Politics and Philosophy: Karl Marx and Friedrich Engels*. Garden City, N.Y.: Doubleday and Co., 1959.

──────── . *Marx and the Intellectuals: A Set of Post-Ideological Essays*. Garden City, N.Y.: Doubleday and Co., 1969.

Fine, Nathan. *Labor and Farmer Parties in the United States 1828–1928*. New York: Rand School of Social Science, 1928.

Fine, Sidney. *Sit-Down: The General Motors Strike of 1936–1937*. Ann Arbor: University of Michigan Press, 1969.

Furlong, W. B. "A 'Boy Wonder' Begins to Wonder." *New York Times Magazine*, November 22, 1959, p. 19.

Galenson, Walter. *The CIO Challenge to the AFL: A History of the American Labor Movement, 1935–1941*. Cambridge: Harvard University Press, 1960.

Goldberg, Arthur J. *AFL-CIO Labor United*. New York: McGraw-Hill, 1956.

Goldman, Ralph M. *The Democratic Party in American Politics*. New York: Macmillan Co., 1966.

Gompers, Samuel. "Invading Labor's Rights." *The American Federationist* 11 (February, 1904).

──────── . "Trade Unions and Liberty." *The American Federationist* 13 (April, 1906).

Gosnell, Harold. *Machine Politics Chicago Model*. Chicago: University of Chicago Press, 1937.

Greenstein, Fred I. *The American Party System and the American People*. Englewood Cliffs, N.J.: Prentice-Hall, 1963.

Greenstone, J. David. *Labor in American Politics*. New York: Alfred A. Knopf, 1969.

Grob, Gerald. *Workers and Utopia*. Evanston: Northwestern University Press, 1961.

Grodzins, Morton. *The American System: A New View of Government in the United States*. Chicago: Rand McNally and Co., 1966.

Haber, William, ed. *Labor in a Changing America*. New York: Basic Books, 1966.

Hadden, Jeffrey K.; Masotti, Louis H.; and Thiessen, Victor. "The Making of Negro Mayors in 1967." *Trans-action*, January/February, 1968, pp. 21–30.

Hare, James M. *With Malice Toward None*. East Lansing: Michigan State University Press, 1972.

Harrington, Michael. *Socialism*. New York: Saturday Review Press, 1972.

Harris, T. G. *Romney's Way*. Englewood Cliffs, N.J.: Prentice-Hall, 1968.

Hartz, Louis. *The Liberal Tradition in America: An Interpretation of American Political Thought Since the Revolution*. New York: Harcourt, Brace, and World, 1955.

Hitchcock, James. "The Intellectuals and the People." *Commentary* 55 (March, 1973): 64–69.

Hoffa, James R. *Hoffa: The Real Story*. New York: Stein and Day, 1975.

Hofstadter, Richard. *The Idea of a Party System: The Rise of Legitimate Opposition in the United States, 1780–1840*. Berkeley: University of California Press, 1969.

Howard, J. Woodford. *Mr. Justice Murphy*. Princeton: Princeton University Press, 1968.

Howe, Irving, and Widick, B. J. *The UAW and Walter Reuther*. New York: Random House, 1949.

Jacob, Herbert, and Vines, Kenneth N., eds. *Politics in the American States: A Comparative Analysis*. Boston: Little, Brown and Co., 1965.

Jacobs, Paul. *The State of the Unions*. New York: Atheneum, 1963.

Josephson, Matthew. *Sidney Hillman: Statesman of American Labor*. Garden City, N.Y.: Doubleday and Co., 1952.

Kariel, Henry S. *The Decline of American Pluralism*. Stanford: Stanford University Press, 1961.

Karson, Marc. *American Labor Unions and Politics, 1900–1918*. Carbondale: Southern Illinois University Press, 1958.

Kemble, Penn, and Muravchik, Josh. "The New Politics and the Democrats." *Commentary*, December, 1972, pp. 78–84.

Key, V. O., Jr. *American State Politics: An Introduction*. New York: Alfred A. Knopf, 1956.

——————. *Politics, Parties, and Pressure Groups*. New York: Thomas Y. Crowell, 1964.

——————. *Public Opinion and American Democracy*. New York: Alfred A. Knopf, 1961.

——————. *The Responsible Electorate: Rationality in Presidential Voting*. Cambridge: Harvard University Press, 1966.

——————. *Southern Politics*. New York: Alfred A. Knopf, 1949.

——————. "A Theory of Critical Elections," *Journal of Politics* 17 (February, 1955): 3–18.

Kornhauser, Arthur, and Sheppard, Harold. *When Labor Votes: A Study of Auto Workers*. New York: University Books, 1956.

Kornhauser, William. *The Politics of Mass Society*. Glencoe, Ill.: Free Press, 1959.

Krock, Arthur. *Memoirs: Sixty Years on the Firing Line*. New York: Funk and Wagnalls, 1968.

Kroll, Jack. "Labor's Political Role," *Annals of the American Academy of Political and Social Science* 274 (March, 1951): 118–22.

——————. "Why Labor Is in Politics." *New York Times Magazine*, October 27, 1946, p. 15.

Latham, Earl. *The Group Basis of Politics: A Study in Basing-Point Legislation*. Ithaca: Cornell University Press, 1952.

Leonard, Richard T. *Report of the Political Action and Legislative Department, UAW-CIO, to the Executive Board*. December, 1946.

Levine, Harold. "Labor in Politics." *Newsweek*, October 25, 1948, pp. 37–38.

Levy, Mark R., and Kramer, Michael S. *The Ethnic Factor: How America's Minorities Decide Elections*. New York: Simon and Schuster, 1972.

Lipset, Seymour M. *Agrarian Socialism: The Cooperative Commonwealth Federation in Saskatchewan, A Study in Political Sociology*. Berkeley: University of California Press, 1959.

——————. "The Election and the National Mood." *Commentary* 55 (January, 1973): 43–50.

——————. *Political Man: The Social Bases of Politics*. Garden City, N.Y.: Doubleday and Co., 1960.

Lipset, Seymour M., and Raab, Earl. *The Politics of Unreason: Right Wing Extremism in America*. New York: Harper and Row, 1970.

Lockard, Duane. *New England State Politics*. Princeton: Princeton University Press, 1959.

Locke, John. *Two Treatises of Government*. New York: Hafner Publishing, 1947.

Lowi, Theodore J. *The End of Liberalism: Ideology, Policy, and the Crisis of Public Authority*. New York: W. W. Norton and Co., 1969.

————. *The Politics of Disorder*. New York: Basic Books, 1971.

————. "The Public Philosophy: Interest Group Liberalism." *American Political Science Review* 61 (March, 1967): 5–24.

————. "Toward Functionalism in Political Science: The Case of Innovation in Party Systems." *American Political Science Review* 57 (September, 1963): 570–83.

Lunt, Richard D. *The High Ministry of Government: The Political Career of Frank Murphy*. Detroit: Wayne State University Press, 1965.

McConnell, Grant. *The Decline of Agrarian Democracy*. Berkeley: University of California Press, 1953.

————. *Private Power and American Democracy*. New York: Alfred A. Knopf, 1966.

McCoy, Charles, and Playford, John. *Apolitical Politics: A Critique of Behavioralism*. New York: Thomas Y. Crowell, 1967.

Machiavelli, Niccolò. *The Prince*. New York: St. Martin's Press, 1964.

McKenzie, Robert, and Silver, Allan. *Angels in Marble: Working Class Conservatives in Urban England*. Chicago: University of Chicago Press, 1968.

McLaughlin, Doris B. *Michigan Labor: A Brief History from 1818 to the Present*. Ann Arbor: Institute of Labor and Industrial Relations, 1970.

McNaughton, Frank. *Mennen Williams of Michigan: Fighter for Progress*. New York: Oceana Publishing, 1960.

MacPherson, C. B. *Democracy in Alberta: Social Credit and the Party System*. Toronto: University of Toronto Press, 1962.

Mansfield, Harvey, Jr. *The Spirit of Liberalism*. Cambridge: Harvard University Press, 1978.

————. *Statesmanship and Party Government*. Chicago: University of Chicago Press, 1965.

Marvitz, Robert J., and Wright, Deil S. *Profile of a Metropolis*. Detroit: Wayne State University Press, 1962.

Marx, Karl. *The German Ideology*. New York: International Publishers, 1968.

Masters, Nicholas A. "The Politics of Union Endorsement of Candidates in the Detroit Area." *Midwest Journal of Political Science* 1 (August, 1957).

Michigan Democratic State Central Committee. *The Michigan Democratic Story 1948–1954*. Lansing, Mich.: Michigan Democratic Party, 1955.

Mollenhoff, C. R. *George Romney: Mormon in Politics*. Des Moines: Meredith Corp., 1968.

Neikind, Claire. "Ringing Doorbells with PAC." *New Republic*, October 25, 1948, pp. 10–14.

Olson, Mancur. *The Logic of Collective Action*. New York: Schocken Books, 1968.

Ortega y Gasset, José. *The Revolt of the Masses*. New York: W. W. Norton and Co., 1960.

Parkin, Frank. *Middle-Class Radicalism: The Social Bases of the British Campaign for Nuclear Disarmament*. New York: Praeger Publishers, 1968.

Patrick, Floyd A. "Organized Labor's Role in American Politics." *Labor Law Journal* 18 (May, 1967): 274–77.

Perlman, Selig. *A Theory of the Labor Movement*. New York: Kelley, 1949.

Peterson, Florence. *American Labor Unions: What They Are and How They Work*. New York: Harper and Row, 1962.

Phillips, Cabell. *The Truman Presidency: The History of a Triumphant Succession*. New York: Macmillan Co., 1966.

Pierce, Neal. *The Megastates of America*. New York: W. W. Norton and Co., 1972.

Polsby, Nelson W. *Community Power and Political Theory*. New Haven: Yale University Press, 1963.

Potter, David M. *People of Plenty: Economic Abundance and the American Character*. Chicago: University of Chicago Press, 1954.

Ranney, Austin. *Curing the Mischiefs of Faction: Party Reform in America*. Berkeley: University of California Press, 1975.

Rappeport, Michael. "Party Alignment: The Biggest Shift in 40 Years." *Washington Monthly*, November, 1971, pp. 19–21.

Raskin, A. H. "The Obsolescent Unions." *Commentary* 36 (July, 1963): 18–25.

Rehmus, Charles M.; McLaughlin, Doris B.; and Nesbitt, Frederick H., eds. *Labor and American Politics: A Book of Readings*. Rev. ed. Ann Arbor: University of Michigan Press, 1978.

Reichley, James. "Philadelphia: 'Good Government' Leads to Moral Frustration." In *Urban Government*, edited by Edward C. Banfield, pp. 357–64. New York: Free Press, 1969.

Reuther, Victor. *The Brothers Reuther and the Story of the UAW: A Memoir*. Boston: Houghton Mifflin Co., 1976.

Reuther, Walter P. "This is Your Fight." *Nation* 162 (January 12, 1946): 35–36.

Riegle, Donald. *O Congress*. New York: Doubleday and Co., 1972.

Riesman, David. "America Moves to the Right." *New York Times Magazine*, October 27, 1968, p. 34.

Rogin, Michael. *The Intellectuals and McCarthy: The Radical Specter*. Cambridge: MIT Press, 1967.

————. "Voluntarism: The Political Functions of an Anti-Political Doctrine." *Industrial and Labor Relations Review* 15 (July, 1962): 521–35.

Ross, Philip. "The Role of Government in Union Growth." *Annals of the American Academy of Political and Social Science*, November, 1963, pp. 74–85.

Rossiter, Clinton. *Parties and Politics in America*. Ithaca: Cornell University Press, 1960.

Rothman, Stanley. "Systematic Political Theory: Observations on the Group Approach." *American Political Science Review* 54 (March, 1960): 15–33.

Sarasohn, Stephen B., and Sarasohn, Vera H. *Political Party Patterns in Michigan*. Detroit: Wayne State University Press, 1957.

Schattschneider, E. E. *Political Parties and Democracy*. New York: Holt, Rinehart and Winston, 1964.

————. *Party Government*. New York: Holt, Rinehart and Winston, 1942.

————. *The Semi-Sovereign People: A Realist's View of Democracy in America*. New York: Holt, Rinehart and Winston, 1960.

Schlesinger, Arthur, Jr. *The Coming of the New Deal*. Boston: Houghton Mifflin Co., 1958.

————. *The Crisis of the Old Order*. Boston: Houghton Mifflin Co., 1957.

————. *The Politics of Upheaval*. Boston: Houghton Mifflin Co., 1967.

Schumpeter, Joseph. *Capitalism, Socialism and Democracy*. New York: Harper and Row, 1962.

Sexton, Patricia Cayo and Sexton, Brendan. *Blue Collars and Hard Hats*. New York: Vintage Books, 1972.

Sheridan, Walter. *The Fall and Rise of Jimmy Hoffa*. New York: Saturday Review Press, 1972.

Shils, Edward. *The Torment of Secrecy: The Background and Consequences of American Security Policies*. Glencoe, Ill.: Free Press; London: William Heinemann, 1956.

Smith, Adam. *An Inquiry into the Nature and Causes of The Wealth of Nations*. New York: E. P. Dutton, 1964.

Sorauf, Frank J. *Party and Representation: Legislative Politics in Pennsylvania*. New York: Atherton Press, 1963.

Stieber, Jack. *Governing the UAW*. New York: John Wiley and Sons, 1962.

Sward, Keith. *The Legend of Henry Ford*. New York: Rinehart, 1948.

Taft, Philip. *The AFL from the Death of Gompers to the Merger*. New York: Harper and Row, 1959.

————. *The AFL in the Time of Gompers*. New York: Harper and Row, 1957.

————. *Organized Labor in American History*. New York: Harper and Row, 1964.

Tocqueville, Alexis de. *Democracy in America*. Edited by Phillips Bradley. New York: Vintage Books, 1945.

————. *The Old Regime and the French Revolution*. Garden City, N.Y.: Doubleday and Co., 1955.

Trotsky, Leon. *The New Course*. Ann Arbor: University of Michigan Press, 1965.

Truman, David. *The Governmental Process: Political Interests and Public Opinion*. New York: Alfred A. Knopf, 1951.

Truman, Harry S. *Years of Trial and Hope*. New York: Doubleday and Co., 1956.

Truman, Margaret. *Harry S. Truman*. New York: William Morrow, 1973.

Ulman, Lloyd. *The Rise of the National Trade Union: The Development and Significance of its Structure, Governing Institutions, and Economic Policies*. Cambridge: Harvard University Press, 1966.

Weinberg, Kenneth G. *Black Victory: Carl Stokes and the Winning of Cleveland*. Chicago: Quadrangle Books, 1968.

Weinstein, James. *The Decline of Socialism in America, 1912–1925*. New York: Vintage Books, 1969.

Weinstein, James, and Eakins, David W., eds. *For a New America: Essays in History and Politics from Studies on the Left, 1959–1967.* New York: Random House, 1970.

White, Theodore H. *The Making of the President 1972.* New York: Atheneum, 1973.
————. *The Making of the President 1964.* New York: Atheneum, 1965.

Widick, B. J. *Detroit: City of Race and Class Violence.* Chicago: Quadrangle Books, 1972.

Wilson, James Q. *The Amateur Democrat: Club Politics in Three Cities.* Chicago: University of Chicago Press, 1962.

————. *Negro Politics: The Search for Leadership.* New York: Free Press, 1960.

Zetterbaum, Marvin. *Tocqueville and the Problem of Democracy.* Stanford: Stanford University Press, 1967.

Index